THE FAMILY WORSHIP BOOK

A Resource Book for Family Devotions

Terry L. Johnson, Editor

Christian Focus Publications

© Terry L. Johnson

ISBN 978-1-85792-401-5

10 9 8 7 6 5 4 3 2 1

Published in 1998
Reprinted in 2003, 2004, 2006 & 2009
by
Christian Focus Publications Ltd.,
Geanies House,
Fearn, Ross-shire,
IV20 1TW, Great Britain

www.christianfocus.com

Cover Design by Alister MacInnes
Printed & Bound by WS Bookwell, Finland

*To Andrew, Samuel, Sally,
Abigail and Benjamin,
members of the "little church"
that meets in our house*

CONTENTS

PREFACE

For years I have been hearing cries from heads of households for help in conducting regular family worship. Their questions have been fundamental: what are we to do and how are we to do it? This work is designed to come to their aid by providing the following;

- An *order of service* for family worship;

- *Resources* in prayers, creeds, commandments, Psalms, hymns and catechisms in a single book;

- *Tables* and *schedules* for Scripture reading, learning Psalms and hymns, and memorizing Scripture.

In addition, we have provided an extended introduction which we hope will persuade families of the duty and benefits of daily family worship, as well as other related life-simplifying commitments. Our prayer is that by again walking these "ancient paths" Christian parents will witness the salvation and sanctification of their covenant children and enjoy the strengthening of their Christian homes.

Chapter One

INTRODUCTION TO FAMILY WORSHIP

The Ancient Paths

Stand by the ways and see and ask for the ancient paths,
Where the good way is, and walk in it;
And you shall find rest for your souls (Jeremiah 6:16)

When I was a young boy, I walked to my public elementary school every school day for seven years. After school, I rode my bike to the ball park for my Little League games. Every Sunday we walked a few blocks to church. The recreation park was a little further away than the ball park and a little closer than the school. Scout Hall was behind the school, so we also rode our bikes, or walked to Boy Scout meetings. Life was simple for us kids and our parents. In the suburbs of Los Angeles, the epitome of the commuter city, we lived life within a mile radius of our home. We even walked to the doctor's office.

Most people used to live this way. Before the automobile, everything had to be within walking distance, or at least horse–and–buggy distance. Communities had to develop accordingly. Each neighborhood had its local grocer, clothier, druggist, school, church, and so on. People knew their neighbors because they couldn't be avoided. One was constantly rubbing shoulders with them as one worked, worshiped, played, ate, and lived in the same area.

I like our cars. I can hardly imagine life without them. But as I was driving to school-work-store-ball game the other day, I kept wondering, is this really a better way of life? Our city, Savannah, Georgia, like every other community in America, now sprawls. We have big malls, big parks, big hospitals, big medical practices, nice roads in every direction, and nice air conditioned cars in which to drive. But is this a more humanly satisfying way to live?

While driving through town one evening, I noted the remarkable differences between poor and middle class neighborhoods. The poor neighborhoods are older, more run-down, and yet abuzz with life. Some folks are sitting out on their porches, rocking and talking. Others are walking on the sidewalks. Still others are congregating on a street corner or at a storefront. What do you see in the middle class neighborhoods? Nothing. Not a soul. Why not? Air-conditioning. In the "poor" neighborhoods the "deprived" have no air-conditioning but do have community. The "affluent" neighborhoods have air-conditioning, but consequently everyone stays inside and minimal human interaction takes place. Who then is truly deprived? From air-conditioned offices to air-conditioned cars to air-conditioned houses, the socially impoverished move about, while the economically impoverished, though sweltering, enjoy a rich community experience.[1]

We are technologically superior to previous generations. But are we losing too much in the process? First we walked, then galloped, the rode on rails together. Now we drive, largely with the window up, and go home to hermetically sealed homes, only coming out to take out the trash or grab the newspaper. Once we entertained ourselves at home by reading books aloud. In the 1920's families gathered around the radio. In the 1950's, they gathered around the T.V. Now there is a T.V. in each room.[2] Computers will only make it worse. Once the home was a castle, a place of refuge for the family. When behind its doors, the family conducted its affairs without interruption and without outside influence. Now one can hardly eat a meal or conduct family worship without the phone ringing. Sacrosanct family time is violated daily. Friends and strangers alike barge right into the middle of the family's most private and intimate moments via technology. Again my question is, is this progress? When does life slow down enough so that we can talk? When do we enjoy our neighborhoods? Where do we experience community? In the last 100 years we have gone from life on a porch with family and neighbors to life in isolation in front of a cathode tube. Is the quality of life improving? Is ours a richer human experience? Frankly, I don't believe it anymore. Call it romanticism. Call it naivete. Call me a Luddite. We have wonderful toys today. But they have cost us too much. Growing prosperity and technological advancement do not necessarily or automatically mark human progress.

I have labored this point because I believe the church has largely failed to recognize the death of family and community or compensate for it. Rather than reaffirm traditional practices that build family life and stimulate community, it has tended to baptize secular trends that do the opposite. The small neighborhood church has given way to the large commuter church. The friendly country parson has been replaced by the suburban CEO/pastor. Older practices such as the "family altar" and the "family pew" have received

---

[1] For a highly effective critique of automobile induced suburban sprawl, read James Howard Kunstler's books *The Geography of Nowhere* (New York: Simon & Schuster, 1993) and the sequel *Home From Nowhere* (New York: Simon & Schuster, 1996). For a "new urbanist" alternative, see Duany, Plater–Zybeck and Speck's *Suburban Nation: The Rise of Sprawl and the Decline of the American Dream* (North Point Press: New York), 2000.

[2] For a powerful critique of television's effects on culture and learning, see Neil Postman, *Amusing Ourselves to Death: Public Discourse in The Age of Show Business* (New York: Penguin, 1985).

token attention, while new programs have been devised that divide families and segregate the ages. In many ways we have become too clever for our own good. We are just as guilty of "chronological arrogance," as C. S. Lewis called it, as the rest of society. Repeatedly tried and proven ways of transmitting the heart and soul of the Christian faith to others have been abandoned in favor of exciting, entertaining, novel, but ineffectual alternatives. We pride ourselves in being modern. We look down our noses at previous generations. We have had a love affair with the novel and the new. Educational, political, social, and religious fads have swept over us again and again, first possessing the field and all right thinking people, and then in a matter of months, fleeing to the curiosity shelf in our cultural museums, replaced by yet another untested novelty. The time has come to admit our error and pause to look back, before we again look ahead.

What we hope to demonstrate in the pages ahead is that by returning to the practices of previous generations we may be able to revitalize the family and the church of today. The "ancient paths" of Sunday worship, Sabbath observance, family worship, and catechizing are where spiritual vitality for the future will be found.

The "Family Pew"

What then is the first key to a Christian family's spiritual health? Though you may not have anticipated our answer, we are quite sure that we are right. The key is not new. It is not novel. It will not reveal long hidden mysteries, disclose any secret formulas, provide any new techniques, or require lengthy or costly counseling.

What is it? Simply, the first and primary key to your family's spiritual health is a commitment to the weekly public worship services of the church. The most important single commitment you have to make to ensure your family's spiritual well-being is to regular, consistent attendance at public worship.

Sound far-fetched? I'll say it even stronger. I have yet to meet a person for whom it could not be said that all of his problems, personal, marital, familial, or vocational would not be solved by such a commitment. I do not believe that the person for whom this is not true exists. By saying so, I do not minimize the seriousness of the problems that people face. Rather I maximize our confidence in the power of the gospel. So I'll say it again: we do not know of anyone of whom it could not be said, if only he were in worship week in and week out, fifty-two weeks a year, year after year, his problems would be basically solved.

That public worship is not generally recognized as playing this central role in spiritual development demonstrates the degree to which modern individualism has rotted the core out of our commitment to Christ. How is it, after all, that we receive the benefits of the death of Christ? How is His grace communicated to us? Does it just drop out of heaven? Or are there means? Yes, there are means. What are they? The *Shorter Catechism* identifies the primary means as follows:

> Q. What are the outward and ordinary means whereby Christ communicateth to us the benefits of redemption?

> A. The outward and ordinary means whereby Christ communicateth to us the benefits of redemption are, his ordinances, especially the Word, sacraments, and prayer; all which are made effectual to the elect for salvation (Q. 88).

The three primary means are the word ("especially the preaching of the Word," says the *Shorter Catechism* #89), the sacraments, and prayer. Now ask yourself, where are these three primary means normally operative? Where is the word preached? Where are the sacraments administered? And as for prayer, yes one can pray in one's closet, but don't forget the special promise of Jesus concerning prayers offered where "two or three have gathered in My name," no doubt, given the context of church discipline in Matthew 18, a reference to organized public worship (Mt 18:15–20). Jesus said,

> *'Again I say to you, that if two of you agree on earth about anything that they may ask, it shall be done for them by My Father who is in heaven...'* *(Matthew 18:19).*

There is a unique efficacy in such public prayers.

When we gather in public worship, we are ushered into the presence of Christ. He is in our midst (Mt 18:20). We do in worship what we were created to do—offer to God intelligent praise. We become more truly human at that point than at any other of human existence. Just as a child is more aware of his identity as a son in the presence of his father, or as a husband is aware of his identity as provider and protector in the presence of his wife, so we are most aware of who we are and what we were created to do as human beings at that point at which we bow in worship before our Creator and Redeemer. We are humbled as we offer to Him our praise and adoration. We are cleansed as we confess our sins. We are built up, torn down, and rebuilt again as we submit to instruction by His word (Eph 4:11ff). We are fed and united to the whole body of Christ by the sacraments. Through the bread and cup we enjoy *koinonia* with Christ and one another (1 Cor 10:16). We access His strength through "all prayer and petition" (Eph 6:18), and are thereby enabled to fight the spiritual battles of life.

The public worship services of the church are our life-line. There we are both purged and fed. There we make soul-saving contact with Christ through His word, sacraments, prayer, and the fellowship of His people. That contact, over the long haul, will change us. It will make us into the kind of people who are able to solve our own problems with the strength that the gospel provides.

The opposite view, that we can prosper spiritually on our own, apart from the public ordinances of the church and the public gatherings of the saints is foolhardy. No, it's worse than that. It is worldliness—worldly individualism, worldly pride, worldly self-sufficiency.

The metaphor of the church as a "body" is employed by the New Testament to represent both our union with Christ and mutual dependence. "The eye cannot say to the hand, 'I have no need of you'" (1 Cor 12:21). We need each other. "We who are many, are one body in Christ, and individually members of one another" (Rom 12:5). We need each other's *gifts* (see Eph 4:11–16; 1 Cor 12–14; Rom 12). We need each other's *graces* (as in the many "one anothers" found throughout the New Testament, such as love one another, be kind to one another, bear one another's burdens, etc.) We need each other's *fellowship*. So we are warned, "Let us consider how to stimulate one another to love and good deeds, not forsaking our own assembling together..." The writer to the Hebrews sees the public assembly as the primary place in which the mutual stimulation to "love and good deeds" takes place. He writes, "not forsaking our own assembling together, as is the habit of some, but encouraging one another; and all the more, as you see the day drawing near" (Heb 10:25).

How does this commitment to public worship relate to the family's spiritual well being? The effect upon parents is clear enough. Spiritually nourished parents make for better families. But the "family pew" has more in mind than sanctifying parents. When your children are brought with you into public worship, they too are sanctified. Your children, from their earliest years, will be ushered along with you into the presence of God. They will be brought under the means of grace and will experience the fellowship of God's people week after week as they mature through childhood. Beyond this, they will sit by you Sunday after Sunday, watching you publicly humble yourself before God and submit to His word. Among their earliest and warmest memories will be those of holding their parents' hands during church, sitting close to their sides, following along in the hymnal, placing money in the offering plate, and bowing their heads in prayer. Do not underestimate the cumulative effect of this witness upon covenant children. No doubt it is considerable, even incalculable.

The key to your own and your family's spiritual health is remarkably simple. Though there is considerable hype to the contrary, it involves no pilgrimages to sacred places. It requires no week-long or weekend retreats, seminars, or special programs. It depends on no special techniques or novel methodologies. You won't have to spend yet another night out. You won't need to add more meetings to an already frantic schedule. The key is to be found in the regular, ordinary, weekly worship services of the church. It is not a glamorous key, but it is the key nonetheless.

The Lord's Day

Let's explore this further. As we have noted, many well-meaning but misinformed leaders in the Christian world would have you running hither, thither, and yon to find the magic formula for spiritual growth. They would have you out every night attending meetings for prayer, study, and fellowship. They thrust before you countless tapes, study books, and methods, techniques, seminars, retreat, and programs, each promising to provide the key to your spiritual well-being and happiness. Our response is—it is not that complicated. Whatever is of fundamental importance for the Christian life has been known in every era and is reproducible in every culture. If a thing is true and necessary, it can be understood and practiced in a primitive, grass-hut civilization, an igloo, and in modern America. This is not to say that the toys of modernity can't help. We make profitable use of the tapes, videos, telephones, fax machines, and computers. We access the modern means of transportation. But we shouldn't lose sight of the greater reality that all that we need to thrive spiritually may be found down the block at our local evangelical church through its regular ministry and worship. In its failure to recognize this, the church today is little better than the world in unnecessarily contributing to the frenetic pace of modern life.

What can we do? Slow down. Stay home. Quit running mindlessly all over town. Limit yourself. And do this: *Commit yourself to the Lord's Day in the Lord's House and little else outside of the home will be necessary for the cultivation of a thriving spiritual life.*

The Puritans referred to the Lord's Day as "the market day of the soul." Six days a week one buys and sells for the sake of one's body. Sunday however we are to "trade" in spiritual commodities for the sake of our souls. All secular affairs are to be set aside. All Christians, after a "due preparing of their hearts, and ordering of their common affairs beforehand," are to "not only observe an holy rest, all the day, from their own works, words, and thoughts about their worldly employments and recreations," but also are to be engaged, "the whole time, in the public and private exercises of His worship, and in the duties of necessity and mercy" (*Westminster Confession of Faith*, XXI. 7). In other places we have argued the biblical case for the continuing obligation to keep the Lord's Day (e.g., our booklet, "Observing the Sabbath"[3]). We won't repeat the case now. Instead we will assume its validity and assert on the basis of it that the key to consistent attendance at public worship (of which we have spoken above as the key to your spiritual well-being) is a commitment to observing the Christian Sabbath. Or to state it negatively, you will never

---

[3]Available from the Independent Presbyterian Church Bookshop, P.O. Box 9266, Savannah, GA 31412-9266. See also Walter Chantry, *Call the Sabbath a Delight* (Edinburgh: The Banner of Truth Trust, 1991), and Joseph Pipa, *The Lord's Day* (Ross-shire, Scotland: Christian Focus Publications Ltd, 1997).

be able to become consistent about attending public worship until you are convinced that Sunday is not just the Lord's Morning, but the Lord's Day.

When the writers of the *Westminster Confession* joined into one chapter "Of Religious Worship and the Sabbath Day," they knew what they were doing. We are the first generation of American Protestants to have forgotten the benefits of the Sabbath command. Prior to the middle of this century, all American Protestant denominations, whether Presbyterian, Methodist, Baptist, or Episcopalian, were Sabbatarian. This was true for over 350 years, dating from the establishment of the Jamestown colony in 1607 until the mid-1960's. For generations it was understood that the Sabbath was made for man, for man's benefit (Mk 2:27, 28). But once again we have become too clever for our own good. We have crammed our schedules full of activity seven days a week. We have lost our Sabbath rest in the process. What have we given up? Hughes Old has recently written, "Any attempt at recovering a Reformed spirituality would do well carefully to study the best of the Puritan literature on the observance of the Lord's Day."[4] How is this so? What is the point?

Essentially it comes down to this. If you are not convinced that the whole of Sunday is the Lord's and not yours, you will not be consistent. You will inevitably allow other matters to interfere. Things will come up. Even the best of us will become three-fifths Christians: three out of five Sundays we will be in church. The other two we will be out of town, watching a ball game, traveling, entertaining out-of-town guests, slightly under the weather, preparing for a busy Monday, out too late on Saturday, and so on. Let me challenge you—count it up. You might be surprised at how much you miss. Though you see yourself as there "every Sunday," even *you* miss two out of five.

Return for Sunday night worship? Forget it. It's once a month at best, even for many of those who are members of the few churches that still conduct Sunday night services. If Sunday is not the Lord's Day, who is going to bother? You might be convinced that it is good to be there, the singing is good, the preaching is, well, the preaching. But if it not the Lord's Day, then one is likely to spend part of the afternoon at the mall, on the ball field, in the garden, cleaning the house, in front of the tube. By Sunday night, one will be too tired, except every fourth Sunday or so when guilt overwhelms inertia. The cumulative effect of this is significant. Instead of the ministry of 104 Sunday services (morning and evening each Sunday) one drops to under 45, 30 Sunday mornings and about 12 Sunday nights. Just like that you have forsaken the assembling of the saints and been deprived of the means of grace

---

[4]Hughes O. Old, *Christianity Today*, "Rescuing Spirituality from the Cloister," June 12, 1994.

on something like 60 occasions in a single year. How do you propose to make it up? The best of us will seek to compensate by adding midweek spiritual commitments. This will help, but only at the cost of hyping-up one's schedule in the process. For most, however, nothing will be done. The loss is absolute.

But, if you are convinced that Sunday is the "market day of the soul," then it changes everything. The questions of the Sunday services is settled—you will be there AM and PM. The fact that the issue is dead, so to speak, has a wonderfully therapeutic effect. It is like the divorce laws pre-no-fault. Because it was tough to get out of marriage, one tended to work it out and in the process find marital happiness. Eliminating options helps. Because Sunday worship is an inflexible given, everything else has to accommodate it. The Fourth Commandment tends thereby to cast its influence over the rest of the week. Life has to be organized around one's Sunday obligations. Shopping, travel, business, yard work, house work, recreation all must be finished by Saturday evening. Sunday must be cleared of all secular obligations. The blessed consequence is not only that one is free to worship twice on the Lord's Day, but one also enjoys guilt-free, refreshing rest from the concerns and labors of life. I find myself regularly falling asleep about three o' clock in the afternoon with chills of gratitude and pleasure for the rest of the Christian Sabbath. Amazingly, even for preachers for whom Sunday is the busiest day of the week, it is also the most restful.

One can understand why the prophets sometimes speak of the abandonment of the whole of Old Testament religion as "profaning the Sabbath" (Ez 20:21; 22:8; 23:38). There is a subtlety to Sabbath observance. Because it excludes secular activity, its "holy rest" comes to dominate all of life. The family's week must be organized around its inactivity. Consequently, it can function as a plumb-line, a litmus test for measuring your commitment to God. Will you submit to the Lordship of Christ in this tangible way, this way that forces you to organize your life, to prepare, to complete your secular affairs, and devote half of "your" weekend to the things of God? Will you "desist from your own ways, from seeking your own pleasure, and speaking your own word" (Is 58:13)? If you will, you will find time for all the things that really count—time for your soul, time for rest, time for the family, and time throughout the week for the rest.

Family Worship

Now we come to the heart of our concern. During the 19th century, as Sunday Schools began to be introduced in North America, resistance was encountered in a number of traditional Presbyterian churches. Their argument? That as the Sunday School was established, it would result in parental neglect of their responsibility for the spiritual training of their children. Were they right? Cause and effect would be difficult to determine. But if they were, it would be an example of the "law of unintended consequences," that is typical of the modern world. Our intentions are wonderful. We mean to improve life by the creation of labor-saving devices, the development of new methods and the provision of supplementary resources. But are we careful to examine the net effect of our innovations? Do they, in the long run, really help? *If the consequence of the proliferation of Christian meetings has been the neglect of daily family worship, then the net spiritual effect of those meetings has been negative.*

Let us assume for a moment that we all understand that the Bible commands that we conduct daily worship in homes. Read the second chapter of this work for an outline of the specifics. This was certainly the conviction of previous generations. For example, the *Westminster Confession of Faith* teaches that worship is to be conducted "in private families daily" (XXI. 6), and the Church of Scotland included in its editions of the *Westminster Standards* a *Directory for Family Worship*, its General Assembly even mandating disciplinary action against heads of households who neglected "this necessary duty."[5] Indeed, many of our Reformed forefathers believed in and practiced family worship *twice* daily (following the pattern of the morning and evening sacrifice). Family worship, they all assumed, was vital to the spiritual development of both parents and children.[6]

But today, one does not hear much about family worship.[7] No, instead we seem to have replaced it with small-group activities. These are the key, we hear again and again, to spiritual growth. Everyone needs to be in a small group. Or, it might be said, everyone needs to be in a discipleship group. Perhaps even, one needs to be involved in both. Maybe one needs to be involved in both, plus the church's prayer meeting, plus visitation, plus the choir, plus committee meetings, etc. You see my point already, I assume. Protestantism has become all but silent on the issue of family worship, a near universal practice in the recent past, and replaced it with meetings that take us out of the home and away from the family. Not only have we given up a proven method of transmitting the faith to the next generation, one that has a built-in format for Bible study, prayer, and singing, but we have done so

---

[5] See appendix 3.

[6] See for example the collection of essays by such worthies as Samuel Davies, Philip Doddridge, Henry Venn, and George Whitefield published under the name, *The Godly Family*, (Pittsburg: Soli Deo Gloria, 1993). See also the essay by Hughes Oliphant Old, "Matthew Henry and the Discipline of Family Prayer," found in *Calvin Studies VII*, Papers Presented at the Colloquium on Calvin Studies at Davidson College, January 28-29, 1994.

[7] Thankfully, there are of late a growing number of exceptions to this claim. For example, the wonderful essay by Douglas F. Kelly, "Family Worship: Biblical, Reformed, and Viable for Today," in Frank J. Smith and David C. Lachman, *Worship in the Presence of God* (Greenville, South Carolina: Greenville Presbyterian Theological Seminary Press, 1992); Kerry Ptacek, *Family Worship: Biblical Basis, Historical Reality, Current Need* (Greenville, South Carolina: Greenville Presbyterian Theological Seminary Press, 1994).

for alternatives that add to our already hectic pace of life and take us away from our spouses, children, and neighbors.

I like small-group Bible studies. I will get more involved with them at a later stage in life, when my children are not so young and my wife and I are able to attend them together. But in the meantime we have a discipleship group, and if you are a parent with children at home, so do you. Everyday little eyes are watching. Sooner than we realize, they become aware of discrepancies between what we say and what we do. The family, in this respect, is the truest of all proving grounds for authentic Christianity. Parents either practice what they preach or become the surest means of sending their children to hell yet devised by man or the devil. Daily family worship forces the issues of Christian piety before the family every 24 hours. It forces parents in the roles of preachers, evangelists, worship leaders, intercessors, and pastors. Who is adequate for this? No one, or course. He who would attempt to be so, must necessarily be forced to his knees. Children growing up with the daily experience of seeing their parents humbled in worship, focusing on spiritual things, submitting to the authority of the word, catechizing and otherwise instructing their children will not easily turn from Christ. Our children should grow up with the voices of their fathers pleading for their souls in prayer ringing in their ears, leading to their salvation, or else haunting them for the rest of their lives.

If your children are in your home for 18 years, you have 6,570 occasions (figuring a six day week) for family worship. If you learn a new Psalm or hymn each month, they will be exposed to 216 in those 18 years. If you read a chapter a day, you will complete the Bible four and a half times in 18 years. Every day (if you follow our format) they will affirm a creed or recite the law. Every day they will confess their sins and plead for mercy. Every day they will intercede on behalf of others. Think in terms of the long view. What is the cumulative impact of just 15 minutes of this each day, day after day, week after week, month after month, year after year, for 18 years? At the rate of six days a week (excluding Sunday), one spends and hour and a half a week in family worship (about the length of a home Bible study), 78 hours a year (about the length of the meeting hours of seven weekend retreats), 1,404 hours over the course of 18 years (about the length of the assembly hours of 40 week-long summer camps, assuming about 30 such hours in an average week-long camp). When you establish your priorities, think in terms of the cumulative effect of this upon your children. Think of the cumulative effect of this upon *you*, after 40 or 60 or 80 years of daily family worship—all this without having to drive anywhere.

Catechism

Finally, we commend the catechizing of children, a grand old Protestant tradition which regrettably has fallen on hard times. Few catechize their children any more. For some, the word itself sounds archaic or like something the Catholics used to do. In actual fact, it is an ancient practice reaching all the way back to the earliest centuries of the church. It was revived in the 16th century by the *Protestant* Reformers so successfully that even the Roman Catholics began to mimic them. Catechisms were written by Luther, Calvin, Bullinger, and nearly all the major Reformers. In keeping with this tradition, the Westminster Assembly produced two catechisms, the *Shorter* for children, and the *Larger* for adults. The former has been the most popular and widely used in the English language since the mid-17th century.

Should you catechize your children? Yes, you should, and for a number of reasons.

1. It is a tried and *proven method of religious instruction*. For generations Protestants have successfully transmitted the content of the Christian faith to their children through Catechisms. This was taken so seriously in Puritan New England that a child could be removed from its parents' custody if they failed to catechize him or her! Admission to the communion table in Scotland for generations was preceded by the successful recitation of the *Shorter Catechism*. It was not uncommon in 19th century Presbyterian homes in America that the *Shorter Catechism* would be completed during a child's sixth year. According to John Leith, 17,000 Presbyterian youth memorized the *Shorter Catechism* and had their names published in the *Christian Observer* in 1928, the year in which he achieved that feat. Education pedagogues come and go. Here is a method that works.

2. It is *simple*. It doesn't require additional resources. Any parent can catechize any child using no more than a small booklet. (In the process, the parent may learn more than the child!) But since the Bible places the responsibility of Christian education squarely upon Christian parents (Deut 6:4ff, Eph 6:1ff), here is a method easily adopted by parents.

3. It is *content-rich*. The old catechisms are rich reservoirs of theological, devotional, and practical content. Fully 40% of the *Shorter Catechism* is concerned with ethics (the Law of God) and nearly 10% with prayer. God, man, sin, Christ, faith, repentance, and so on are all given succinct, accurate definitions. Children nurtured on the catechism will be formidable theologians in an age of irrationalism and general mindlessness.

Here are a couple of practical reasons as well.

1. Memory is a faculty that should be developed. One might liken memory to a muscle—it grows when exercised and shrinks when neglected. J. A. Motyer, former Principal of Trinity College, Bristol, and lecturer in Old Testament and Hebrew once said that he noticed a significant change in the capacity of his students to learn Hebrew declensions. What was typically learned upon first hearing by students in the 1930's and 40's was the labor of a week in the 1970's and 80's. Obviously, it is a great asset in life to have what we call a "good memory." What has often not been understood is that having such is more a matter of work than nature.

2. Memorizing logical, structured, conceptual material like the *Shorter Catechism* actually contributes to mental development. J. S. Mill, no friend of orthodox Christianity, claimed in his famous essay, *On Liberty*, that the Scots had become mental philosophers of the first order through their study of the Bible and the *Shorter Catechism*. Douglas Kelly, noting the work of Scottish theologian T. F. Torrance, states that "children brought up on the Catechism have a greater capacity for conceptual thinking (as opposed to merely pictorial thinking) than those who never memorized it."[8] It provides matter (theological matter!) for building the mental framework within which rational thought can take place. While not superior to the memorization of Scripture, this does explain why the Catechisms are to be memorized alongside of Scripture.

The Anglo-Catholic essayist, J. A. Froude, who spoke of "the Scottish peasant as the most remarkable man in Europe," traced the dignity, intellect, and character of the typical Scottish peasant up to that time, "as largely flowing from the memorization of the *Shorter Catechism*," says Douglas Kelly again.[9] Let the educational fads come and go. Concentrate on a method that has stood the test of time.[10]

A Simpler Life

Now pull together the various threads. Instead of spiritual concerns contributing to an already frantic pace of life, the family should commit itself to the time-proven, biblically-based means of spiritual nurture—public and family worship. In these settings great Psalms and hymns are sung, children are catechized, sins are confessed, and the Scriptures are read and taught. Instead of running all over town, children and parents heading out in every direction, commitments are focused upon the Lord's Day services and daily

---

[8]Douglas F. Kelly, "The Westminster Shorter Catechism," Carson and Hall (ed), in *To Glorify and Enjoy God*, (Edinburgh: The Banner of Truth Trust, 1994), p. 124.

[9]Ibid., p. 125.

[10]Regarding the concern that children don't understand what they are memorizing, David Calhoun, in his *History of Princeton Seminary, Volume 1: Faith and Learning (1812-1868)*, (Edinburgh: The Banner of Truth Trust, 1994), records the following comments of Robert Hamill Nassau, career medical missionary in Africa. After noting his ability to answer Dr. Hodges' classroom questions in the language of the *Shorter Catechism*, he said,

> "I thus had a reply for any one who objected to children being taught Catechism, on the ground that they could not understand it. Of course, they did not. Neither had I, in my childhood. But memorizing is easy in childhood. With that Catechism in memory it was an advantage to have its splendid 'form of words' when I reached an age at which I *could* understand them" (p. 363).

worship at home. Life is simplified! Not only will we be using means that are more fruitful than the modern alternatives, and more likely to result in the salvation and sanctification of covenant children and parents alike, but the pace of life will slow, allowing more rather than less time for families to be together. Public worship, family worship, the Lord's Day, and catechizing are the "ancient paths" in which we will find "rest" for our souls.

Chapter Two

MAKING THE COMMITMENT TO
FAMILY WORSHIP

Are you interested at this point but wondering how to proceed? You may be in need of three kinds of reinforcement: First, you may need to be more fully convinced that this is something that you *must* do; Second, you may need practical, *"how-to"* help in establishing a routine; Third, you may need help in *what* to do and why. Let us explore these issues.

More Reasons Why

Let us return now to the Biblical, theological, historical, and practical arguments for family worship as a necessary and important discipline for your family. The reasons may be outlined as follows:

1. *Biblical*—The original church was the family and the original worship was family worship. Undoubtedly this was true before the fall. Afterward, while there was yet but one family we read "then men began to call upon the name of the Lord" (Gen. 4:26). Later, Abraham was directed to "command his children and his household after him to keep the way of the Lord" (Gen. 18:19). Job "rose up early in the morning and offered burnt offerings according to the number of his children...." (Job 1:5). The norm prior to the instituting of public worship under Moses was family-based worship. "The families of the Patriarchs were all the churches God had in the world for the time," says Thomas Manton in his "Epistle to the Reader" of *The Westminster Confession of Faith*. However even public ordinances once introduced did not supersede family worship. Families continued to be directed, to "teach [the commandments] to your children" (Deut. 6:7). The Psalmist says that God commands fathers "that they should teach [the praises of the Lord] to their children," and that each succeeding generation should "arise and tell them to their children, that they should put their confidence in God, not forget the works of God, but keep His commandments" (Ps 78:4-7). As we move into the New Testament, Timothy seems to have been taught at home by his grandmother and mother (2 Tim. 1:5, 3:15); Jesus encouraged the gathering of two or three (Matt. 18:20); and parents are exhorted to rear their children in the "discipline and instruction of the Lord" (Eph. 6:1-4). Among the early

church fathers, both Clement and Tertullian strongly commend family worship, giving us some indication of the persistence of the practice in the earliest centuries of the church.[11]

2. *Theological*—David based his devotional practice upon that of the temple. The morning and evening sacrifices provided the pattern for his prayers, which he offered morning and evening, and to which he even applied the language of sacrifice (Pss. 5:3 and 141:2; cf Ps. 51:16, 17). We continue this worship pattern in the New Testament, like David, substituting sacrificial animals with "a sacrifice of praise... the fruit of our lips" (Heb. 13:15). It is our Christian duty to worship God daily.

3. *Historical*—While the Medieval church held daily mass based on the preceding principle, Protestants moved daily worship into the home, where godly fathers served as "priests" in their homes. Thus the pattern in the best Protestant homes became that of daily private (personal) devotions and daily family worship. "What the liturgy of the hours was for monks of the Middle Ages, the discipline of family prayer was for the Puritans," says Hughes Old. "The Puritans," he continues, "whether on the Connecticut frontiers or in the heart of London, whether they were Cambridge scholars or Shropshire cotters, gave great importance to maintaining a daily discipline of family prayer."[12] For generations outstanding Protestant devotional writers, from Richard Baxter to Matthew Henry to Philip Dodderidge to Charles Spurgeon, have vigorously promoted it. We would be wise to heed and foolish to ignore their counsel.

4. *Practical*—There are a number of good reasons for having daily family worship as well:

   i) it gives parents a daily opportunity to model humble dependence upon God;

   ii) it ensures daily intercessory prayer on behalf of the family's needs;

   iii) it provides a daily setting for reading and instruction from the Bible (see Deut. 6:7ff);

   iv) it provides a forum for reinforcing the memorization of the fixed forms of public worship (eg. Creeds, Doxology, Lord's Prayer, etc.).

   v) it draws the family together at least once daily, no mean achievement in today's hectic and fragmented world;

---

[11]See Ptacek, *Family Worship*,pp. 40ff.

[12]Old, *Calvin Studies*, p. 69.

"The families of Christians should be little churches," says Richard Baxter.[13] Each day the family should assemble to offer God its praise, to hear His word, to give thanks for His mercies.

Getting Started

Do you wish you and your family were having regular family worship, but aren't? Wondering how to get started? We would like to make the following recommendations to help you along.

1. *Remember, there is nothing to getting started like actually getting started.* Doesn't sound helpful? We're making a point—like everything else that is valuable but requires discipline and sacrifice (losing weight, stopping drinking, getting an education, staying married, attending worship services), it finally comes down to doing it. Start! Do it!

2. *Settle on a routine that will work most days of the week.* For example, at the breakfast table, or at the dinner table, or at bedtime, etc. Let it become as regular and habitual as brushing your teeth. The older authors (eg. J. W. Alexander in *Thoughts on Family Worship*)[14] strongly suggests a fixed time throughout the week, for example 6:30 each morning or 5:30 each evening.

3. *Adjust for irregularities.* If Monday and Thursday nights one of you is out, then have your family worship in the mornings on those days. Plan ahead and make this adjustment a part of the routine. Thus, Tuesday, Wednesday, Friday and Saturday, family worship might be in the evenings. Monday and Thursday it might be in the mornings. Sunday it is at church morning and evening. This irregular schedule may not be as desirable as the fixed time, but it may be the best that can be done in today's world.

4. *Persevere.* If you miss once, don't despair, but don't miss twice, either. Persist and your routine will become routine!

Admittedly the matter of discipline and routine is neither common nor popular today. Yet Scripture urges us to "redeem the time, for the days are evil" (Eph 5:16). The Psalmist exhorts us to "number our days" (Ps 90:12). Time is a gift of God. We have been given a limited amount of it. Once it is past it is gone. Consequently sound stewardship requires that we make every day count that God gives to us. Such is only possible if we bring order to our lives and plan for our priorities. Life must be lived *intentionally*. We will never

---

[13]Old, *Calvin Studies*, p. 85, n25. The quotation is from Baxter's *Christian Directory*.

[14]J.W. Alexander, *Thoughts on Family Worship* (1847), was bound together with B.M. Palmer, *The Family in its Civil and Churchly Aspects* (1876) and published as *The Family* (Harrisonburg, Va.: Sprinkle Publications), 1981.

regularly do what we don't set out intentionally to do. J.I. Packer's summation of the Puritan (ie. Biblical) outlook on order in family life is right to the point:

> Puritan teachers thought humane family life, in which Christian love and joy would find full and free expression, could not be achieved till the ordered pattern they envisage—the regular authority-structure and daily routine—had been firmly established. Their passion to please God expressed itself in an ardor for order; their vision of the good and godly life was of a planned, well-thought-out flow of activities in which all obligations were recognized and met, and time was found for everything that mattered: for personal devotion, for family worship, for household tasks, for wage-earning employment, for intimacy with spouse and children, for Sabbath rest, and whatever else one's calling or callings required.[15]

If this "ardor for order" is characteristic of us as well, we will find time for daily family devotions.

Suggested Elements

We are convinced that family worship ought to be *worship*, not games, not entertainment, not a discussion (though discussion may occur), not "family time" (though the family is together), but a devotional exercise. Consequently, even in a family with young children, the elements in family worship ought to be those of public worship (minus the sacraments) adapted for the more informal family setting, but still predominantly serious and substantial. Furthermore, such an approach will have the salutary effect of family and public worship reinforcing and building upon one another. Family worship that employs the commonly used elements and forms of public worship (eg. Creed, Doxology, Lord's Prayer, Ten Commandments, etc.) will hasten memorization and enable active participation of small children in the "family pew" at a very young age.

The following list of elements provides an outline of the kinds of things that you might do, adapting the particulars to the needs of your family (ages of your children, etc.).

1. *Singing*—Start to sing Psalms and hymns to your children on the day you bring them home from the hospital. By age two they will begin to pick up the tunes and some words; by age four they will be able to sing a host of hymns and Psalms such as those being suggested in this work. On Saturday sing the Sunday hymns in preparation for the Lord's Day. chapter VIII of this work provides a selection of the best hymns and Psalms for family use. For a larger collection, our recommended songbooks are:

---

[15]J.I. Packer, *A Quest for Godliness* (Wheaton: Crossway Books, 1990). p. 273.

Trinity Hymnal[16]
Trinity Psalter or *Trinity Psalter Music Edition*[17]

2. *Prayer*—Teach them to bow their heads, fold their hands, and 1) pray ACTS, the whole range of **A**-doration, **C**-onfession, **T**-hanksgiving, and **S**-upplication ("Our Father in heaven, we worship you, we praise you... we confess our sins... we thank you for Jesus who died for our sins... bless Mommy and Daddy," etc.); and 2) pray the Lord's Prayer, which by age four or so they may have committed to memory. For examples of family prayers, see the following:

Matthew Henry, *A Method for Prayer* (Greenville: Reformed Academic Press, 1994), pp 214-241.

The Directory for Family Worship, Section IX (Found in chapter VII of this work).

3. *Confession of Faith*—Begin with the Apostles' Creed; once mastered, go on to the Children's Catechism, then the Shorter Catechism (the catechisms may be found in chapter VI of this work). The Law of God and the Beatitudes may be used either as preparation for prayer or an affirmation of faith.

4. *Teaching*—Get a good Bible story book as a guide and read or tell the stories in such a way as makes them live. Remember that much of the Biblical revelation is in the form of stories. Use them. As children get older, move from children's versions to adult. We have found the following to be useful and edifying children's "Bibles." They are listed in order of sophistication, from the simplest to the more mature:

Read-Aloud Bible Stories, Vols. 1–4 (Chicago: Moody Press, 1982–1995).

Twenty basic Bible stories, beautifully illustrated, appeals to all ages, even the very youngest. Ages 1–4.

The Beginner's Bible (Sisters, Oregon: Questar Publishers, 1991).

Provides good overview of Bible stories, though the happy-face pictures tend to undermine themes of sin and judgment. Ages 2–6.

The Bible in Pictures for Little Eyes (Chicago: Moody Press, 1956).

Combines texts written by the *Living Bible's* Kenneth Taylor with beautiful artwork from previous generations. Contains 184 stories which when read in combination with suggested Scripture reading are very effective. Ages 4-12.

---

[16]Philadelphia, Pennsylvania: Great Commission Publications, Inc,. 1990.

[17]Pittsburgh, Pennsylvania: Crown and Covenant Publications, 1994; Pittsburgh: Crown and Covenant, 1999.

The Children's Daily Devotional Bible (Nashville: Thomas Nelson Publishers, 1996).

> Two-hundred sixty Scripture portions, Contemporary English Version, organized for fifty-two weeks, five readings per week. As with the others, beautifully illustrated. Ages 4+ (when read aloud).

The Children's Story Bible (Edinburgh: The Banner of Truth Trust; Grand Rapids: Eerdmans Publishing Co, 1935).

> A classic, written by Catherine F. Vos, wife of Princeton theologian Gerhardus Vos. Ages 8-12.

There may also be occasions when thematic studies are desirable. The following are recommended for family devotions:

Sinclair B. Ferguson, *The Big Book of Questions and Answers* (Ross-shire, Scotland: Christian Focus Publications Ltd, 1997).

Sinclair B. Ferguson, *The Big Book of Questions and Answers about Jesus* (Ross-shire, Scotland: Christian Focus Publications Ltd, 2000).

> Using a question and answer format, illustrations, and interactive material, seventy-seven questions are asked and answered spanning creation, fall, redemption, and Christian living. Excellent. Ages 5 and older.

Stephen Barcliff, *My Best Bible Word Book Ever* (Sisters, Oregon: Questar Publishers, Inc., 1992).

> Forty-five lessons are placed in Biblical order with detailed illustrations portraying life in Bible times. Extra pages of illustrations of weapons, musical instruments, tools and so on are included. Very good for helping young ones visualize the meaning of Bible words. Ages 4 and older.

Sandy Silverthorne, *The Awesome Book of Bible Facts* (Eugene, Oregon: Harvest Book Publishers, 1994). Forty-seven lessons arranged by order of appearance in Bible, loaded with facts, comparison between Biblical phenomena and the modern world, and humorously illustrated.

These suggestions are not exhaustive and no doubt other excellent alternatives are available. It needs to be said as well, that most reading of the (adult) Bible itself, has still proven to be the most edifying of devotional exercises for our family. The children's editions tend to edit-out controversial or "negative" matters (*e.g.*, divorce) from which some of our most stimulating discussions have come.

By using these elements in daily family worship you will be providing regular spiritual instruction for your family as well as preparing them for the public worship services of the church. At an early age, your children will be able to join in with the congregation and repeat the parts that they have learned at home. In the process, the public worship service becomes the focal point of your week. Your family devotions lead up to it. The service itself becomes a "family time," when parents model public devotion to God, and children learn to worship Him.

Chapter Three

AN OUTLINE FOR FAMILY WORSHIP

1. **Call to Worship/Prayer of Praise**
   The Creator
   His Attributes
   The Redeemer
   The Holy Spirit
   Our Need of and Longing For God

2. **Psalm and Hymns**
   Psalm/Hymn of the Month
   Psalms/Hymns for Review

3. **Creeds and Commandments**
   Apostles' Creed
   Nicene Creed
   The Law of God
   The Beatitudes

4. **Scripture Reading**

5. **Prayers of Confession, Intercession and Thanksgiving**
   Scriptural Encouragements to Prayer
   Scriptural Expressions of Confession and Pleas for Forgiveness
   Scriptural Promises of Pardon
   Scriptural Petitions
   The Lord's Prayer

6. **Ascriptions of Praise**
   Doxology
   Gloria Patri

7. **Benediction**
   Aaronic
   Apostolic

Chapter Four

ORDER FOR FAMILY WORSHIP

An abundance of resources is provided under each of the following headings. Notice first, that these helps are mainly biblical. Under the heading of each of the prayers (Praise, Confession, Intercession) follows a long list of Scripture texts which may provide suitable devotional language. Here again we are consciously attempting to revive a venerable practice of evangelical Protestantism, that of enriching prayer with Scriptural expressions and allusions. For generations Protestants were taught to pray by studying works such as Matthew Henry's *A Method for Prayer*[18] and Isaac Watt's *A Guide to Prayer*.[19] An edition of each is still in print and highly recommended, while an outline and summary of the latter is provided in chapter VII's "Historical Resources". A more recent work, *Handbook to Prayer: Praying Scripture Back to God* by Kenneth Boa, is an excellent guide to learning to pray in the language of the Bible, which we highly recommend.[20] Scripture-enriched prayers are particularly effective as means of grace because faith comes by hearing the word of God: scriptural praise inspires, scriptural confession humbles, scriptural assurance soothes, scriptural petitions encourage, scriptural promises strengthen.

Second, it is our intent that family worship *need not last more than 15 to 20 minutes*. Of course, it may always be longer, but it is not wise to be overly ambitious. A quarter of an hour each day is better than one hour every two weeks. The "service" should move briskly (but not hurriedly) from an opening prayer or call, to the singing of several Psalms and hymns, to the reciting of *one* of the creeds or "commandments," followed by the reading of Scripture. Then the family kneels for a comprehensive prayer of confession and intercession that concludes with the Lord's Prayer. Finally, the service is concluded with the Doxology or Gloria Patri and a benediction. This order may easily be expanded, contracted, or otherwise altered according to circumstances.

---

[18]Matthew Henry, *A Method for Prayer*, ed. J. Ligon Duncan, III (Greenville, South Carolina: Reformed Academic Press, 1994 [1716]).

[19]Isaac Watts, *A Guide to Prayer* (Edinburgh: The Banner of Truth Trust, 2001 [1715]).

[20] Kenneth Boa, *Handbook to Prayer: Praying Scripture Back to God* (Atlanta: Trinity House Publishers, 1993).

1.   Call to Worship/Prayer of Praise

One or more of the following texts may be used as calls to worship or as building blocks out of which a prayer of praise may be constructed. This reading and/or prayer sets the tone for the occasion, marking a serious transition from other activities to worship.

> The Lord is near to all who call upon Him, to all who call upon Him in truth. (Ps 145:18)

> For thus says the high and exalted One Who lives forever, whose name is Holy, "I dwell on a high and holy place, and also with the contrite and lowly of spirit . . ." (Is 57:15a)

> But the Lord is in His holy temple. Let all the earth be silent before Him. (Hab 2:20)

> For from the rising of the sun even to its setting, My name will be great among the nations, and in every place incense is going to be offered in My name, and a grain offering that is pure; for My name will be great among the nations, says the Lord of hosts. (Mal 1:11)

> God is spirit, and those who worship Him must worship in spirit and truth. (Jn 4:24)

> I urge you therefore, brethren, by the mercies of God, to present your bodies a living and holy sacrifice, acceptable to God, which is your spiritual service of worship. (Rom 12:1)

> Therefore, since we receive a kingdom which cannot be shaken, let us show gratitude, by which we may offer to God an acceptable service with reverence and awe. (Heb 12:28)

The Creator

> O Lord, our Lord, how majestic is Thy name in all the earth, who hast displayed Thy splendor above the heavens! (Ps 8:1)

> The heavens are telling of the glory of God; and their expanse is declaring the work of His hands. (Ps 19:1)

> The earth is the Lord's and all it contains, the world, and those who dwell in it. For He has founded it upon the seas, and established it upon the rivers. (Ps 24:1, 2)

> Lord, Thou hast been our dwelling place in all generations. Before the mountains were born, or Thou didst give birth to the earth and the world, even from everlasting to everlasting, Thou art God. (Ps 90:1)

> Come, let us worship and bow down; let us kneel before the Lord our Maker. For He is our God, and we are the people of His pasture, and the sheep of His hand. (Ps 95:6, 7a)

Our help is in the name of the Lord who made heaven and earth. (Ps 124:8)

Worthy are Thou, our Lord and our God, to receive glory and honor and power; for Thou didst create all things, and because of Thy will they existed, and were created. (Rev 4:11)

His Attributes

The Lord, the Lord God, compassionate and gracious, slow to anger, and abounding in lovingkindness and truth; who keeps lovingkindness for thousands, who forgives iniquity, transgression and sin; yet He will by no means leave the guilty unpunished, visiting the iniquity of the fathers on the children and on the grandchildren to the third and fourth generations. (Ex 34:6b, 7)

Thine, O Lord, is the greatness and the power and the glory and the victory and the majesty, indeed everything that is in the heavens and the earth; Thine is the dominion, O Lord, and Thou dost exalt Thyself as head over all. Both riches and honor come from Thee, and Thou dost rule over all, and in Thy hand is power and might; and it lies in Thy hand to make great, and to strengthen everyone. Now therefore, our God, we thank Thee, and praise Thy glorious name. (1 Chr 29:11-13)

Behold, the nations are like a drop from a bucket, and are regarded as a speck of dust on the scales; all the nations are as nothing before Him, they are regarded by Him as less than nothing and meaningless. (Is 40:15a, 17)

Ah, Lord God! Behold, Thou hast made the heavens and the earth by Thy great power and by Thine outstretched arm! Nothing is too difficult for Thee, who showest lovingkindness to thousands, but repayest the iniquity of the fathers into the bosom of their children after them, O great and mighty God. The Lord of hosts is His name; great in counsel and mighty in deed, whose eyes are open to all the ways of the sons of men, giving to everyone according to his ways and according to the fruit of his deeds. (Jer 32:17-19)

The Lord's lovingkindnesses indeed never cease, for His compassions never fail. They are new every morning; great is Thy faithfulness. (Lam 3:22,23)

Oh, the depth of the riches both of the wisdom and knowledge of God! How unsearchable are His judgments and unfathomable His ways! For who has known the mind of the Lord, or who became His counselor? Or who has first given to Him that it might be paid back to Him again? For from Him and through Him and to Him are all things. To Him be the glory forever. Amen. (Rom 11:33-36)

Now to the King eternal, immortal, invisible, the only God, be honor and glory forever and ever. Amen. (1 Tim 1:17)

He is the blessed and only Sovereign, the King of kings and Lord of lords; who alone possesses immortality and dwells in unapproachable light; whom no man has seen or can see. To Him be honor and eternal dominion! Amen. (1 Tim 6:15, 16)

Every good thing bestowed and every perfect gift is from above, coming down from the Father of lights, with whom there is no variation, or shifting shadow. (Jas 1:17)

And there is no creature hidden from His sight, but all things are open and laid bare to the eyes of Him with whom we have to do. (Heb 4:13)

Holy, Holy, Holy, is the Lord God, the Almighty, who was and who is and who is to come. (Rev 4:8b)

"God is a Spirit, infinite, eternal, and unchangeable in His being, wisdom, power, holiness, justice, goodness, and truth." (Shorter Catechism Q #4)

The Redeemer

Blessed be the God and Father of our Lord Jesus Christ, who has blessed us with every spiritual blessing in the heavenly places in Christ, just as He chose us in Him before the foundation of the world, that we should be holy and blameless before Him. In love He predestined us to adoption as sons through Jesus Christ to Himself, according to the kind intention of His will, to the praise of the glory of His grace, which He freely bestowed on us in the Beloved. (Eph 1:3–6)

For He delivered us from the domain of darkness, and transferred us to the kingdom of His beloved Son, in whom we have redemption, the forgiveness of sins. And He is the image of the invisible God, the first-born of all creation. For by Him all things were created, both in the heavens and on earth, visible and invisible, whether thrones or dominions or rulers or authorities all things have been created by Him and for Him. And He is before all things, and in Him all things hold together. He is also head of the body, the church; and He is the beginning, the first-born from the dead; so that He Himself might come to have first place in everything. For it was the Father's good pleasure for all the fulness to dwell in Him, and through Him to reconcile all things to Himself, having made peace through the blood of His cross; through Him, I say, whether things on earth or things in heaven. (Col 1:13–20)

Worthy art Thou to take the book, and to break its seals; for Thou wast slain, and didst purchase for God with Thy blood men from every tribe and tongue and people and nation. And Thou hast made them to be a kingdom and priests to our God; and they will reign upon the earth ... Worthy is the Lamb that was slain to receive power and riches and wisdom and might and honor and glory and blessing ... To Him who sits on the throne, and to the Lamb, be blessing and honor and glory and dominion forever and ever. (Rev 5:9, 10, 12, 13b)

He is the Prince of Peace (Is 9:6), the Prince of Life, the Holy and Righteous One (Acts 3:15, 16), the Word of God, who was in the beginning with God, who was God, through whom all things came into being and apart from whom nothing came into being that has come into being. In Him was life; and the life was the light of men; and who became flesh and dwelt among us and we beheld His glory, glory as the only begotten from the Father, full of grace and truth (Jn 1:1–4, 14); the Son of God (Rom 1:4), our Lord and God (Jn 20:28), who is over all, God blessed forever (Rom 9:5). In Him are hidden all the treasures of wisdom and knowledge; in Him all the fullness of Deity dwells in bodily form (Col 2:3, 9). He is heir of all things, the radiance of His glory and the exact representation of His nature. He upholds all things by the word of His power (Heb 1:2,3). He is the Bread of Life (Jn 6:35), the Light of the world (Jn 8:12), the Resurrection and the Life (Jn 11:25), the Good Shepherd (Jn 10:11), the Vine (Jn 15:1, 5), the Way, the Truth and the Life (Jn 14:6), the Alpha and Omega, the beginning and the end (Rev 21:6), the root and the offspring of David, the bright morning star (Rev 21:18). He is the Savior of the World (1 Jn 4:14); the Lamb of God who takes away the sin of the world (Jn 1:28); Immanuel, God with us, who saves His people from their sins (Mt 1:21–23), who loves us, and released us from our sins by His blood, and made us to be a kingdom, priests to His God and father (Rev 1:6); He gave His life a ransom for many (Mk 10:45); He bore our sins in His body on the cross (1 Pet 2:24); though He knew no sin He became sin that we might become the righteousness of God in Him (2 Cor 5:21); He is the only mediator between God and man (1 Tim 2:5); our Advocate with the Father, Jesus Christ the righteous (1 Jn 2:1); who always lives to make intercession for us (Heb 7:25); the same yesterday and today, yes and forever. (Heb 13:8)

The Holy Spirit

He is the Eternal Spirit, the Breath of the Almighty (Heb 9:14; Job 32:8). He is the Holy Spirit of promise, by whom we are sealed in Christ and who is given as a pledge of our inheritance (Eph 1:13,14). He is the Spirit of understanding, of counsel and strength

(Is 11:2), of wisdom and of revelation (Eph 1:17), the Helper, the Spirit of Truth who abides with us and is in us, who teaches us all things, and leads us into all truth (Jn 14:16, 17, 25; 16:13); who searches all things, and convicts the world concerning sin, and righteousness, and judgment; who glorifies Christ and discloses the things of Christ (1 Cor 2:10; Jn 16:8, 14). By Him we are born again (Jn 3:l), are enabled to say Jesus is Lord (1 Cor 12:3), are baptized, are gifted for the common good (1 Cor 12:7, 13), whose fruit is godliness (Gal 5:22, 23), and by whom we walk, are led, and in whom we live, and who intercedes for us. (Gal 5:16, 18, 25; Rom 8:26, 27)

Our Need of and Longing for God

I love Thee, O Lord, my strength. The Lord is my rock and my fortress and my deliverer, my God, my rock, in whom I take refuge; my shield and the horn of my salvation, my stronghold. I call upon the Lord, who is worthy to be praised, and I am saved from my enemies. (Ps 18:1–3)

One thing I have asked from the Lord, that I shall seek: that I may dwell in the house of the Lord all the days of my life, to behold the beauty of the Lord, and to meditate in His temple ... When Thou didst say, "Seek My face," my heart said to Thee, "Thy face, O Lord, I shall seek". (Ps 27:4, 8)

As the deer pants for the water brooks, so my soul pants for Thee, O God. My soul thirsts for God, for the living God. (Ps 42:1–2a)

God is our refuge and strength, a very present help in trouble. (Ps 46:1)

O God, Thou are my God; I shall seek Thee earnestly; my soul thirsts for Thee, my flesh yearns for Thee, in a dry and weary land where there is no water. Thus I have beheld Thee in the sanctuary, to see Thy power and Thy glory. Because Thy lovingkindness is better than life, my lips shall praise Thee. So I will bless Thee as long as I live; I will lift up my hands in Thy name. (Ps 63:1–4)

Whom have I in heaven but Thee? And besides Thee, I desire nothing on earth. My flesh and my heart may fail, but God is the strength of my heart and my portion forever ... But as for me, the nearness of God is my good; I have made the Lord God my refuge, that I may tell of all Thy works. (Ps 73:25–26, 28)

How lovely are Thy dwelling places, O Lord of hosts! My soul longed and even yearned for the courts of the Lord; my heart and my flesh sing for joy to the living God ... How blessed are those who dwell in Thy house! ... For a day in Thy courts is better than a thousand outside. I would rather stand at the threshold of the house of my God, than dwell in the tents of wickedness. For the Lord God is a sun and shield; the Lord gives grace and glory; no good thing does He withhold from those who walk uprightly. O Lord of hosts, how blessed is the man who trusts in Thee! (Ps 84: 1, 2, 4, 10–12)

...We have waited for Thee eagerly; Thy name, even Thy memory, is the desire of our souls. At night my soul longs for Thee, indeed, my spirit within me seeks Thee diligently... (Is 26:8b–9a)

Oh, that Thou wouldst rend the heavens and come down. Bow Thy heavens, O Lord, and come down. (Is 64:1a; Ps 144:5a)

2.   Psalms and Hymns

We have provided the texts of 60 Psalms and 60 hymns in chapter VIII, enough for a new selection each month over a ten year period. We suggest alternating between hymns and Psalms month by month, and have provided tables outlining usage over a 10–year period.

Monthly—*select one for singing each day in a given month*

For review—*continually review first stanzas of those Psalms/hymns that you have learned*

3.   Creeds and Commandments

Use one of the following texts. Vary to avoid formalism. Repeat to facilitate memorization.

Apostles' Creed[21]

I believe in God the Father Almighty, Maker of heaven and earth:

And in Jesus Christ his only Son, our Lord; who was conceived by the Holy Ghost, born of the Virgin Mary, suffered under Pontius Pilate, was crucified, dead, and buried; he descended into hell; the third day he arose again from the dead; he ascended into heaven, and sitteth on the right hand of God the Father Almighty; from thence he shall come to judge the quick and the dead.

---

[21]Although not written by the apostles, the Apostles' Creed is a concise summary of their teachings. It originated as a baptismal confession, probably in the second century, and developed into its present form by the sixth or seventh century. Though not specifically commended by the Westminster Assembly for use in public worship, it was bound with the *Confession* and *Catechisms*.

I believe in the Holy Ghost; the holy catholic church; the communion of saints; the forgiveness of sins; the resurrection of the body; and the life everlasting. Amen.

Nicene Creed[22]

We believe in one God, the Father Almighty, Maker of heaven and earth, of all things visible and invisible.

And in one Lord Jesus Christ, the only-begotten Son of God, begotten of his Father before all worlds, God of God, Light of Light, very God of very God, begotten, not made, being of one substance with the Father; by whom all things were made; who for us and for our salvation came down from heaven, and was incarnate by the Holy Spirit of the virgin Mary, and was made man; and was crucified also for us under Pontius Pilate; he suffered and was buried; and the third day he rose again according to the Scriptures, and ascended into heaven, and is seated at the right hand of the Father; and he shall come again, with glory, to judge both the living and the dead; whose kingdom shall have no end.

And we believe in the Holy Spirit, the Lord and giver of life, who proceeds from the Father and the Son; who with the Father and the Son together is worshiped and glorified; who spoke by the prophets; and we believe in one holy catholic and apostolic church; we acknowledge on baptism for the remission of sins; and we look for the resurrection of the dead, and the life of the world to come. Amen.

Westminster Creed[23]

I believe man's chief end is to glorify God, and to enjoy him forever;

I believe God is a Spirit, infinite, eternal, and unchangeable, in his being, wisdom, power, holiness, justice, goodness, and truth; I believe there is but one true and living God; that there are three persons in the Godhead: the Father, the Son, and the Holy Ghost; and that these three are one God, the same in substance, equal in power and glory; I believe God has foreordained whatever comes

---

[22]The Nicene Creed originated at the Council of Nicea (325), and an expanded form was adopted by the Council of Chalcedon (451). It was formulated to answer heresies that denied the biblical doctrine of the Trinity and of the dual nature of Christ.

[23]Composed mainly out of language found in the *Shorter Catechism*.

to pass; that God made all things of nothing, by the word of His power, in the space of six days, and all very good; and that God preserves and governs all His creatures and all their actions.

I believe our first parents, though created in knowledge, righteousness, and holiness, sinned against God, by eating the forbidden fruit; and that their fall brought mankind into an estate of sin and misery; I believe God determined, out of His mere good pleasure, to deliver His elect out of the estate of sin and misery, and to bring them into an estate of salvation by a Redeemer; I believe the only Redeemer of God's elect is the Lord Jesus Christ, who, being the eternal Son of God, became man, and so was, and continues to be, God and man in two distinct natures, and one person, forever; I believe Christ, as our Redeemer, executes the office of a prophet, of a priest, and of a king. I believe He underwent the miseries of this life, the wrath of God, the cursed death of the cross, and burial, offering Himself as a sacrifice to satisfy divine justice, and reconcile us to God; I believe He rose again from the dead on the third day, ascended up into heaven, sits at the right hand of God, the Father, and is coming to judge the world at the last day.

I believe we are made partakers of the redemption purchased by Christ, by the effectual application of it to us by his Holy Spirit; I believe God requires of us faith in Jesus Christ, and repentance unto life to escape the wrath and curse of God due to us for sin; I believe by His free grace we are effectually called, justified, and sanctified, and gathered into the visible church, out of which there is no ordinary possibility of salvation; I believe that we also are given *in this life* such accompanying benefits as assurance of God's love, peace of conscience, joy in the Holy Ghost, increase of grace, and perseverance therein to the end; that *at death*, we are made perfect in holiness, and immediately pass into glory; and our bodies, being still united in Christ, rest in their graves, till the resurrection; and *at the resurrection*, we shall be raised up in glory, we shall openly be acknowledged and acquitted in the day of judgment, and made perfectly blessed in the full enjoying of God to all eternity.

The Law of God (Exodus 20:1-17)[24]

Leader: God spake all these words, saying, I am the LORD thy God, which have brought thee out of the land of Egypt, out of the house of bondage.

All (Read in unison the bold or as time permits, the entire text):

I. **Thou shalt have no other gods before me.**

II. **Thou shalt not make unto thee any graven image,**
or any likeness of any thing that is in heaven above, or that is in the earth beneath, or that is in the water under the earth: thou shalt not bow down thyself to them, nor serve them: for I the LORD thy God am a jealous God, visiting the iniquity of the fathers upon the children unto the third and fourth generation of them that hate me; and showing mercy unto thousands of them that love me, and keep my commandments.

III. **Thou shalt not take the Name of the LORD thy God in vain;**
for the LORD will not hold him guiltless that taketh his Name in vain.

IV. **Remember the Sabbath day, to keep it holy.**
Six days shalt thou labor, and do all thy work: but the seventh day is the Sabbath of the LORD thy God; in it thou shalt not do any work, thou, nor thy son, nor thy daughter, thy man-servant, nor thy maid-servant, nor thy cattle, nor thy stranger that is within thy gates; for in six days the LORD made heaven and earth, the sea, and all that in them is, and rested the seventh day: wherefore the LORD blessed the Sabbath day, and hallowed it.

V. **Honor thy father and thy mother:**
that thy days may be long upon the land which the LORD thy God giveth thee.

VI. **Thou shalt not kill.**

VII. **Thou shalt not commit adultery.**

---

[24]The Law of God is read because "through the law comes the knowledge of sin (Romans 3:20)." The Apostle Paul testifies, "I would not have come to know sin except through the Law" (Romans 7:7). Thus the Law shows us our sin and consequently our need of Christ. Again the Apostle says, "The Law has become our tutor to lead us to Christ, that we may be justified by faith" (Galatians 3:24). The Law of God as found in the Ten Commandments, and further summarized by Jesus in the Two Commandments shows us our peril and our need of Christ for salvation.

VIII. **Thou shalt not steal.**

IX. **Thou shalt not bear false witness**
against thy neighbor.

X. **Thou shalt not covet**
thy neighbor's house, thou shalt not covet thy neighbor's
wife, nor his man-servant, nor his maid-servant, nor his
ox, nor his donkey, nor any thing that is thy neighbor's.

**Hear also the words of our Lord Jesus, how he saith: Thou
shalt love the Lord thy God with all thy heart, and with
all thy soul, and with all thy mind. This is the first and
great commandment. And the second is like unto it: Thou
shalt love thy neighbor as thyself. On these two
commandments hang all the law and the prophets.
(Matthew 22:37-40)**

The Beatitudes (Matthew 5:1-10)[25]

Leader: When Jesus saw the multitude, He went up on the
mountain; and after He sat down, His disciples came to
Him, and He began teaching them, saying:

All: **Blessed are the poor in spirit:**

For theirs is the kingdom of heaven.

Blessed are those who mourn:

For they shall be comforted.

Blessed are the meek:

For they shall inherit the earth.

Blessed are those who hunger and thirst after righteousness:

For they shall be filled.

Blessed are the merciful:

For they shall obtain mercy.

---

[25]Given that there are no mountains in Galilee, the opening words, "Jesus went up
to the mountain," are probably an implicit reference to Moses and Mt. Sinai. Jesus is
seen as delivering a "new" law, which is not a new law at all, but an explanation of
the old law. The Beatitudes are character descriptions of God's people, which when
measured against our performance, lead us like the law to Christ for mercy.

Blessed are the pure in heart:

For they shall see God.

Blessed are the peacemakers:

For they shall be called the children of God.

Blessed are those who are persecuted for righteousness' sake:

For theirs is the kingdom of heaven, (Matthew 5:1-10).

4. Scripture Reading

Read as much as is appropriate given time constraints and the makeup of the family. Progress through the whole Bible should be made over time. A table for such is provided in chapter VI's "Family Resources."

5. Prayers of Confession, Intercession, and Thanksgiving

This is a comprehensive prayer that begins with the confession of sin, then gives thanks for the assurance of pardon, and concludes with petitions and thanksgivings. Relate your petitions to the concerns of the family. Let your children hear you pleading with God for their souls; for their sanctification and growth; for their healing when afflicted; for the church and their part in its ministry; and for the nation.

Scriptural Encouragements to Prayer

Ask, and it shall be given to you; seek, and you shall find; knock, and it shall be opened to you. For everyone who asks receives, and he who seeks finds, and to him who knocks it shall be opened. (Mt 7:7,8)

If you then, being evil, know how to give good gifts to your children, who much more shall your heavenly Father give the Holy Spirit to those who ask Him? (Lk 11:13)

And whatever you ask in My name, that will I do, that the Father may be glorified in the Son. If you ask Me anything in My name, I will do it. (Jn 14:13,14)

And this is the confidence which we have before Him, that, if we ask anything according to His will, He hears us. And if we know that He hears us in whatever we ask, we know that we have the requests which we have asked from Him. (1 Jn 5:14,15)

Be anxious for nothing, but in everything by prayer and supplication with thanksgiving let your requests be made known to God. And the peace of God, which surpasses all comprehension, shall guard your hearts and your minds in Christ Jesus. (Phil 4:6,7)

You do not have because you do not ask. (Jas 4:2b)

Therefore, He had to be made like His brethren in all things that He might become a merciful and faithful high priest in things pertaining to God, to make propitiation for the sins of the people. For since He Himself was tempted in that which He has suffered, He is able to come to the aid of those who are tempted. (Heb 2:17,18)

For we do not have a high priest who cannot sympathize with our weaknesses, but one who has been tempted in all things as we are, yet without sin. Let us therefore draw near with confidence to the throne of grace, that we may receive mercy and may find grace to help in time of need. (Heb 4:15, 16)

Since therefore, brethren, we have confidence to enter the holy place by the blood of Jesus, by a new and living way which He inaugurated for us through the veil, that is, His flesh, and since we have a great priest over the house of God, let us draw near with a sincere heart in full assurance of faith, having our hearts sprinkled clean from an evil conscience and our bodies washed with pure water. (Heb 10:19–22)

Scriptural Expressions of Confession and Pleas for Forgiveness

Do Thou pardon our iniquity and our sin, and take us as Thine own possession. (Ex 34:9)

Pardon, I pray, the iniquities of this people, according to the greatness of Thy lovingkindness. (Num 14:19)

...Be sure your sin will find you out. (Num 32:23)

Acquit me of hidden faults. Also keep back Thy servant from presumptuous sins; let them not rule over me; then I shall be blameless, and I shall be acquitted of great transgressions. (Ps 19:12,13)

Do not remember the sins of my youth or my transgressions; According to Thy lovingkindness remember Thou me, for Thy goodness' sake, O Lord... For Thy name's sake, O Lord, pardon my iniquity, for it is great. (Ps 25:7,11)

Be gracious to me, O LORD, for I am in distress; my eye is wasted away from grief, my soul and my body also. For my life is spent with sorrow, and my years with sighing; my strength has failed because of my iniquity, and my body has wasted away. (Ps 31:9, 10)

There is no health in my bones because of my sin. For my iniquities are gone over my head; as a heavy burden they weigh too much for me. (Ps 38:3b, 4)

For I confess my iniquity; I am full of anxiety because of my sin. (Ps. 38:18)

Deliver me from all my transgressions;… (Ps. 39:8a)

For evils beyond number have surrounded me; my iniquities have overtaken me, so that I am not able to see; they are more numerous than the hairs of my head; and my heart has failed me. (Ps. 40:12)

As for me, I said, "O Lord, be gracious to me; heal my soul, for I have sinned against Thee." (Ps. 41:4)

Be gracious to me, O God, according to Thy lovingkindness; according to the greatness of Thy compassion blot out my transgressions. Wash me thoroughly from my iniquity, and cleanse me from my sin. For I know my transgressions, and my sin is ever before me. Against Thee, Thee only, I have sinned, and done what is evil in Thy sight. (Psalm 51:1–4a)

Behold, I was brought forth in iniquity, and in sin my mother conceived me. …Purify me with hyssop, and I shall be clean; wash me, and I shall be whiter than snow…Hide Thy face from my sins, and blot out all my iniquities…Deliver me from bloodguiltiness, O God, Thou God of my salvation. (Ps 51:5, 7, 9, 14a)

Create in me a clean heart, O God, and renew a steadfast spirit within me. Do not cast me away from Thy presence, and do not take Thy Holy Spirit from me. Restore to me the joy of Thy salvation, and sustain me with a willing spirit…O Lord, open my lips, that my mouth may declare Thy praise. For Thou dost not delight in sacrifice, otherwise I would give it; Thou art not pleased with burnt offering. The sacrifices of God are a broken spirit; a broken and a contrite heart, O God, Thou wilt not despise. (Ps 51:10–12, 15–17)

O God, it is Thou who dost know my folly, and my wrongs are not hidden from Thee. (Ps 69:5)

Help us, O God of our salvation, for the glory of Thy name; and deliver us, and forgive our sins, for Thy name's sake. (Ps 79:9)

We have sinned like our fathers, we have committed iniquity, we have behaved wickedly. (Ps 106:6)

If Thou, Lord, shouldst mark iniquities, O Lord, who could stand? But there is forgiveness with Thee. (Ps 130:3–4a)

Search me, O God, and know my heart; try me and know my anxious thoughts; and see if there be any hurtful way in me, and lead me in the everlasting way. (Ps 139:23, 24; cf. 2 Ch 6:36-38)

We have sinned, committed iniquity, acted wickedly, and rebelled, even turning aside from Thy commandments and ordinances...Open shame belongs to us, O Lord...because we have sinned against Thee. To the Lord our God belong compassion and forgiveness, for we have rebelled against Him; nor have we obeyed the voice of the Lord our God, to walk in His teachings which He set before us through His servants the prophets. Indeed all Israel has transgressed the Law and turned aside, not obeying Thy voice. ...So now, our God, listen to the prayer of Thy servant and to his supplications, and for Thy sake, O Lord, let Thy face shine on Thy desolate sanctuary. O my God, incline Thine ear and hear! Open Thine eyes and see our desolations and the city which is called by Thy name; for we are not presenting our supplications before Thee on account of any merits of our own, but on account of Thy great compassion. O Lord, hear! O Lord, forgive! O Lord, listen and take action! For Thine own sake, O my God, do not delay, because Thy city and Thy people are called by Thy name. (Dan 9:5, 8–11a, 17–19)

O my God, I am ashamed and embarrassed to lift up my face to Thee, my God, for our iniquities have risen above our heads, and our guilt has grown even to the heavens. (Ezra 9:6)

'We have acted very corruptly against Thee and have not kept the commandments, nor the statutes, nor the ordinances which Thou didst command Thy servant Moses.' (Neh 1:7)

Thou art just in all that has come upon us; for Thou hast dealt faithfully, but we have acted wickedly. For our kings, our leaders, our priests, and our fathers have not kept Thy law or paid attention to Thy commandments and Thine admonitions with which Thou has admonished them. (Neh 9:33, 34)

And the son said to him, 'Father, I have sinned against heaven and in your sight; I am no longer worthy to be called your son.' (Lk 15:21)

But the tax-gatherer, standing some distance away, was even unwilling to lift up his eyes to heaven, but was beating his breast, saying, 'God be merciful to me, the sinner!' (Lk 18:13)

'... [F]or her sins have piled up as high as heaven, and God has remembered her iniquities.' (Rev 18:5)

Scriptural Promises of Pardon

How blessed is he whose transgression is forgiven, whose sin is covered! How blessed is the man to whom the Lord does not impute iniquity, and in whose spirit there is no deceit! (Ps 32:1, 2),

I acknowledged my sin to Thee, and my iniquity I did not hide; I said, 'I will confess my transgression to the Lord"; And Thou didst forgive the guilt of my sin'. (Ps 32:5)

Thou didst forgive the iniquity of Thy people; Thou didst cover all their sin. (Ps 85:2)

For Thou, Lord, art good, and ready to forgive, and abundant in lovingkindness to all who call upon Thee. Give ear, O Lord, to my prayer; and give heed to the voice of my supplications! (Ps 86:5, 6)

The Lord is compassionate and gracious, slow to anger and abounding in lovingkindness. He has not dealt with us according to our sins, nor rewarded us according to our iniquities. For as high as the heavens are above the earth, so great is His lovingkindness toward those who fear Him. As far as the east is from the west, so far has He removed our transgressions from us. (Ps 103:8, 10–12)

For Thou hast cast all my sins behind Thy back. (Is 38:17b)

I, even I, am the one who wipes out your transgressions for My own sake; and I will not remember your sins. (Is 43:25)

'I have wiped out your transgresions like a thick cloud, and your sins like a heavy mist. Return to Me, for I have redeemed you.' (Is 44:22)

But He was pierced through for our transgressions, He was crushed for our iniquities; the chastening for our wellbeing fell upon Him, and by His scourging we are healed. All of us like sheep have gone astray, each of us has turned to his own way; but the Lord has caused the iniquity of us all to fall on Him. (Is 53:5, 6)

'But this is the covenant which I will make with the house of Israel after those days', declares the Lord, 'I will put My law within them, and on their heart, I will write it; and I will be their God, and they shall be My people. And they shall not each again, each man his neighbor and each man his brother, saying, 'Know the Lord,' for they shall all know Me, from the least of them to the greatest of them,' declares the Lord, 'for I will forgive their iniquity, and their sin I will remember no more'. (Jer 31:33–34)

He will again have compassion on us; He will tread our iniquities underfoot. Yes, Thou wilt cast all their sins into the depths of the sea. (Micah 7:19)

Therefore having been justified by faith, we have peace with God through our Lord Jesus Christ. (Rom 5:1)

For the wages of sin is death, but the free gift of God is eternal life in Christ Jesus our Lord. (Rom 6:23)

There is therefore now no condemnation for those who are in Christ Jesus. (Rom 8:1)

For by grace you have been saved through faith; and that not of yourselves, it is the gift of God; not as a result of works, that no one should boast. (Eph 2:8, 9)

It is a trustworthy statement, deserving full acceptance, that Christ Jesus came into the world to save sinners, among whom I am foremost of all. (1 Tim 1:15)

For we also once were foolish ourselves, disobedient, deceived, enslaved to various lusts and pleasures, spending our life in malice and envy, hateful, hating one another. But when the kindness of God our Savior and His love for mankind appeared, He saved us, not on the basis of deeds which we have done in righteousness, but according to His mercy, by the washing of regeneration and renewing by the Holy Spirit. (Tit 3:5–7)

And He Himself bore our sins in His body on the cross, that we might die to sin and live in righteousness; for by His wounds you were healed. (1 Pet 2:24)

For Christ also died for sins once for all, the just for the unjust, in order that He might bring us to God, having been put to death in the flesh, but made alive in the spirit. (1 Pet 3:18)

If we say that we have no sin, we are deceiving ourselves, and the truth is not in us. If we confess our sins, He is faithful and righteous to forgive us our sins and to cleanse us from all unrighteousness. (1 Jn 1:8, 9)

My little children, I am writing these things to you that you may not sin. And if anyone sins, we have an advocate with the Father,

Jesus Christ the righteous; and He Himself is the propitiation for our sins; and not for ours only, but also for those of the whole world. (1 Jn 2:1, 2; cf. Rev. 1:5, 5:9)

Scriptural Petitions[26]

i.   Civil authorities:

First of all, then, I urge that entreaties and prayers, petitions and thanksgivings, be made on behalf of all men, for kings and all who are in authority, in order that we may lead a tranquil and quiet life in all godliness and dignity. (1 Tim 2:1, 2)

ii.   Christian ministry and mission:

And seeing the multitudes, He felt compassion for them, because they were distressed and downcast like sheep without a shepherd. Then He said to His disciples, "The harvest is plentiful, but the workers are few. Therefore beseech the Lord of the harvest to send out workers into His harvest." (Mt 9:36–38)

iii.   Salvation of all men:

First of all, then, I urge that entreaties and prayers, petitions and thanksgivings, be made on behalf of all men…. This is good and acceptable in the sight of God our Savior, who desires all men to be saved and to come to the knowledge of the truth. (1 Tim 2:1, 34)

iv.   Sanctification of the Saints:

With all prayer and petition pray at all times in the Spirit, and with this in view, be on the alert with all perseverance and petition for all the saints. (Eph 6:18)

And this I pray, that your love may abound still more and more in real knowledge and all discernment, so that you may approve the things that are excellent, in order to be sincere and blameless until the day of Christ; having been filled with the fruit of righteousness which comes through Jesus Christ, to the glory and praise of God. (Phil 1:9–11)

For this reason also, since the day we heard of it, we have not ceased to pray for you and to ask that you may be filled with the

---

[26]Scripture encourages petitions according to these five categories. The early church made use of them. The Reformers in the 16th century revived their use for public worship (see *Leading in Worship*, p. 10, n. 15). They provide a useful guide for the family's intercessions.

knowledge of His will in all spiritual wisdom and understanding, so that you may walk in a manner worthy of the Lord, to please Him in all respects, bearing fruit in every good work and increasing in the knowledge of God; strengthened with all power, according to His glorious might, for the attaining of all steadfastness and patience. (Col 1:9–11; cf., Eph 1:15–23)

v. Comfort and healing of the afflicted:

Is anyone among you suffering? Let him pray. Is anyone among you cheerful? Let him sing praises. Is anyone among you sick? Let him call for the elders of the church, and let them pray over him, anointing him with oil in the name of the Lord; and the prayer offered in faith will restore the one who is sick, and the Lord will raise him up, and if he has committed sins, they will be forgiven him. Therefore, confess your sins to one another, and pray for one another, so that you may be healed. The effective prayer of a righteous man can accomplish much. Elijah was a man with a nature like ours, and he prayed earnestly that it might not rain; and it did not rain on the earth for three years and six months. And he prayed again, and the sky poured rain, and the earth produced its fruit. (Jas 5:13–18; cf 2 Cor 1:3–11)

The Lord's Prayer

Our Father, who art in Heaven, Hallowed be Thy name. Thy kingdom come. Thy will be done on earth as it is in heaven. Give us this day our daily bread. And forgive us our debts, as we forgive our debtors. And lead us not into temptation, but deliver us from evil: For Thine is the kingdom, and the power, and the glory, for ever. Amen.

6. Ascriptions of Praise

Use one of the following:

Doxology

Praise God from whom all blessings flow; praise him, all creatures here below; praise him above ye heavenly host; praise Father, Son, and Holy Ghost. Amen. (Tune: Old Hundredth)

Praise God from whom all blessings flow; praise him, all creatures here below: alleluia, alleluia! Praise him above ye heavenly host; praise Father, Son, and Holy Ghost: alleluia, alleluia, alleluia, alleluia, alleluia! Amen. (Tune: Lasst uns Erfreuen)

Gloria Patri

Glory be to the Father, and to the Son and to the Holy Ghost; as it was in the beginning, is now and ever shall be, world without end. Amen. Amen. (Tune: Greatorex)

Laud and honor to the Father; laud and honor to the Son; laud and honor to the Spirit, ever Three and ever One; One in might, and One in glory, while unending ages run. (Tune: Regent Square)

7.   Benediction

The head of the household may now use one of the following benedictory prayers, pronouncing the Lord's blessing upon the family:

Aaronic

"The LORD bless you and keep you; the LORD make His face shine upon you, and be gracious to you; the LORD lift up His countenance upon you, and give you peace" (Num 6:24–26).

Apostolic

The grace of the Lord Jesus Christ, and the love of God, and the fellowship of the Holy Spirit, be with you all (2 Cor 13:14).

Chapter Five

A SAMPLE FOR FAMILY WORSHIP

The following is an example of how an actual session of family worship might go (and actually does at our house), with almost limitless variation.

1. Call to Worship/Prayer of Praise

Begin with a "gathering song" or move immediately into a prayer of praise.

All: **"God is so good"** (repeat 3 times)

　　　　"He's so good to me"

Leader: Join with me in prayer as we seek the presence and favor of our God.

O Lord, we have come to worship and bow down, and kneel before You the Lord our Maker, for You are our God, and we are the people of Your pasture, the sheep of Your hand. Our family has gathered to worship You in Spirit and in truth; we have come to praise You with reverence and awe. Receive our adoration through our Advocate with the Father, Jesus Christ the Righteous, in whose name we pray. Amen. (Ps 95:6, 7; Jn 4:23, 24; Heb 12:28; I Jn 2:1)

2. Psalms and Hymns

Leader: Let's sing our Psalm of the Month.

All: **"The Lord's my Shepherd, I'll not want..." (Psalm 23)**

Leader: Can someone help us start Psalm 68?

All: **"Let God arise and scattered far be all His enemies..." (Psalm 68:1ff)**

Leader: Who remembers last month's hymn of the month?

All: **"Rejoice, the Lord is King, your Lord and King adore..."**

Leader: Let's do one more—"When I Survey"

All: **"When I survey the wondrous cross..."**

3. Creeds and Commandments

Leader: What is today? Monday? What do we recite on Monday, Wednesday, and Friday?

All: **The Apostles' Creed** (Tuesday, Thursday, Saturday we do the Ten Commandments)

All: **"I believe in God the Father Almighty..."**

4. Scripture Reading

Leader: Where did we leave off in our Bible reading? We'll pick up where we left off. Listen now, this is God's Word.

Leader: What does the Bible mean when it says that? What should we do? How should we act? Isn't God good to say such things as that?! Isn't He wonderful?! I need never worry, need I?!

5. Prayers of Confession and Intercession

Leader: Let's join together in prayer.

We thank You our God for what we've just learned about You in Your word. You are a holy God. Your eyes are too pure to look upon evil. You are light, and in You there is no darkness at all. We confess that we have sinned against You in our thoughts, words, and deeds, in the evil we have done, and the good we've left undone. We have transgressed Your law, broken Your commandments, disregarded Your will, and fallen short of Your glory. We've been naughty, demanding, selfish, deceitful, and ungrateful. Forgive our sins. Blot out our transgressions. Tread our iniquities under foot and cast them into the depths of the sea. Hide our sins behind Your back. Remove them as far as the east is from the west and remember them no more. (Is 6:3; Hab 1:3; 1 Jn 1:5; Rom 3:23; Ps 51:1ff; Mic 7:19; Is 43:25; Ps 103:12; Jer 31:34).

Grant us the gift of Your Holy Spirit. Wash and cleanse our hearts Make us new creatures in Christ Jesus. May the old things pass away and all things become new. Make us like Christ, even imitators of God as beloved children. Help us to walk in love even as He is love. O Lord, regenerate and sanctify our children even as

You have promised to be a God to us and our children (2 Cor 5:17; Eph 5:1f; Gen 17:7).

We pray for the sick (names) that they might be healed. We pray for the events of the day/week (review them) and seek Yor help and blessing. We pray for our nation and its leaders. We pray for our church and its ministry. We pray for Your protection, guidance and care, even as we give thanks for Your bountiful provision. Be our refuge and strength. Be our shepherd and guide. Lead us in the paths of righteousness. Never leave or forsake us, even as You promise to be with us always even to the end of the age. We pray as Jesus taught us to pray, saying together (Jas 5:13ff; Ps 46:1; Ps 23:1ff; Heb 13:5; Mt 28:20),

All: **"Our Father, who art in heaven..."**

6. Ascription of Praise

All: **"Praise God from whom all blessings flow...""**

7. Benediction

Leader: "The Lord bless you, and keep you; The Lord make His face shine on you, and be gracious to you; the Lord lift up His countenance on you, and give you peace." (Num 6:24–26).

Chapter Six

FAMILY RESOURCES

1. Family Bible Reading Record

The following table of Bible readings is provided to help guide the family in its Bible readings as well as record and track what has been read. Note the following:

1. A total of 1083 chapters or sections are designated for family reading, 776 Old Testament, 307 New Testament.

2. We recommend that a number of chapters be omitted because they are ill-suited to family worship due to their contents or repetition. This includes 57 chapters from the Levitical instructions found between Exodus 21 through Deuteronomy, 9 chapters from Joshua, 77 chapters through harmonizing Samuel/Kings and Chronicles, 9 chapters from Ezekiel, and about 30 chapters through harmonizing the Synoptic gospels, for a total of about 185 chapters. Of course these may be profitably read on other occasions.

3. The boxes □□□ are provided for checking off (✓) chapters or sections as they are read for the first, second, and third times.

4. The length of the passage to be read is left to each family to determine. Because of such variables as ages and comprehension levels of family members the amount typically read cannot be standardized. We note that a full chapter, on many occasions, will prove to be too much. Often chapters will need to be divided, or certain portions read over in a cursory fashion while focusing on key paragraphs.

5. It may be wise to vary the type of Scripture (narrative, poetic, didactic, wisdom), that the family reads rather than reading straight through from Genesis to Revelation.

GENESIS

☐☐☐ 1. Genesis 1
☐☐☐ 2. Genesis 2
☐☐☐ 3. Genesis 3
☐☐☐ 4. Genesis 4
(omit 5)
☐☐☐ 5. Genesis 6
☐☐☐ 6. Genesis 7
☐☐☐ 7. Genesis 8
☐☐☐ 8. Genesis 9, 10
☐☐☐ 9. Genesis 11
☐☐☐ 10. Genesis 12
☐☐☐ 11. Genesis 13
☐☐☐ 12. Genesis 14
☐☐☐ 13. Genesis 15
☐☐☐ 14. Genesis 16
☐☐☐ 15. Genesis 17
☐☐☐ 16. Genesis 18
☐☐☐ 17. Genesis 19
☐☐☐ 18. Genesis 20
☐☐☐ 19. Genesis 21
☐☐☐ 20. Genesis 22
☐☐☐ 21. Genesis 23
☐☐☐ 22. Genesis 24
☐☐☐ 23. Genesis 25
☐☐☐ 24. Genesis 26
☐☐☐ 25. Genesis 27
☐☐☐ 26. Genesis 28
☐☐☐ 27. Genesis 29
☐☐☐ 28. Genesis 30
☐☐☐ 29. Genesis 31
☐☐☐ 30. Genesis 32
☐☐☐ 31. Genesis 33
☐☐☐ 32. Genesis 34
☐☐☐ 33. Genesis 35, 36
☐☐☐ 34. Genesis 37
☐☐☐ 35. Genesis 38
☐☐☐ 36. Genesis 39
☐☐☐ 37. Genesis 40
☐☐☐ 38. Genesis 41
☐☐☐ 39. Genesis 42

☐☐☐ 40. Genesis 43
☐☐☐ 41. Genesis 44
☐☐☐ 42. Genesis 45
☐☐☐ 43. Genesis 46
☐☐☐ 44. Genesis 47
☐☐☐ 45. Genesis 48
☐☐☐ 46. Genesis 49
☐☐☐ 47. Genesis 50

EXODUS

☐☐☐ 48. Exodus 1
☐☐☐ 49. Exodus 2
☐☐☐ 50. Exodus 3
☐☐☐ 51. Exodus 4
☐☐☐ 52. Exodus 5
☐☐☐ 53. Exodus 6
☐☐☐ 54. Exodus 7
☐☐☐ 55. Exodus 8
☐☐☐ 56. Exodus 9
☐☐☐ 57. Exodus 10
☐☐☐ 58. Exodus 11
☐☐☐ 59. Exodus 12
☐☐☐ 60. Exodus 13
☐☐☐ 61. Exodus 14
☐☐☐ 62. Exodus 15
☐☐☐ 63. Exodus 16
☐☐☐ 64. Exodus 17
☐☐☐ 65. Exodus 18
☐☐☐ 66. Exodus 19
☐☐☐ 67. Exodus 20
(omit 21–23)
☐☐☐ 68. Exodus 24
(omit 25–31)
☐☐☐ 69. Exodus 32
☐☐☐ 70. Exodus 33
☐☐☐ 71. Exodus 34
(omit 35–39)
☐☐☐ 72. Exodus 40

LEVITICUS

(omit 1-10)
☐☐☐ 73. Leviticus 11
(omit 12-27)

NUMBERS

(omit 1-9)
☐☐☐ 74. Numbers 10
☐☐☐ 75. Numbers 11
☐☐☐ 76. Numbers 12
☐☐☐ 77. Numbers 13
☐☐☐ 78. Numbers 14
(omit 15)
☐☐☐ 79. Numbers 16
☐☐☐ 80. Numbers 17, 20
☐☐☐ 81. Numbers 21
☐☐☐ 82. Numbers 22
☐☐☐ 83. Numbers 23
☐☐☐ 84. Numbers 24
☐☐☐ 85. Numbers 25
(omit 26–36)

DEUTERONOMY

☐☐☐ 86. Deuteronomy 1
☐☐☐ 87. Deuteronomy 2
☐☐☐ 88. Deuteronomy 3
☐☐☐ 89. Deuteronomy 4
☐☐☐ 90. Deuteronomy 5
☐☐☐ 91. Deuteronomy 6
☐☐☐ 92. Deuteronomy 7
☐☐☐ 93. Deuteronomy 8
☐☐☐ 94. Deuteronomy 9
☐☐☐ 95. Deuteronomy 10
☐☐☐ 96. Deuteronomy 11
(omit 12)
☐☐☐ 97. Deuteronomy 13
(omit 14)
☐☐☐ 98. Deuteronomy 15
☐☐☐ 99. Deuteronomy 16
☐☐☐ 100. Deuteronomy 17
(omit 18, 19)

☐☐☐ 101. Deuteronomy 20
☐☐☐ 102. Deuteronomy 21
☐☐☐ 103. Deuteronomy 22
☐☐☐ 104. Deuteronomy 23
☐☐☐ 105. Deuteronomy 24
☐☐☐ 106. Deuteronomy 25
☐☐☐ 107. Deuteronomy 26
☐☐☐ 108. Deuteronomy 27
☐☐☐ 109. Deuteronomy 28
☐☐☐ 110. Deuteronomy 29
☐☐☐ 111. Deuteronomy 30
☐☐☐ 112. Deuteronomy 31
☐☐☐ 113. Deuteronomy 32
☐☐☐ 114. Deuteronomy 33
☐☐☐ 115. Deuteronomy 34

JOSHUA

☐☐☐ 116. Joshua 1
☐☐☐ 117. Joshua 2
☐☐☐ 118. Joshua 3
☐☐☐ 119. Joshua 4
☐☐☐ 120. Joshua 5
☐☐☐ 121. Joshua 6
☐☐☐ 122. Joshua 7
☐☐☐ 123. Joshua 8
☐☐☐ 124. Joshua 9
☐☐☐ 125. Joshua 10
☐☐☐ 126. Joshua 11
(omit 12,13)
☐☐☐ 127. Joshua 14
(omit 15–21)
☐☐☐ 128. Joshua 22
☐☐☐ 129. Joshua 23
☐☐☐ 130. Joshua 24

JUDGES

☐☐☐ 131. Judges 1
☐☐☐ 132. Judges 2
☐☐☐ 133. Judges 3
☐☐☐ 134. Judges 4

☐☐☐ 135. Judges 5
☐☐☐ 136. Judges 6
☐☐☐ 137. Judges 7
☐☐☐ 138. Judges 8
☐☐☐ 139. Judges 9
☐☐☐ 140. Judges 10
☐☐☐ 141. Judges 11
☐☐☐ 142. Judges 12
☐☐☐ 143. Judges 13
☐☐☐ 144. Judges 14
☐☐☐ 145. Judges 15
☐☐☐ 146. Judges 16
☐☐☐ 147. Judges 17
☐☐☐ 148. Judges 18
☐☐☐ 149. Judges 19
☐☐☐ 150. Judges 20
☐☐☐ 151. Judges 21

RUTH

☐☐☐ 152. Ruth 1
☐☐☐ 153. Ruth 2
☐☐☐ 154. Ruth 3
☐☐☐ 155. Ruth 4

1 SAMUEL

☐☐☐ 156. 1 Samuel 1
☐☐☐ 157. 1 Samuel 2
☐☐☐ 158. 1 Samuel 3
☐☐☐ 159. 1 Samuel 4
☐☐☐ 160. 1 Samuel 5
☐☐☐ 161. 1 Samuel 6
☐☐☐ 162. 1 Samuel 7
☐☐☐ 163. 1 Samuel 8
☐☐☐ 164. 1 Samuel 9
☐☐☐ 165. 1 Samuel 10
☐☐☐ 166. 1 Samuel 11
☐☐☐ 167. 1 Samuel 12
☐☐☐ 168. 1 Samuel 13
☐☐☐ 169. 1 Samuel 14
☐☐☐ 170. 1 Samuel 15
☐☐☐ 171. 1 Samuel 16

☐☐☐ 172. 1 Samuel 17
☐☐☐ 173. 1 Samuel 18
☐☐☐ 174. 1 Samuel 19
☐☐☐ 175. 1 Samuel 20
☐☐☐ 176. 1 Samuel 21
☐☐☐ 177. 1 Samuel 22
☐☐☐ 178. 1 Samuel 23
☐☐☐ 179. 1 Samuel 24
☐☐☐ 180. 1 Samuel 25
☐☐☐ 181. 1 Samuel 26
☐☐☐ 182. 1 Samuel 27
☐☐☐ 183. 1 Samuel 28
☐☐☐ 184. 1 Samuel 29
☐☐☐ 185. 1 Samuel 30
☐☐☐ 186. 1 Samuel 31

HARMONY OF 2 SAMUEL & 1 CHRONICLES

☐☐☐ 187. 2 Samuel 1
☐☐☐ 188. 2 Samuel 2
☐☐☐ 189. 2 Samuel 3
☐☐☐ 190. 2 Samuel 4
☐☐☐ 191. 2 Samuel 5
☐☐☐ 192. 2 Samuel 6
☐☐☐ 193. 1 Chron 6
☐☐☐ 194. 2 Samuel 7
☐☐☐ 195. 2 Samuel 8
☐☐☐ 196. 2 Samuel 9
☐☐☐ 197. 2 Samuel 10
☐☐☐ 198. 2 Samuel 11
☐☐☐ 199. 2 Samuel 12
☐☐☐ 200. 2 Samuel 13
☐☐☐ 201. 2 Samuel 14
☐☐☐ 202. 2 Samuel 15
☐☐☐ 203. 2 Samuel 16
☐☐☐ 204. 2 Samuel 17
☐☐☐ 205. 2 Samuel 18
☐☐☐ 206. 2 Samuel 19
☐☐☐ 207. 2 Samuel 20
☐☐☐ 208. 2 Samuel 21
☐☐☐ 209. 2 Samuel 22

☐☐☐ 210. 2 Samuel 23
☐☐☐ 211. 2 Samuel 24
☐☐☐ 212. 1Chron 22
☐☐☐ 213. 1Chron 28
☐☐☐ 214. 1Chron 29

HARMONY OF
1 & 2 KINGS AND
2 CHRONICLES

☐☐☐ 215. 1 Kings 1
☐☐☐ 216. 1 Kings 2
☐☐☐ 217. 1 Kings 3
☐☐☐ 218. 1 Kings 4
☐☐☐ 219. 1 Kings 5
☐☐☐ 220. 1 Kings 6
☐☐☐ 221. 1 Kings 7
☐☐☐ 222. 2 Chron 5
☐☐☐ 223. 2 Chron 6
☐☐☐ 224. 1 Kings 8
☐☐☐ 225. 1 Kings 9
☐☐☐ 226. 1 Kings 10
☐☐☐ 227. 1 Kings 11
☐☐☐ 228. 1 Kings 12
☐☐☐ 229. 1 Kings 13
☐☐☐ 230. 1 Kings 14
☐☐☐ 231. 2 Chron 12
☐☐☐ 232. 2 Chron 13
☐☐☐ 233. 1 Kings 15
☐☐☐ 234. 2 Chron 14
☐☐☐ 235. 2 Chron 15
☐☐☐ 236. 2 Chron 16
☐☐☐ 237. 1 Kings 16
☐☐☐ 238. 2 Chron 17
☐☐☐ 239. 1 Kings 17
☐☐☐ 240. 1 Kings 18
☐☐☐ 241. 1 Kings 19
☐☐☐ 242. 1 Kings 20
☐☐☐ 243. 1 Kings 21
☐☐☐ 244. 1 Kings 22
☐☐☐ 245. 2 Chron 19
☐☐☐ 246. 2 Chron 20

☐☐☐ 247. 2 Kings 1
☐☐☐ 248. 2 Kings 2
☐☐☐ 249. 2 Kings 3
☐☐☐ 250. 2 Kings 4
☐☐☐ 251. 2 Kings 5
☐☐☐ 252. 2 Kings 6
☐☐☐ 253. 2 Kings 7
☐☐☐ 254. 2 Kings 8
☐☐☐ 255. 2 Kings 9
☐☐☐ 256. 2 Kings 10
☐☐☐ 257. 2 Kings 11
☐☐☐ 258. 2 Kings 12
☐☐☐ 259. 2 Kings 13
☐☐☐ 260. 2 Kings 14
☐☐☐ 261. 2 Kings 15
☐☐☐ 262. 2 Chron 26
☐☐☐ 263. 2 Chron 28
☐☐☐ 264. 2 Kings 16
☐☐☐ 265. 2 Kings 17
☐☐☐ 266. 2 Chron 29
☐☐☐ 267. 2 Chron 30
☐☐☐ 268. 2 Chron 31
☐☐☐ 269. 2 Kings 18
☐☐☐ 270. 2 Kings 19
☐☐☐ 271. 2 Kings 20
☐☐☐ 272. 2 Kings 21
☐☐☐ 273. 2 Kings 22
☐☐☐ 274. 2 Kings 23
☐☐☐ 275. 2 Chron 35
☐☐☐ 276. 2 Kings 24
☐☐☐ 277. 2 Kings 25

EZRA

☐☐☐ 278. Ezra 1
(omit 2)
☐☐☐ 279. Ezra 3
☐☐☐ 280. Ezra 4
☐☐☐ 281. Ezra 5
☐☐☐ 282. Ezra 6
☐☐☐ 283. Ezra 7
☐☐☐ 284. Ezra 8

☐☐☐ 285. Ezra 9
☐☐☐ 286. Ezra 10

NEHEMIAH

☐☐☐ 287. Nehemiah 1
☐☐☐ 288. Nehemiah 2
☐☐☐ 289. Nehemiah 3
☐☐☐ 290. Nehemiah 4
☐☐☐ 291. Nehemiah 5
☐☐☐ 292. Nehemiah 6
(omit 7)
☐☐☐ 293. Nehemiah 8
☐☐☐ 294. Nehemiah 9
☐☐☐ 295. Nehemiah 10
(omit 11, 12)
☐☐☐ 296. Nehemiah 13

ESTHER

☐☐☐ 297. Esther 1
☐☐☐ 298. Esther 2
☐☐☐ 299. Esther 3
☐☐☐ 300. Esther 4
☐☐☐ 301. Esther 5
☐☐☐ 302. Esther 6
☐☐☐ 303. Esther 7
☐☐☐ 304. Esther 8
☐☐☐ 305. Esther 9, 10

JOB

☐☐☐ 306. Job 1
☐☐☐ 307. Job 2
☐☐☐ 308. Job 3
☐☐☐ 309. Job 4
☐☐☐ 310. Job 5
☐☐☐ 311. Job 6
☐☐☐ 312. Job 7
☐☐☐ 313. Job 8
☐☐☐ 314. Job 9
☐☐☐ 315. Job 10
☐☐☐ 316. Job 11
☐☐☐ 317. Job 12

☐☐☐ 318. Job 13
☐☐☐ 319. Job 14
☐☐☐ 320. Job 15
☐☐☐ 321. Job 16
☐☐☐ 322. Job 17
☐☐☐ 323. Job 18
☐☐☐ 324. Job 19
☐☐☐ 325. Job 20
☐☐☐ 326. Job 21
☐☐☐ 327. Job 22
☐☐☐ 328. Job 23
☐☐☐ 329. Job 24
☐☐☐ 330. Job 25, 26
☐☐☐ 331. Job 27
☐☐☐ 332. Job 28
☐☐☐ 333. Job 29
☐☐☐ 334. Job 30
☐☐☐ 335. Job 31
☐☐☐ 336. Job 32
☐☐☐ 337. Job 33
☐☐☐ 338. Job 34
☐☐☐ 339. Job 35
☐☐☐ 340. Job 36
☐☐☐ 341. Job 37
☐☐☐ 342. Job 38
☐☐☐ 343. Job 39
☐☐☐ 344. Job 40
☐☐☐ 345. Job 41
☐☐☐ 346. Job 42

PSALMS

☐☐☐ 347. Psalm 1
☐☐☐ 348. Psalm 2
☐☐☐ 349. Psalm 3
☐☐☐ 350. Psalm 4
☐☐☐ 351. Psalm 5
☐☐☐ 352. Psalm 6
☐☐☐ 353. Psalm 7
☐☐☐ 354. Psalm 8
☐☐☐ 355. Psalm 9
☐☐☐ 356. Psalm 10

☐☐☐ 357. Psalm 11
☐☐☐ 358. Psalm 12
☐☐☐ 359. Psalm 13
☐☐☐ 360. Psalm 14
☐☐☐ 361. Psalm 15
☐☐☐ 362. Psalm 16
☐☐☐ 363. Psalm 17
☐☐☐ 364. Psalm 18
☐☐☐ 365. Psalm 19
☐☐☐ 366. Psalm 20
☐☐☐ 367. Psalm 21
☐☐☐ 368. Psalm 22
☐☐☐ 369. Psalm 23
☐☐☐ 370. Psalm 24
☐☐☐ 371. Psalm 25
☐☐☐ 372. Psalm 26
☐☐☐ 373. Psalm 27
☐☐☐ 374. Psalm 28
☐☐☐ 375. Psalm 29
☐☐☐ 376. Psalm 30
☐☐☐ 377. Psalm 31
☐☐☐ 378. Psalm 32
☐☐☐ 379. Psalm 33
☐☐☐ 380. Psalm 34
☐☐☐ 381. Psalm 35
☐☐☐ 382. Psalm 36
☐☐☐ 383. Psalm 37
☐☐☐ 384. Psalm 38
☐☐☐ 385. Psalm 39
☐☐☐ 386. Psalm 40
☐☐☐ 387. Psalm 41
☐☐☐ 388. Psalms 42, 43
☐☐☐ 389. Psalm 44
☐☐☐ 390. Psalm 45
☐☐☐ 391. Psalm 46
☐☐☐ 392. Psalm 47
☐☐☐ 393. Psalm 48
☐☐☐ 394. Psalm 49
☐☐☐ 395. Psalm 50
☐☐☐ 396. Psalm 51
☐☐☐ 397. Psalm 52

☐☐☐ 398. Psalm 53
☐☐☐ 399. Psalm 54
☐☐☐ 400. Psalm 55
☐☐☐ 401. Psalm 56
☐☐☐ 402. Psalm 57
☐☐☐ 403. Psalm 58
☐☐☐ 404. Psalm 59
☐☐☐ 405. Psalm 60
☐☐☐ 406. Psalm 61
☐☐☐ 407. Psalm 62
☐☐☐ 408. Psalm 63
☐☐☐ 409. Psalm 64
☐☐☐ 410. Psalm 65
☐☐☐ 411. Psalm 66
☐☐☐ 412. Psalm 67
☐☐☐ 413. Psalm 68
☐☐☐ 414. Psalm 69
☐☐☐ 415. Psalm 70
☐☐☐ 416. Psalm 71
☐☐☐ 417. Psalm 72
☐☐☐ 418. Psalm 73
☐☐☐ 419. Psalm 74
☐☐☐ 420. Psalm 75
☐☐☐ 421. Psalm 76
☐☐☐ 422. Psalm 77
☐☐☐ 423. Psalm 78
☐☐☐ 424. Psalm 79
☐☐☐ 425. Psalm 80
☐☐☐ 426. Psalm 81
☐☐☐ 427. Psalm 82
☐☐☐ 428. Psalm 83
☐☐☐ 429. Psalm 84
☐☐☐ 430. Psalm 85
☐☐☐ 431. Psalm 86
☐☐☐ 432. Psalm 87
☐☐☐ 433. Psalm 88
☐☐☐ 434. Psalm 89
☐☐☐ 435 Psalm 90
☐☐☐ 436. Psalm 91
☐☐☐ 437. Psalm 92
☐☐☐ 438. Psalm 93

☐☐☐ 439. Psalm 94
☐☐☐ 440. Psalm 95
☐☐☐ 441. Psalm 96
☐☐☐ 442. Psalm 97
☐☐☐ 443. Psalm 98
☐☐☐ 444. Psalm 99
☐☐☐ 445. Ps 100,101
☐☐☐ 446. Psalm 102
☐☐☐ 447. Psalm 103
☐☐☐ 448. Psalm 104
☐☐☐ 449. Psalm 105
☐☐☐ 450. Psalm 106
☐☐☐ 451. Psalm 107
☐☐☐ 452. Psalm 108
☐☐☐ 453. Psalm 109
☐☐☐ 454. Psalm 110
☐☐☐ 455. Psalm 111
☐☐☐ 456. Psalm 112
☐☐☐ 457. Psalm 113
☐☐☐ 458. Psalm 114
☐☐☐ 459. Psalm 115
☐☐☐ 460. Psalm 116
☐☐☐ 461. Psalm 117
☐☐☐ 462. Psalm 118
☐☐☐ 463. Psalm 119
☐☐☐ 464. Psalm 120
☐☐☐ 465. Psalm 121
☐☐☐ 466. Ps 122,123
☐☐☐ 467. Ps 124,125
☐☐☐ 468. Ps 126,127
☐☐☐ 469. Ps 128,129
☐☐☐ 470. Ps 130,131
☐☐☐ 471. Psalm 132
☐☐☐ 472. Ps 133,134
☐☐☐ 473. Psalm 135
☐☐☐ 474. Psalm 136
☐☐☐ 475. Psalm 137
☐☐☐ 476. Psalm 138
☐☐☐ 477. Psalm 139
☐☐☐ 478. Psalm 140
☐☐☐ 479. Psalm 141

☐☐☐ 480. Psalm 142
☐☐☐ 481. Psalm 143
☐☐☐ 482. Psalm 144
☐☐☐ 483. Psalm 145
☐☐☐ 484. Psalm 146
☐☐☐ 485. Psalm 147
☐☐☐ 486. Psalm 148
☐☐☐ 487. Ps 149,150

PROVERBS

☐☐☐ 488. Proverbs 1
☐☐☐ 489. Proverbs 2
☐☐☐ 490. Proverbs 3
☐☐☐ 491. Proverbs 4
☐☐☐ 492. Proverbs 5
☐☐☐ 493. Proverbs 6
☐☐☐ 494. Proverbs 7
☐☐☐ 495. Proverbs 8
☐☐☐ 496. Proverbs 9
☐☐☐ 497. Proverbs 10
☐☐☐ 498. Proverbs 11
☐☐☐ 499. Proverbs 12
☐☐☐ 500. Proverbs 13
☐☐☐ 501. Proverbs 14
☐☐☐ 502. Proverbs 15
☐☐☐ 503. Proverbs 16
☐☐☐ 504. Proverbs 17
☐☐☐ 505. Proverbs 18
☐☐☐ 506. Proverbs 19
☐☐☐ 507. Proverbs 20
☐☐☐ 508. Proverbs 21
☐☐☐ 509. Proverbs 22
☐☐☐ 510. Proverbs 23
☐☐☐ 511. Proverbs 24
☐☐☐ 512. Proverbs 25
☐☐☐ 513. Proverbs 26
☐☐☐ 514. Proverbs 27
☐☐☐ 515. Proverbs 28
☐☐☐ 516. Proverbs 29
☐☐☐ 517. Proverbs 30
☐☐☐ 518. Proverbs 31

ECCLESIASTES

☐☐☐ 519. Ecclesiastes 1
☐☐☐ 520. Ecclesiastes 2
☐☐☐ 521. Ecclesiastes 3
☐☐☐ 522. Ecclesiastes 4
☐☐☐ 523. Ecclesiastes 5
☐☐☐ 524. Ecclesiastes 6
☐☐☐ 525. Ecclesiastes 7
☐☐☐ 526. Ecclesiastes 8
☐☐☐ 527. Ecclesiastes 9
☐☐☐ 528. Ecclesiastes 10
☐☐☐ 529. Ecclesiastes 11
☐☐☐ 530. Ecclesiastes 12

SONG OF SOLOMON

☐☐☐ 531. Song of Sol 1
☐☐☐ 532. Song of Sol 2
☐☐☐ 533. Song of Sol 3
☐☐☐ 534. Song of Sol 4
☐☐☐ 535. Song of Sol 5
☐☐☐ 536. Song of Sol 6
☐☐☐ 537. Song of Sol 7
☐☐☐ 538. Song of Sol 8

ISAIAH

☐☐☐ 539. Isaiah 1
☐☐☐ 540. Isaiah 2
☐☐☐ 541. Isaiah 3
☐☐☐ 542. Isaiah 4
☐☐☐ 543. Isaiah 5
☐☐☐ 544. Isaiah 6
☐☐☐ 545. Isaiah 7
☐☐☐ 546. Isaiah 8
☐☐☐ 547. Isaiah 9
☐☐☐ 548. Isaiah 10
☐☐☐ 549. Isaiah 11
☐☐☐ 550. Isaiah 12
☐☐☐ 551. Isaiah 13
☐☐☐ 552. Isaiah 14
☐☐☐ 553. Isaiah 15

□□□ 554. Isaiah 16
□□□ 555. Isaiah 17
□□□ 556. Isaiah 18
□□□ 557. Isaiah 19
□□□ 558. Isaiah 20,21
□□□ 559. Isaiah 22
□□□ 560. Isaiah 23
□□□ 561. Isaiah 24
□□□ 562. Isaiah 25
□□□ 563. Isaiah 26
□□□ 564. Isaiah 27
□□□ 565. Isaiah 28
□□□ 566. Isaiah 29
□□□ 567. Isaiah 30
□□□ 568. Isaiah 31
□□□ 569. Isaiah 32
□□□ 570. Isaiah 33
□□□ 571. Isaiah 34
□□□ 572. Isaiah 35
□□□ 573. Isaiah 36
□□□ 574. Isaiah 37
□□□ 575. Isaiah 38
□□□ 576. Isaiah 39
□□□ 577. Isaiah 40
□□□ 578. Isaiah 41
□□□ 579. Isaiah 42
□□□ 580. Isaiah 43
□□□ 581. Isaiah 44
□□□ 582. Isaiah 45
□□□ 583. Isaiah 46
□□□ 584. Isaiah 47
□□□ 585. Isaiah 48
□□□ 586. Isaiah 49
□□□ 587. Isaiah 50
□□□ 588. Isaiah 51
□□□ 589. Isaiah 52
□□□ 590. Isaiah 53
□□□ 591. Isaiah 54
□□□ 592. Isaiah 55
□□□ 593. Isaiah 56
□□□ 594. Isaiah 57

□□□ 595. Isaiah 58
□□□ 596. Isaiah 59
□□□ 597. Isaiah 60
□□□ 598. Isaiah 61
□□□ 599. Isaiah 62
□□□ 600. Isaiah 63
□□□ 601. Isaiah 64
□□□ 602. Isaiah 65
□□□ 603. Isaiah 66

JEREMIAH
□□□ 604. Jeremiah 1
□□□ 605. Jeremiah 2
□□□ 606. Jeremiah 3
□□□ 607. Jeremiah 4
□□□ 608. Jeremiah 5
□□□ 609. Jeremiah 6
□□□ 610. Jeremiah 7
□□□ 611. Jeremiah 8
□□□ 612. Jeremiah 9
□□□ 613. Jeremiah 10
□□□ 614. Jeremiah 11
□□□ 615. Jeremiah 12
□□□ 616. Jeremiah 13
□□□ 617. Jeremiah 14
□□□ 618. Jeremiah 15
□□□ 619. Jeremiah 16
□□□ 620. Jeremiah 17
□□□ 621. Jeremiah 18
□□□ 622. Jeremiah 19
□□□ 623. Jeremiah 20
□□□ 624. Jeremiah 21
□□□ 625. Jeremiah 22
□□□ 626. Jeremiah 23
□□□ 627. Jeremiah 24
□□□ 628. Jeremiah 25
□□□ 629. Jeremiah 26
□□□ 630. Jeremiah 27
□□□ 631. Jeremiah 28
□□□ 632. Jeremiah 29
□□□ 633. Jeremiah 30

□□□ 634. Jeremiah 31
□□□ 635. Jeremiah 32
□□□ 636. Jeremiah 33
□□□ 637. Jeremiah 34
□□□ 638. Jeremiah 35
□□□ 639. Jeremiah 36
□□□ 640. Jeremiah 37
□□□ 641. Jeremiah 38
□□□ 642. Jeremiah 39
□□□ 643. Jeremiah 40
□□□ 644. Jeremiah 41
□□□ 645. Jeremiah 42
□□□ 646. Jeremiah 43
□□□ 647. Jeremiah 44
□□□ 648. Jeremiah 45
□□□ 649. Jeremiah 46
□□□ 650. Jeremiah 47
□□□ 651. Jeremiah 48
□□□ 652. Jeremiah 49
□□□ 653. Jeremiah 50
□□□ 654. Jeremiah 51

LAMENTATIONS
□□□ 655. Lamen 1
□□□ 656. Lamen 2
□□□ 657. Lamen 3
□□□ 658. Lamen 4
□□□ 659. Lamen 5

EZEKIEL
□□□ 660. Ezekiel 1
□□□ 661. Ezekiel 2
□□□ 662. Ezekiel 3
□□□ 663. Ezekiel 4
□□□ 664. Ezekiel 5
□□□ 665. Ezekiel 6
□□□ 666. Ezekiel 7
□□□ 667. Ezekiel 8
□□□ 668. Ezekiel 9
□□□ 669. Ezekiel 10
□□□ 670. Ezekiel 11

☐☐☐ 671. Ezekiel 12
☐☐☐ 672. Ezekiel 13
☐☐☐ 673. Ezekiel 14
☐☐☐ 674. Ezekiel 15
☐☐☐ 675. Ezekiel 16
☐☐☐ 676. Ezekiel 17
☐☐☐ 677. Ezekiel 18
☐☐☐ 678. Ezekiel 19
☐☐☐ 679. Ezekiel 20
☐☐☐ 680. Ezekiel 21
☐☐☐ 681. Ezekiel 22
☐☐☐ 682. Ezekiel 23
☐☐☐ 683. Ezekiel 24
☐☐☐ 684. Ezekiel 25
☐☐☐ 685. Ezekiel 26
☐☐☐ 686. Ezekiel 27
☐☐☐ 687. Ezekiel 28
☐☐☐ 688. Ezekiel 29
☐☐☐ 689. Ezekiel 30
☐☐☐ 690. Ezekiel 31
☐☐☐ 691. Ezekiel 32
☐☐☐ 692. Ezekiel 33
☐☐☐ 693. Ezekiel 34
☐☐☐ 694. Ezekiel 35
☐☐☐ 695. Ezekiel 36
☐☐☐ 696. Ezekiel 37
☐☐☐ 697. Ezekiel 38
☐☐☐ 698. Ezekiel 39
(omit 40–48)

DANIEL

☐☐☐ 699. Daniel 1
☐☐☐ 700. Daniel 2
☐☐☐ 701. Daniel 3
☐☐☐ 702. Daniel 4
☐☐☐ 703. Daniel 5
☐☐☐ 704. Daniel 6
☐☐☐ 705. Daniel 7
☐☐☐ 706. Daniel 8
☐☐☐ 707. Daniel 9

☐☐☐ 708. Daniel 10
☐☐☐ 709. Daniel 11
☐☐☐ 710. Daniel 12

HOSEA

☐☐☐ 711. Hosea 1
☐☐☐ 712. Hosea 2,3
☐☐☐ 713. Hosea 4
☐☐☐ 714. Hosea 5
☐☐☐ 715. Hosea 6
☐☐☐ 716. Hosea 7
☐☐☐ 717. Hosea 8
☐☐☐ 718. Hosea 9
☐☐☐ 719. Hosea 10
☐☐☐ 720. Hosea 11
☐☐☐ 721. Hosea 12
☐☐☐ 722. Hosea 13
☐☐☐ 723. Hosea 14

JOEL

☐☐☐ 724. Joel 1
☐☐☐ 725. Joel 2
☐☐☐ 726. Joel 3

AMOS

☐☐☐ 727. Amos 1
☐☐☐ 728. Amos 2
☐☐☐ 729. Amos 3
☐☐☐ 730. Amos 4
☐☐☐ 731. Amos 5
☐☐☐ 732. Amos 6
☐☐☐ 733. Amos 7
☐☐☐ 734. Amos 8
☐☐☐ 735. Amos 9

OBADIAH

☐☐☐ 736. Obadiah 1

JONAH

☐☐☐ 737. Jonah 1

☐☐☐ 738. Jonah 2
☐☐☐ 739. Jonah 3
☐☐☐ 740. Jonah 4

MICAH

☐☐☐ 741. Micah 1
☐☐☐ 742. Micah 2
☐☐☐ 743. Micah 3
☐☐☐ 744. Micah 4
☐☐☐ 745. Micah 5
☐☐☐ 746. Micah 6
☐☐☐ 747. Micah 7

NAHUM

☐☐☐ 748. Nahum 1
☐☐☐ 749. Nahum 2
☐☐☐ 750. Nahum 3

HABAKKUK

☐☐☐ 751. Habakkuk 1
☐☐☐ 752. Habakkuk 2
☐☐☐ 753. Habakkuk 3

ZEPHANIAH

☐☐☐ 754. Zephaniah 1
☐☐☐ 755. Zephaniah 2
☐☐☐ 756. Zephaniah 3

HAGGAI

☐☐☐ 757. Haggai 1
☐☐☐ 758. Haggai 2

ZECHARIAH

☐☐☐ 759. Zechariah 1
☐☐☐ 760. Zechariah 2
☐☐☐ 761. Zechariah 3
☐☐☐ 762. Zechariah 4
☐☐☐ 763. Zechariah 5
☐☐☐ 764. Zechariah 6
☐☐☐ 765. Zechariah 7

☐☐☐ 766. Zechariah 8
☐☐☐ 767. Zechariah 9
☐☐☐ 768. Zechariah 10
☐☐☐ 769. Zechariah 11
☐☐☐ 770. Zechariah 12
☐☐☐ 771. Zechariah 13
☐☐☐ 772. Zechariah 14

MALACHI

☐☐☐ 773. Malachi 1
☐☐☐ 774. Malachi 2
☐☐☐ 775. Malachi 3
☐☐☐ 776. Malachi 4

HARMONY OF THE SYNOPTIC GOSPELS

☐☐☐ Matthew
☐☐☐ Mark
☐☐☐ Luke

Birth Narratives
☐☐☐ 1. Lk 1:5-25
☐☐☐ 2. Lk 1:26-38
☐☐☐ 3. Lk 1:39-56
☐☐☐ 4. Lk 1:57- 80
☐☐☐ 5. Mt 1:18-25
☐☐☐ 6. Lk 2:1-20
☐☐☐ 7. Lk 2:21-39
☐☐☐ 8. Mt 2:1-12
☐☐☐ 9. Mt 2:13-23
☐☐☐ 10 Lk 2:40-52

Public Ministry
☐☐☐ 11. Lk 3:1-23
☐☐☐ 12. Mt 3:13-17; 4:1-11
☐☐☐ 13. Lk 4:16-31
☐☐☐ 14. Mt 4:13-22
☐☐☐ 15. Lk 5:1-11
☐☐☐ 16. Mk 1:21-45

☐☐☐ 17. Mk 2:1-12
☐☐☐ 18. Mk 2:13-17
☐☐☐ 19. Mk 2:18-3:6
☐☐☐ 20. Mk 3:7-19
☐☐☐ 21. Mt 5:1-12
☐☐☐ 22. Mt 5:13-20
☐☐☐ 23. Mt 5:21-37
☐☐☐ 24. Mt 5:38-48
☐☐☐ 25. Mt 6:1-15
☐☐☐ 26. Mt 6:16-24
☐☐☐ 27. Mt 6:25-34
☐☐☐ 28. Mt 7:1-6
☐☐☐ 29. Mt 7:7-12
☐☐☐ 30. Mt 7:13-23
☐☐☐ 31. Mt 7:24-29
☐☐☐ 32. Mt 8:1-13
☐☐☐ 33. Lk 7:11-17
☐☐☐ 34. Lk 7:18-35
☐☐☐ 35. Mt 11:20-30
☐☐☐ 36. Lk 7:36-50
☐☐☐ 37. Mt 12:22-37
☐☐☐ 38. Mt 12:38-45
☐☐☐ 39. Mt 12:46-50
☐☐☐ 40. Mt 13:1-23
☐☐☐ 41. Mk 4:21-29
☐☐☐ 42. Mt 13:24-35
☐☐☐ 43. Mt 13:36-53
☐☐☐ 44. Mt 8:18-34
☐☐☐ 45. Mk 5:21-43
☐☐☐ 46. Mt 9:27-34
☐☐☐ 47. Mt 13:54-58
☐☐☐ 48. Mt 9:35-11:1
☐☐☐ 49. Mk 6:14-29
☐☐☐ 50. Mk 6:30-44
☐☐☐ 51. Mt 14:22-36
☐☐☐ 52. Mk 7:1-23
☐☐☐ 53. Mk 7:24-8:9
☐☐☐ 54. Mk 8:10-26
☐☐☐ 55. Mt 16:13-20
☐☐☐ 56. Mt 16:21-28
☐☐☐ 57. Mt 17:1-13

☐☐☐ 58. Mk 9:14-32
☐☐☐ 59. Mt 17:24–18:14
☐☐☐ 60. Mt 18:15-35
☐☐☐ 61. Lk 9:57-10:24
☐☐☐ 62. Lk 10:25-37
☐☐☐ 63. Lk 10:38-42
☐☐☐ 64. Lk 11:1-13
☐☐☐ 65. Lk 11:14-36
☐☐☐ 66. Lk 11:37-54
☐☐☐ 67. Lk 12:1-12
☐☐☐ 68. Lk 12:13-21
☐☐☐ 69. Lk 12:22-34
☐☐☐ 70. Lk 12:35-48
☐☐☐ 71. Lk 12:49-59
☐☐☐ 72. Lk 13:1-9
☐☐☐ 73. Lk 13:10-21
☐☐☐ 74. Lk 13:22-35
☐☐☐ 75. Lk 14:1-24
☐☐☐ 76. Lk 14:25-35
☐☐☐ 77. Lk 15:1-32
☐☐☐ 78. Lk 16:1-18
☐☐☐ 79. Lk 16:19-31
☐☐☐ 80. Lk 17:1-10
☐☐☐ 81. Lk 17:11-19
☐☐☐ 82. Lk 17:20-37
☐☐☐ 83. Lk 8:1-14
☐☐☐ 84. Mt 19:1-12
☐☐☐ 85. Mt 19:13-30
☐☐☐ 86. Mt 20:1-16
☐☐☐ 87. Mt 20:17-34
☐☐☐ 88. Lk 19:1-10
☐☐☐ 89. Lk 19:11-28

The Last Week
☐☐☐ 90. Mt 21:1-17
☐☐☐ 91. Mt 21:18-27
☐☐☐ 92. Mt 21:28-46
☐☐☐ 93. Mt 22:1-14
☐☐☐ 94. Mt 22:15-22
☐☐☐ 95. Mt 22:23-33
☐☐☐ 96. Mt 22:34-46

□□□ 97. Mt 23:1-22
□□□ 98. Mt 23:23-39
□□□ 99. Mt 24:1-14
□□□ 100. Mt 24:15-35
□□□ 101. Mt 24:36-51
□□□ 102. Mt 25:1-13
□□□ 103. Mt 25:14-30
□□□ 104. Mt 25:31-36

Betrayal and Crucifixion
□□□ 105. Mt 26:1-13
□□□ 106. Mt 26:14-35
□□□ 107. Lk 22:24-38
□□□ 108. Mt 26:36-46
□□□ 109. Mt 26:47-56
□□□ 110. Mt 26:57-75

Resurrection
□□□ 111. Mt 27:1-26
□□□ 112. Mt 27:27-56
□□□ 113. Mt 27:57-66
□□□ 114. Lk 24:1-12
□□□ 115. Lk 24:13-35
□□□ 116. Lk 24:36-53
□□□ 117. Mt 28:11-20

JOHN
□□□ 118. John 1
□□□ 119. John 2
□□□ 120. John 3
□□□ 121. John 4
□□□ 122. John 5
□□□ 123. John 6
□□□ 124. John 7
□□□ 125. John 8
□□□ 126. John 9
□□□ 127. John 10
□□□ 128. John 11
□□□ 129. John 12
□□□ 130. John 13
□□□ 131. John 14

□□□ 132. John 15
□□□ 133. John 16
□□□ 134. John 17
□□□ 135. John 18
□□□ 136. John 19
□□□ 137. John 20
□□□ 138. John 21

ACTS
□□□ 139. Acts 1
□□□ 140. Acts 2
□□□ 141. Acts 3
□□□ 142. Acts 4
□□□ 143. Acts 5
□□□ 144. Acts 6
□□□ 145. Acts 7
□□□ 146. Acts 8
□□□ 147. Acts 9
□□□ 148. Acts 10
□□□ 149. Acts 11
□□□ 150. Acts 12
□□□ 151. Acts 13
□□□ 152. Acts 14
□□□ 153. Acts 15
□□□ 154. Acts 16
□□□ 155. Acts 17
□□□ 156. Acts 18
□□□ 157. Acts 19
□□□ 158. Acts 20
□□□ 159. Acts 21
□□□ 160. Acts 22
□□□ 161. Acts 23
□□□ 162. Acts 24
□□□ 163. Acts 25
□□□ 164. Acts 26
□□□ 165. Acts 27
□□□ 166. Acts 28

ROMANS
□□□ 167. Romans 1
□□□ 168. Romans 2

□□□ 169. Romans 3
□□□ 170. Romans 4
□□□ 171. Romans 5
□□□ 172. Romans 6
□□□ 173. Romans 7
□□□ 174. Romans 8
□□□ 175. Romans 9
□□□ 176. Romans 10
□□□ 177. Romans 11
□□□ 178. Romans 12
□□□ 179. Romans 13
□□□ 180. Romans 14
□□□ 181. Romans 15
□□□ 182. Romans 16

1 CORINTHIANS
□□□ 183. 1 Cor 1
□□□ 184. 1 Cor 2
□□□ 185. 1 Cor 3
□□□ 186. 1 Cor 4
□□□ 187. 1 Cor 5
□□□ 188. 1 Cor 6
□□□ 189. 1 Cor 7
□□□ 190. 1 Cor 8
□□□ 191. 1 Cor 9
□□□ 192. 1 Cor 10
□□□ 193. 1 Cor 11
□□□ 194. 1 Cor 12
□□□ 195. 1 Cor 13
□□□ 196. 1 Cor 14
□□□ 197. 1 Cor 15
□□□ 198. 1 Cor 16

2 CORINTHIANS
□□□ 199. 2 Cor 1
□□□ 200. 2 Cor 2
□□□ 201. 2 Cor 3
□□□ 202. 2 Cor 4
□□□ 203. 2 Cor 5
□□□ 204. 2 Cor 6
□□□ 205. 2 Cor 7

☐☐☐ 206. 2 Cor 8
☐☐☐ 207. 2 Cor 9
☐☐☐ 208. 2 Cor 10
☐☐☐ 209. 2 Cor 11
☐☐☐ 210. 2 Cor 12
☐☐☐ 211. 2 Cor 13

GALATIANS
☐☐☐ 212. Galatians 1
☐☐☐ 213. Galatians 2
☐☐☐ 214. Galatians 3
☐☐☐ 215. Galatians 4
☐☐☐ 216. Galatians 5
☐☐☐217. Galatians 6

EPHESIANS
☐☐☐ 218. Ephesians 1
☐☐☐ 219. Ephesians 2
☐☐☐ 220. Ephesians 3
☐☐☐ 221. Ephesians 4
☐☐☐ 222. Ephesians 5
☐☐☐ 223. Ephesians 6

PHILIPPIANS
☐☐☐ 224. Phil 1
☐☐☐ 225. Phil 2
☐☐☐ 226. Phil 3
☐☐☐ 227. Phil 4

COLOSSIANS
☐☐☐ 228. Colossians 1
☐☐☐ 229. Colossians 2
☐☐☐ 230. Colossians 3
☐☐☐ 231. Colossians 4

1 THESSALONIANS
☐☐☐ 232. 1 Thess 1
☐☐☐ 233. 1 Thess 2
☐☐☐ 234. 1 Thess 3
☐☐☐ 235. 1 Thess 4

☐☐☐ 236. 1 Thess 5

2 THESSALONIANS
☐☐☐ 237. 2 Thess 1
☐☐☐ 238. 2 Thess 2
☐☐☐ 239. 2 Thess 3

1 TIMOTHY
☐☐☐ 240. 1 Timothy 1
☐☐☐ 241. 1 Timothy 2
☐☐☐ 242. 1 Timothy 3
☐☐☐ 243. 1 Timothy 4
☐☐☐ 244. 1 Timothy 5

2 TIMOTHY
☐☐☐ 245. 2 Timothy 1
☐☐☐ 246. 2 Timothy 2
☐☐☐ 247. 2 Timothy 3
☐☐☐ 248. 2 Timothy 4

TITUS
☐☐☐ 249. Titus 1
☐☐☐ 250. Titus 2
☐☐☐ 251. Titus 3

PHILEMON
☐☐☐ 252. Philemon 1

HEBREWS
☐☐☐ 253. Hebrews 1
☐☐☐ 254. Hebrews 2
☐☐☐ 255. Hebrews 3
☐☐☐ 256. Hebrews 4
☐☐☐ 257. Hebrews 5
☐☐☐ 258. Hebrews 6
☐☐☐ 259. Hebrews 7
☐☐☐ 260. Hebrews 8
☐☐☐ 261. Hebrews 9
☐☐☐ 262. Hebrews 10
☐☐☐ 263. Hebrews 11

☐☐☐ 264. Hebrews 12
☐☐☐ 265. Hebrews 13

JAMES
☐☐☐ 266. James 1
☐☐☐ 267. James 2
☐☐☐ 268. James 3
☐☐☐ 269. James 4
☐☐☐ 270. James 5

1 PETER
☐☐☐ 271. 1 Peter 1
☐☐☐ 272. 1 Peter 2
☐☐☐ 273. 1 Peter 3
☐☐☐ 274. 1 Peter 4
☐☐☐ 275. 1 Peter 5

2 PETER
☐☐☐ 276. 2 Peter 1
☐☐☐ 277. 2 Peter 2
☐☐☐ 278. 2 Peter 3

1 JOHN
☐☐☐ 279. 1 John 1
☐☐☐ 280. 1 John 2
☐☐☐ 281. 1 John 3
☐☐☐ 282. 1 John 4
☐☐☐ 283. 1 John 5

2 JOHN
☐☐☐ 284. 2 John 1

3 JOHN
☐☐☐ 285. 3 John 1

JUDE
☐☐☐ 286. Jude 1

REVELATION

☐☐☐ 287. Revelation 1
☐☐☐ 288. Revelation 2
☐☐☐ 289. Revelation 3
☐☐☐ 290. Revelation 4
☐☐☐ 291. Revelation 5
☐☐☐ 292. Revelation 6
☐☐☐ 293. Revelation 7
☐☐☐ 293. Revelation 8

☐☐☐ 294. Revelation 9
☐☐☐ 295. Revelation10
☐☐☐ 296. Revelation11
☐☐☐ 298. Revelation12
☐☐☐ 299. Revelation13
☐☐☐ 300. Revelation 14
☐☐☐ 301. Revelation 15
☐☐☐ 302. Revelation 16

☐☐☐ 303. Revelation 17
☐☐☐ 304. Revelation 18
☐☐☐ 305. Revelation 19
☐☐☐ 306. Revelation 20
☐☐☐ 307. Revelation 21
☐☐☐ 308. Revelation 22

2. Catechism for Young Children

The following catechism was prepared by Mr. Joseph P. Engles (1793-1861), lifelong grammar school headmaster and later publishing agent of the Presbyterian Board of Publication. It was originally published in 1840 as an introduction to the *Shorter Catechism* and included an opening charge "to parents and teachers." As to the importance of the religious education of the young he wrote,

> You have an awfully responsible office in being entrusted with the training of immortal spirits for the service of God on earth and for glory in heaven. The temporal welfare and the eternal salvation not only of your own children, but of future generations, may depend upon your faithfulness in the discharge of this duty. The prosperity, and even the continuance, of the church of God on earth are connected with the religious education of the rising generation. To aid you in this all-important task, the following little work has been written, and is humbly offered for your acceptance.

As to the manner in which catechizing is conducted he counseled,

> Endeavor to impress the minds of the dear children with the importance of **understanding** what they learn. Be not satisfied with the verbal accuracy of their answers. Encourage them to ask and be ready to answer questions for information, while you gently check a spirit of idle curiosity. Endeavor to make what most children consider an irksome task a pleasing and profitable study.[27]

Question 1

Q. *Who made you?*

A. God.

Question 2

Q. *What else did God make?*

A. God made all things.

Question 3

Q. *Why did God make you and all things?*

A. For his own glory.

Question 4

Q. *How can you glorify God?*

A. By loving him and doing what he commands

---

[27]*Catechism for Young Children, Being an Introduction to the Shorter Catechism* (Philadelphia: Presbyterian Board of Publication and Sabbath-School Work, 1840).

Question 5

Q. *Why ought you to glorify God?*

A. Because he made me and takes care of me.

Question 6

Q. *Are there more gods than one?*

A. There is only one God.

Question 7

Q. *In how many persons does this one God exist?*

A. In three persons.

Question 8

Q. *What are they?*

A. The Father, the Son, and the Holy Ghost.

Question 9

Q. *What is God?*

A. God is a Spirit, and has not a body like men.

Question 10

Q. *Where is God?*

A. God is everywhere.

Question 11

Q. *Can you see God?*

A. No; I cannot see God, but he always sees me.

Question 12

Q. *Does God know all things?*

A. Yes; nothing can be hid from God.

Question 13

Q. *Can God do all things?*

A. Yes; God can do all his holy will.

Question 14

Q. *Where do you learn how to love and obey God?*

A. In the Bible alone.

Question 15

Q. *Who wrote the Bible?*

A. Holy men who were taught by the Holy Spirit.

Question 16

Q. *Who were our first parents?*

A. Adam and Eve.

Question 17

Q. *Of what were our first parents made?*

A. God made the body of Adam out of the ground, and formed Eve from the body of Adam.

Question 18

Q. *What did God give Adam and Eve besides bodies?*

A. He gave them souls that could never die.

Question 19

Q. *Have you a soul as well as body?*

A. Yes; I have a soul that can never die.

Question 20

Q. *How do you know that you have a soul?*

A. Because the Bible tells me so.

Question 21

Q. *In what condition did God make Adam and Eve?*

A. He made them holy and happy.

Question 22

Q. *What is a covenant?*

A. An agreement between two or more persons.

Question 23

Q. *What covenant did God make with Adam?*

A. The covenant of works.

Question 24

Q. *What was Adam bound to do by the covenant of works?*

A. To obey God perfectly.

Question 25

Q. *What did God promise in the covenant of works?*

A. To reward Adam with life if he obeyed him.

Question 26

Q. *What did God threaten in the covenant of works?*

A. To punish Adam with death if he disobeyed.

Question 27

Q. *Did Adam keep the covenant of works?*

A. No; he sinned against God.

Question 28

Q. *What is sin?*

A. Sin is any want of conformity unto, or transgression of, the law of God.

Question 29

Q. *What is meant by want of conformity?*

A. Not being or doing what God requires.

Question 30

Q. *What is meant by transgression?*

A. Doing what God forbids.

Question 31

Q. *What was the sin of our first parents?*

A. Eating the forbidden fruit.

Question 32

Q. *Who tempted them to this sin?*

A. The devil tempted Eve, and she gave the fruit to Adam.

Question 33

Q. *What befell our first parents when they had sinned?*

A. Instead of being holy and happy, they became sinful and miserable.

Question 34

Q. *Did Adam act for himself alone in the covenant of works?*

A. No; he represented all his posterity.

Question 35

Q. *What effect had the sin of Adam on all mankind?*

A. All mankind are born in a state of sin and misery.

Question 36

Q. *What is that sinful nature which we inherit from Adam called?*

A. Original sin.

Question 37

Q. *What does every sin deserve?*

A. The wrath and curse of God.

Question 38

Q. *Can anyone go to heaven with this sinful nature?*

A. No; our hearts must be changed before we can be fit for heaven.

Question 39

Q. *What is a change of heart called?*

A. Regeneration.

Question 40

Q. *Who can change a sinner's heart?*

A. The Holy Spirit alone.

Question 41

Q. *Can anyone be saved through the covenant of works?*

A. None can be saved through the covenant of works.

Question 42

Q. *Why can none be saved through the covenant of works?*

A. Because all have broken it, and are condemned by it.

Question 43

Q. *With whom did God the Father make the covenant of grace?*

A. With Christ, his eternal Son.

Question 44

Q. *Whom did Christ represent in the covenant of grace?*

A. His elect people.

Question 45

Q. *What did Christ undertake in the covenant of grace?*

A. To keep the whole law for his people, and to suffer the punishment due to their sins.

Question 46

Q. *Did our Lord Jesus Christ ever commit the least sin?*

A. No; he was holy, harmless, and undefiled.

Question 47

Q. *How could the Son of God suffer?*

A. Christ, the Son of God, became man that he might obey and suffer in our nature.

Question 48

Q. *What is meant by the Atonement?*

A. Christ's satisfying divine justice, by his sufferings and death, in the place of sinners.

Question 49

Q. *What did God the Father undertake in the covenant of grace?*

A. To justify and sanctify those for whom Christ should die.

Question 50

Q. *What is justification?*

A. It is God's forgiving sinners, and treating them as if they had never sinned.

Question 51

Q. *What is sanctification?*

A. It is God's making sinners holy in heart and conduct.

Question 52

Q. *For whom did Christ obey and suffer?*

A. For those whom the Father had given him.

Question 53

Q. *What kind of life did Christ live on earth?*

A. A life of poverty and suffering.

Question 54

Q. *What kind of death did Christ die?*

A. The painful and shameful death of the cross.

Question 55

Q. *Who will be saved?*

A. Only those who repent of sin, believe in Christ, and lead holy lives.

Question 56

Q. *What is it to repent?*

A. To be sorry for sin, and to hate and forsake it because it is displeasing to God.

Question 57

Q. *What is it to believe or have faith in Christ?*

A. To trust in Christ alone for salvation.

Question 58

Q. *Can you repent and believe in Christ by your own power?*

A. No; I can do nothing good without the help of God's Holy Spirit.

Question 59

Q. *How can you get the help of the Holy Spirit?*

A. God has told us that we must pray to him for the Holy Spirit.

Question 60

Q. *How long ago is it since Christ died?*

A. More than nineteen hundred years.

Question 61

Q. *How were pious persons saved before the coming of Christ?*

A. By believing in a Savior to Come.

Question 62

Q. *How did they show their faith?*

A. By offering sacrifices on God's altar.

Question 63

Q. *What did these sacrifices represent?*

A. Christ, the Lamb of God, who was to die for sinners.

Question 64

Q. *What offices has Christ?*

A. Christ has three offices.

Question 65

Q. *What are they?*

A. The offices of a prophet, of a priest, and of a king.

Question 66

Q. *How is Christ a prophet?*

A. Because he teaches us the will of God.

Question 67

Q. *How is Christ a priest?*

A. Because he died for our sins and pleads with God for us.

Question 68

Q. *How is Christ a king?*

A. Because he rules over us and defends us.

Question 69

Q. *Why do you need Christ as a prophet?*

A. Because I am ignorant.

Question 70

Q. *Why do you need Christ as a priest?*

A. Because I am guilty.

Question 71

Q. *Why do you need Christ as a king?*

A. Because I am weak and helpless.

Question 72

Q. *How many commandments did God give on Mount Sinai?*

A. Ten commandments.

Question 73

Q. *What are the ten commandments sometimes called?*

A. The Decalogue.

Question 74

Q. *What do the first four commandments teach?*

A. Our duty to God.

Question 75

Q. *What do the last six commandments teach?*

A. Our duty to our fellow men.

Question 76

Q. What *is the* sum of the ten commandments?

A. To love God with all my heart, and my neighbor as myself.

Question 77

Q. *Who is your neighbor?*

A. All my fellow men are my neighbors.

Question 78

Q. *Is God pleased with those who love and obey him?*

A. Yes; he says, "I love them that love me."

Question 79

Q. *Is God displeased with those who do not love and obey him?*

A. Yes; "God is angry with the wicked every day."

Question 80

Q. *What is the first commandment?*

A. The first commandment is, Thou shalt have no other gods before me.

Question 81

Q. *What does the first commandment teach us?*

A. To worship God alone.

Question 82

Q. *What is the second commandment?*

A. The second commandment is, Thou shalt not make unto thee any graven image, or any likeness of anything that is in heaven above, or that is in the earth beneath, or that is in the water under the earth; thou shalt not bow down thyself to them, nor serve them: for I, the Lord thy God, am a jealous God, visiting the iniquity of the fathers upon the children unto the third and fourth generation of them that hate me; and showing mercy unto thousands of them that love me, and keep my commandments.

Question 83

Q. *What does the second commandment teach us?*

A. To worship God in a proper manner, and to avoid idolatry.

Question 84

Q. *What is the third commandment?*

A. The third commandment is, Thou shalt not take the name of the Lord thy God in vain: for the Lord will not hold him guiltless that taketh his name in vain

Question 85

Q. *What does the third commandment teach us?*

A. To reverence God's name, word, and works.

Question 86

Q. *What is the fourth commandment?*

A. The fourth commandment is, Remember the Sabbath day to keep it holy. Six days shalt thou labor, and do all thy work, but the seventh day is the Sabbath of the Lord thy God; in it thou shalt not do any work, thou, nor thy son, nor thy daughter, nor thy manservant, nor thy maidservant, nor thy cattle, nor thy stranger that is within thy gates: for in six days the Lord made heaven and earth, the sea, and all that in them is, and rested the seventh day; wherefore the Lord blessed the Sabbath Day, and hallowed it.

Question 87

Q. *What does the fourth commandment teach us?*

A. To keep the Sabbath holy.

Question 88

Q. *What day of the week is the Christian Sabbath?*

A. The first day of the week, called the Lord's day.

Question 89

Q. *Why is it called the Lord's day?*

A. Because on that day Christ rose from the dead.

Question 90

Q. *How should the Sabbath be spent?*

A. In prayer and praise, in hearing and reading God's Word, and in doing good to our fellow men.

Question 91

Q. *What is the fifth commandment?*

A. The fifth commandment is, Honor thy father and thy mother, that thy days may be long upon the land which the Lord thy God giveth thee.

Question 92

Q. *What does the fifth commandment teach us?*

A. To love and obey our parents and teachers.

Question 93

Q. *What is the sixth commandment?*

A. The sixth commandment is, Thou shalt not kill.

Question 94

Q. *What does the sixth commandment teach us?*

A. To avoid angry passions.

Question 95

Q. *What is the seventh commandment?*

A. The seventh commandment is, Thou shalt not commit adultery.

Question 96

Q. *What does the seventh commandment teach us?*

A. To be pure in heart, language, and conduct.

Question 97

Q. *What is the eighth commandment?*

A. The eighth commandment is, Thou shalt not steal.

Question 98

Q. *What does the eighth commandment teach us?*

A. To be honest and industrious

Question 99

Q. *What is the ninth commandment?*

A. The ninth commandment is, Thou shalt not bear false witness against thy neighbor.

Question 100

Q. *What does the ninth commandment teach us?*

A. To tell the truth.

Question 101

Q. *What is the tenth commandment?*

A. The tenth commandment is, Thou shalt not covet thy neighbor's house, thou shalt not covet thy neighbor's wife, nor his manservant, nor his maidservant, nor his ox, nor his ass, nor anything that is thy neighbor's.

Question 102

Q. *What does the tenth commandment teach us?*

A. To be content with our lot.

Question 103

Q. *Can any man keep these ten commandments perfectly?*

A. No mere man, since the fall of Adam, ever did or can keep the ten commandments perfectly.

Question 104

Q. *Of what use are the ten commandments to us?*

A. They teach us our duty, and show our need of a Savior.

Question 105

Q. *What is prayer?*

A. Prayer is asking God for things which he has promised to give.

Question 106

Q. *In whose name should we pray?*

A. Only in the name of Christ.

Question 107

Q. *What has Christ given us to teach us how to pray?*

A. The Lord's Prayer.

Question 108

Q. *Repeat the Lord's Prayer.*

A. Our Father which art in heaven, Hallowed be thy name. Thy kingdom come. Thy will be done in earth, as it is in heaven. Give us this day our daily bread. And forgive us our debts, as we forgive our debtors. And lead us not into temptation, but deliver us from evil: For thine is the kingdom, and the power, and the glory, forever. Amen.

Question 109

Q. *How many petitions are there in the Lord's Prayer?*

A. Six.

Question 110

Q. *What is the first petition?*

A. "Hallowed be thy name."

Question 111

Q. *What do we pray for in the first petition?*

A. That God's name may be honored by us and all men.

Question 112

Q. *What is the second petition?*

A. "Thy kingdom come."

Question 113

Q. *What do we pray for in the second petition?*

A. That the gospel may be preached in all the world, and believed and obeyed by us and all men.

Question 114

Q. *What is the third petition?*

A. "Thy will be done in earth, as it is in heaven."

Question 115

Q. *What do we pray for in the third petition?*

A. That men on earth may serve God as the angels do in heaven.

Question 116

Q. *What is the fourth petition?*

A. "Give us this day our daily bread."

Question 117

Q. *What do we pray for in the fourth petition?*

A. That God would give us all things needful for our bodies and souls.

Question 118

Q. *What is the fifth petition?*

A. "And forgive us our debts, as we forgive our debtors."

Question 119

Q. *What do we pray for in the fifth petititon?*

A. That God would pardon our sins for Christ's sake, and enable us to forgive those who have injured us.

Question 120

Q. *What is the sixth petition?*

A. "And lead us not into temptation, but deliver us from evil."

Question 121

Q. *What do we pray for in the sixth petition?*

A. That God would keep us from sin.

Question 122

Q. *How many sacraments are there?*

A. Two.

Question 123

Q. *What are they?*

A. Baptism and the Lord's Supper.

Question 124

Q. *Who appointed these sacraments?*

A. The Lord Jesus Christ.

Question 125

Q. *Why did Christ appoint these sacraments?*

A. To distinguish his disciples from the world, and to comfort and strengthen them.

Question 126

Q. *What sign is used in baptism?*

A. The washing with water.

Question 127

Q. *What does this signify?*

A. That we are cleansed from sin by the blood of Christ.

Question 128

Q. *In whose name are we baptized?*

A. In the name of the Father, and of the Son, and of the Holy Ghost.

Question 129

Q. *Who are to be baptized?*

A. Believers and their children.

Question 130

Q. *Why should infants be baptized?*

A. Because they have a sinful nature and need a Savior.

Question 131

Q. *Does Christ care for little children?*

A. Yes; for he says, "Suffer the little children to come unto me, and forbid them not: for of such is the kingdom of God."

Question 132

Q. *To what does your baptism bind you?*

A. To be a true follower of Christ.

Question 133

Q. *What is the Lord's Supper?*

A. The eating of bread and drinking of wine in remembrance of the sufferings and death of Christ.

Question 134

Q. *What does the bread represent?*

A. The body of Christ, broken for our sins

Question 135

Q. *What does the wine represent?*

A. The blood of Christ, shed for our salvation.

Question 136

Q. *Who should partake of the Lord's Supper?*

A. Only those who repent of their sins, believe in Christ for salvation, and love their fellow men.

Question 137

Q. *Did Christ remain in the tomb after his crucifixion?*

A. No; he rose from the tomb on the third day after his death.

Question 138

Q. *Where is Christ now?*

A. In heaven, interceding for sinners.

Question 139

Q. *Will he come again?*

A. Yes; at the last day Christ will come to judge the world.

Question 140

Q. *What becomes of men at death?*

A. The body returns to dust, and the soul goes into the world of spirits.

Question 141

Q. *Will the bodies of the dead be raised to life again?*

A. Yes; "the trumpet shall sound, and the dead shall be raised."

Question 142

Q. *What will become of the wicked in the day of judgment?*

A. They shall be cast into hell.

Question 143

Q. *What is hell?*

A. A place of dreadful and endless torment.

Question 144

Q. *What will become of the righteous?*

A. They shall be taken to heaven.

Question 145

Q. *What is heaven?*

A. A glorious and happy place, where the righteous shall be forever with the Lord.

3. The Shorter Catechism

For over three hundred years the *Shorter Catechism* has been the most widely used and beloved catechism amongst English–speaking peoples. The assembly of Puritan divines that produced the *Westminster Confession of Faith* (1646) also produced a *Larger Catechism* (1648) for the instruction of the mature, and a *Shorter Catechism* (1647) for "such as are of weaker capacity." Noted for its brevity, precision and thoroughness, it has been profitably employed by generations of Baptists, Congregationalists, as well as Presbyterians. Following its introductory questions (numbers 1–3), the main body of the catechism divides into the two categories indicated by the third of the introductory questions: what man is to believe concerning God (questions 4–39), and what duty God requires of man (questions 40–107).[28]

Question 1

Q. *What is the chief end of man?*

A. Man's chief end is to glorify God, and to enjoy him forever.

Question 2

Q. *What rule hath God given to direct us how we may glorify and enjoy him?*

A. The Word of God, which is contained in the Scriptures of the Old and New Testaments, is the only rule to direct us how we may glorify and enjoy him.

Question 3

Q. *What do the Scriptures principally teach?*

A. The Scriptures principally teach, what man is to believe concerning God, and what duty God requires of man.

Question 4

Q. *What is God?*

A. God is a Spirit, infinite, eternal, and unchangeable, in his being, wisdom, power, holiness, justice, goodness, and truth.

Question 5

Q. *Are there more Gods than one?*

A. There is but one only, the living and true God.

---

[28]Christian Focus publishes a splendid, pocket-sized edition of the *Shorter Catechism* with explanatory notes: *The Shorter Catechism with Explanatory Notes and Review Questions*, by Roderick Lawson.

Question 6

Q. *How many persons are there in the Godhead?*

A. There are three persons in the Godhead: the Father, the Son, and the Holy Ghost; and these three are one God, the same in substance, equal in power and glory.

Question 7

Q. *What are the decrees of God?*

A. The decrees of God are, his eternal purpose, according to the counsel of his will, whereby, for his own glory, he hath foreordained whatsoever comes to pass.

Question 8

Q. *How doth God execute his decrees?*

A. God executeth his decrees in the works of creation and providence.

Question 9

Q. *What is the work of creation?*

A. The work of creation is, God's making all things of nothing, by the word of his power, in the space of six days, and all very good.

Question 10

Q. *How did God create man?*

A. God created man male and female, after his own image, in knowledge, righteousness, and holiness, with dominion over the creatures.

Question 11

Q. *What are God's works of providence?*

A. God's works of providence are, his most holy, wise, and powerful preserving and governing all his creatures, and all their actions.

Question 12

Q. *What special act of providence did God exercise towards man in the estate wherein he was created?*

A. When God had created man, he entered into a covenant of life with him, upon condition of perfect obedience; forbidding him to eat of the tree of the knowledge of good and evil, upon pain of death.

Question 13

Q. *Did our first parents continue in the estate wherein they were created?*

A. Our first parents, being left to the freedom of their own will, fell from the estate wherein they were created, by sinning against God.

Question 14

Q. *What is sin?*

A. Sin is any want of conformity unto, or transgression of, the law of God.

Question 15

Q. *What was the sin whereby our first parents fell from the estate wherein they were created?*

A. The sin whereby our first parents fell from the estate wherein they were created, was their eating the forbidden fruit.

Question 16

Q. *Did all mankind fall in Adam's first transgression?*

A. The covenant being made with Adam, not only for himself, but for his posterity; all mankind, descending from him by ordinary generation, sinned in him, and fell with him, in his first transgression.

Question 17

Q. *Into what estate did the fall bring mankind?*

A. The fall brought mankind into an estate of sin and misery.

Question 18

Q. *Wherein consists the sinfulness of that estate whereinto man fell?*

A. The sinfulness of that estate whereinto man fell, consists in the guilt of Adam's first sin, the want of original righteousness, and the corruption of his whole nature, which is commonly called original sin; together with all actual transgressions which proceed from it.

Question 19

Q. *What is the misery of that estate whereinto man fell?*

A. All mankind by their fall lost communion with God, are under his wrath and curse, and so made liable to all the miseries of this life, to death itself, and to the pains of hell forever.

Question 20

Q. *Did God leave all mankind to perish in the estate of sin and misery?*

A. God, having out of his mere good pleasure, from all eternity, elected some to everlasting life, did enter into a covenant of grace to deliver them out of the estate of sin and misery, and to bring them into an estate of salvation by a Redeemer.

Question 21

Q. *Who is the Redeemer of God's elect?*

A. The only Redeemer of God's elect is the Lord Jesus Christ, who, being the eternal Son of God, became man, and so was, and continueth to be, God and man in two distinct natures, and one person, forever.

Question 22

Q. *How did Christ, being the Son of God, become man?*

A. Christ, the Son of God, became man, by taking to himself a true body, and a reasonable soul, being conceived by the power of the Holy Ghost, in the womb of the virgin Mary, and born of her, yet without sin.

Question 23

Q. *What offices doth Christ execute as our Redeemer?*

A. Christ, as our Redeemer, executeth the offices of a prophet, of a priest, and of a king, both in his estate of humiliation and exaltation.

Question 24

Q. *How doth Christ execute the office of a prophet?*

A. Christ executeth the office of a prophet, in revealing to us, by his Word and Spirit, the will of God for our salvation.

Question 25

Q. *How doth Christ execute the office of a priest?*

A. Christ executeth the office of a priest, in his once offering up of himself a sacrifice to satisfy divine justice, and reconcile us to God, and in making continual intercession for us.

Question 26

Q. *How doth Christ execute the office of a king?*

A. Christ executeth the office of a king, in subduing us to himself, in ruling and defending us, and in restraining and conquering all his and our enemies.

Question 27

Q. *Wherein did Christ's humiliation consist?*

A. Christ's humiliation consisted in his being born, and that in a low condition, made under the law, undergoing the miseries of this life, the wrath of God, and the cursed death of the cross; in being buried, and continuing under the power of death for a time.

Question 28

Q. *Wherein consisteth Christ's exaltation?*

A. Christ's exaltation consisteth in his rising again from the dead on the third day, in ascending up into heaven, in sitting at the right hand of God the Father, and in coming to judge the world at the last day.

Question 29

Q. *How are we made partakers of the redemption purchased by Christ?*

A. We are made partakers of the redemption purchased by Christ, by the effectual application of it to us by his Holy Spirit.

Question 30

Q. *How doth the Spirit apply to us the redemption purchased by Christ?*

A. The Spirit applieth to us the redemption purchased by Christ, by working faith in us, and thereby uniting us to Christ in our effectual calling.

Question 31

Q. *What is effectual calling?*

A. Effectual calling is the work of God's Spirit, whereby, convincing us of our sin and misery, enlightening our minds in the knowledge of Christ, and renewing our wills, he doth persuade and enable us to embrace Jesus Christ, freely offered to us in the gospel.

Question 32

Q. *What benefits do they that are effectually called partake of in this life?*

A. They that are effectually called do in this life partake of justification, adoption, and sanctification, and the several benefits which in this life do either accompany or flow from them.

Question 33

Q. *What is justification?*

A. Justification is an act of God's free grace, wherein he pardoneth all our sins, and accepteth us as righteous in his sight, only for the righteousness of Christ imputed to us, and received by faith alone.

Question 34

Q. *What is adoption?*

A. Adoption is an act of God's free grace, whereby we are received into the number, and have a right to all the privileges, of the sons of God.

Question 35

Q. *What is sanctification?*

A. Sanctification is the work of God's free grace, whereby we are renewed in the whole man after the image of God, and are enabled more and more to die unto sin, and live unto righteousness.

Question 36

Q. *What are the benefits which in this life do accompany or flow from justification, adoption, and sanctification?*

A. The benefits which in this life do accompany or flow from justification, adoption, and sanctification, are, assurance of God's love, peace of conscience, joy in the Holy Ghost, increase of grace, and perseverance therein to the end.

Question 37

Q. *What benefits do believers receive from Christ at death?*

A. The souls of believers are at their death made perfect in holiness, and do immediately pass into glory; and their bodies, being still united in Christ, do rest in their graves, till the resurrection.

Question 38

Q. *What benefits do believers receive from Christ at the resurrection?*

A. At the resurrection, believers, being raised up in glory, shall be openly acknowledged and acquitted in the day of judgment, and made perfectly blessed in the full enjoying of God to all eternity.

Question 39

Q. *What is the duty which God requireth of man?*

A. The duty which God requireth of man, is obedience to his revealed will.

Question 40

Q. *What did God at first reveal to man for the rule of his obedience?*

A. The rule which God at first revealed to man for his obedience, was the moral law.

Question 41

Q. *Wherein is the moral law summarily comprehended?*

A. The moral law is summarily comprehended in the ten commandments.

Question 42

Q. *What is the sum of the ten commandments?*

A. The sum of the ten commandments is, to love the Lord our God with all our heart, with all our soul, with all our strength, and with all our mind; and our neighbor as ourselves.

Question 43

Q. *What is the preface to the ten commandments?*

A. The preface to the ten commandments is in these words, I am the Lord thy God, which have brought thee out of the land of Egypt, out of the house of bondage.

Question 44

Q. *What doth the preface to the ten commandments teach us?*

A. The preface to the ten commandments teacheth us, that because God is the Lord, and our God, and Redeemer, therefore we are bound to keep all his commandments.

Question 45

Q. *Which is the first commandment?*

A. The first commandment is, Thou shalt have no other gods before me.

Question 46

Q. *What is required in the first commandment?*

A. The first commandment requireth us to know and acknowledge God to be the only true God, and our God; and to worship and glorify him accordingly.

Question 47

Q. *What is forbidden in the first commandment?*

A. The first commandment forbiddeth the denying, or not worshiping and glorifying, the true God as God, and our God; and the giving of that worship and glory to any other, which is due to him alone.

Question 48

Q. *What are we specially taught by these words before me in the first commandment?*

A. These words before me in the first commandment teach us, that God, who seeth all things, taketh notice of, and is much displeased with, the sin of having any other god.

Question 49

Q. *Which is the second commandment?*

A. The second commandment is, Thou shalt not make unto thee any graven image, or any likeness of anything that is in heaven above, or that is in the earth beneath, or that is in the water under the earth: Thou shalt not bow down thyself to them, nor serve them: for I the Lord thy God am a jealous God, visiting the iniquity of the fathers upon the children unto the third and fourth generation of them that hate me; and showing mercy unto thousands of them that love me, and keep my commandments.

Question 50

Q. *What is required in the second commandment?*

A. The second commandment requireth the receiving, observing, and keeping pure and entire, all such religious worship and ordinances as God hath appointed in his Word.

Question 51

Q. *What is forbidden in the second commandment?*

A. The second commandment forbiddeth the worshiping of God by images, or any other way not appointed in his Word.

Question 52

Q. *What are the reasons annexed to the second commandment?*

A. The reasons annexed to the second commandment are, God's sovereignty over us, his propriety in us, and the zeal he hath to his own worship.

Question 53

Q. *Which is the third commandment?*

A. The third commandment is, Thou shalt not take the name of the Lord thy God in vain: for the Lord will not hold him guiltless that taketh his name in vain.

Question 54

Q. *What is required in the third commandment?*

A. The third commandment requireth the holy and reverend use of God's names, titles, attributes, ordinances, Word, and works.

Question 55

Q. *What is forbidden in the third commandment?*

A. The third commandment forbiddeth all profaning or abusing of anything whereby God maketh himself known.

Question 56

Q. *What is the reason annexed to the third commandment?*

A. The reason annexed to the third commandment is, that however the breakers of this commandment may escape punishment from men, yet the Lord our God will not suffer them to escape his righteous judgment.

Question 57

Q. *Which is the fourth commandment?*

A. The fourth commandment is, Remember the sabbath day to keep it holy. Six days shalt thou labor, and do all thy work: but the seventh day is the sabbath of the Lord thy God: in it thou shalt not do any work, thou, nor thy son, nor thy daughter, thy manservant, nor thy maidservant, nor thy cattle, nor thy stranger that is within thy gates: For in six days the Lord made heaven and earth, the sea, and all that in them is, and rested the seventh day: wherefore the Lord blessed the sabbath day, and hallowed it.

Question 58

Q. *What is required in the fourth commandment?*

A. The fourth commandment requireth the keeping holy to God such set times as he hath appointed in his Word; expressly one whole day in seven, to be a holy sabbath to himself.

Question 59

Q. *Which day of the seven hath God appointed to be the weekly sabbath?*

A. From the beginning of the world to the resurrection of Christ, God appointed the seventh day of the week to be the weekly sabbath; and the first day of the week ever since, to continue to the end of the world, which is the Christian sabbath.

Question 60

Q. *How is the sabbath to be sanctified?*

A. The sabbath is to be sanctified by a holy resting all that day, even from such worldly employments and recreations as are lawful on other days; and spending the whole time in the public and private exercises of God's worship, except so much as is to be taken up in the works of necessity and mercy.

Question 61

Q. *What is forbidden in the fourth commandment?*

A. The fourth commandment forbiddeth the omission, or careless performance, of the duties required, and the profaning the day by idleness, or doing that which is in itself sinful, or by unnecessary thoughts, words, or works, about our worldly employments or recreations.

Question 62

Q. *What are the reasons annexed to the fourth commandment?*

A. The reasons annexed to the fourth commandment are, God's allowing us six days of the week for our own employments, his challenging a special propriety in the seventh, his own example, and his blessing the sabbath day.

Question 63

Q. *Which is the fifth commandment?*

A. The fifth commandment is, Honor thy father and thy mother: that thy days may be long upon the land which the Lord thy God giveth thee.

Question 64

Q. *What is required in the fifth commandment?*

A. The fifth commandment requireth the preserving the honor, and performing the duties, belonging to everyone in their several places and relations,
as superiors, inferiors, or equals.

Question 65

Q. *What is forbidden in the fifth commandment?*

A. The fifth commandment forbiddeth the neglecting of, or doing anything
against, the honor and duty which belongeth to everyone in their several
places and relations.

Question 66

Q. *What is the reason annexed to the fifth commandment?*

A. The reason annexed to the fifth commandment is, a promise of long life and
prosperity (as far as it shall serve for God's glory and their own good) to all
such as keep this commandment.

Question 67

Q. *Which is the sixth commandment?*

A. The sixth commandment is, Thou shalt not kill.

Question 68

Q. *What is required in the sixth commandment?*

A. The sixth commandment requireth all lawful endeavors to preserve our
own life, and the life of others.

Question 69

Q. *What is forbidden in the sixth commandment?*

A. The sixth commandment forbiddeth the taking away of our own life, or the
life of our neighbor, unjustly, or whatsoever tendeth thereunto.

Question 70

Q. *Which is the seventh commandment?*

A. The seventh commandment is, Thou shalt not commit adultery.

Question 71

Q. *What is required in the seventh commandment?*

A. The seventh commandment requireth the preservation of our own and our
neighbor's chastity, in heart, speech, and behavior.

Question 72

Q. *What is forbidden in the seventh commandment?*

A. The seventh commandment forbiddeth all unchaste thoughts, words, and actions.

Question 73

Q. *Which is the eighth commandment?*

A. The eighth commandment is, Thou shalt not steal.

Question 74

Q. *What is required in the eighth commandment?*

A. The eighth commandment requireth the lawful procuring and furthering the wealth and outward estate of ourselves and others.

Question 75

Q. *What is forbidden in the eighth commandment?*

A. The eighth commandment forbiddeth whatsoever doth, or may, unjustly hinder our own, or our neighbor's, wealth or outward estate.

Question 76

Q. *Which is the ninth commandment?*

A. The ninth commandment is, Thou shalt not bear false witness against thy neighbor.

Question 77

Q. *What is required in the ninth commandment?*

A. The ninth commandment requireth the maintaining and promoting of truth between man and man, and of our own and our neighbor's good name, especially in witness bearing.

Question 78

Q. *What is forbidden in the ninth commandment?*

A. The ninth commandment forbiddeth whatsoever is prejudicial to truth, or injurious to our own, or our neighbor's, good name.

Question 79

Q. *Which is the tenth commandment?*

A. The tenth commandment is, Thou shalt not covet thy neighbor's house, thou shalt not covet thy neighbor's wife, nor his manservant, nor his maidservant, nor his ox, nor his ass, nor anything that is thy neighbor's.

Question 80

Q. *What is required in the tenth commandment?*

A. The tenth commandment requireth full contentment with our own condition, with a right and charitable frame of spirit toward our neighbor, and all that is his.

Question 81

Q. *What is forbidden in the tenth commandment?*

A. The tenth commandment forbiddeth all discontentment with our own estate, envying or grieving at the good of our neighbor, and all inordinate motions and affections to anything that is his.

Question 82

Q. *Is any man able perfectly to keep the commandments of God?*

A. No mere man, since the fall, is able in this life perfectly to keep the commandments of God, but doth daily break them in thought, word, and deed.

Question 83

Q. *Are all transgressions of the law equally heinous?*

A. Some sins in themselves, and by reason of several aggravations, are more heinous in the sight of God than others.

Question 84

Q. *What doth every sin deserve?*

A. Every sin deserveth God's wrath and curse, both in this life, and that which is to come.

Question 85

Q. *What doth God require of us, that we may escape his wrath and curse, due to us for sin?*

A. To escape the wrath and curse of God, due to us for sin, God requireth of us faith in Jesus Christ, repentance unto life, with the diligent use of all the outward means whereby Christ communicateth to us the benefits of redemption.

Question 86

Q. *What is faith in Jesus Christ?*

A. Faith in Jesus Christ is a saving grace, whereby we receive and rest upon him alone for salvation, as he is offered to us in the gospel.

Question 87

Q. *What is repentance unto life?*

A. Repentance unto life is a saving grace, whereby a sinner, out of a true sense of his sin, and apprehension of the mercy of God in Christ, doth, with grief and hatred of his sin, turn from it unto God, with full purpose of, and endeavor after, new obedience.

Question 88

Q. *What are the outward and ordinary means whereby Christ communicateth to us the benefits of redemption?*

A. The outward and ordinary means whereby Christ communicateth to us the benefits of redemption are, his ordinances, especially the Word, sacraments,and prayer; all which are made effectual to the elect for salvation.

Question 89

Q. *How is the Word made effectual to salvation?*

A. The Spirit of God maketh the reading, but especially the preaching, of the Word, an effectual means of convincing and converting sinners, and of building them up in holiness and comfort, through faith, unto salvation.

Question 90

Q. *How is the Word to be read and heard, that it may become effectual to salvation?*

A. That the Word may become effectual to salvation, we must attend thereunto with diligence, preparation, and prayer; receive it with faith and love, lay it up in our hearts, and practice it in our lives.

Question 91

Q. *How do the sacraments become effectual means of salvation?*

A. The sacraments become effectual means of salvation, not from any virtue in them, or in him that doth administer them; but only by the blessing of Christ, and the working of his Spirit in them that by faith receive them.

Question 92

Q. *What is a sacrament?*

A. A sacrament is a holy ordinance instituted by Christ; wherein, by sensible signs, Christ, and the benefits of the new covenant, are represented, sealed, and applied to believers.

Question 93

Q. *Which are the sacraments of the New Testament?*

A. The sacraments of the New Testament are, Baptism, and the Lord's Supper.

Question 94

Q. *What is Baptism?*

A. Baptism is a sacrament, wherein the washing with water in the name of the Father, and of the Son, and of the Holy Ghost, doth signify and seal our ingrafting into Christ, and partaking of the benefits of the covenant of grace, and our engagement to be the Lord's.

Question 95

Q. *To whom is Baptism to be administered?*

A. Baptism is not to be administered to any that are out of the visible church, till they profess their faith in Christ, and obedience to him; but the infants of such as are members of the visible church are to be baptized.

Question 96

Q. *What is the Lord's Supper?*

A. The Lord's Supper is a sacrament, wherein, by giving and receiving bread and wine, according to Christ's appointment, his death is showed forth; and the worthy receivers are, not after a corporal and carnal manner, but by faith, made partakers of his body and blood, with all his benefits, to their spiritual nourishment, and growth in grace.

Question 97

Q. *What is required for the worthy receiving of the Lord's Supper?*

A. It is required of them that would worthily partake of the Lord's Supper, that they examine themselves of their knowledge to discern the Lord's body, of their faith to feed upon him, of their repentance, love, and new obedience; lest, coming unworthily, they eat and drink judgment to themselves.

Question 98

Q. *What is prayer?*

A. Prayer is an offering up of our desires unto God, for things agreeable to his will, in the name of Christ, with confession of our sins, and thankful acknowledgment of his mercies.

Question 99

Q. *What rule hath God given for our direction in prayer?*

A. The whole Word of God is of use to direct us in prayer; but the special rule of direction is that form of prayer which Christ taught his disciples, commonly called the Lord's Prayer.

Question 100

Q. *What doth the preface of the Lord's Prayer teach us?*

A. The preface of the Lord's Prayer, which is, Our Father which art in heaven, teacheth us to draw near to God with all holy reverence and confidence, as children to a father, able and ready to help us; and that we should pray with and for others.

Question 101

Q. *What do we pray for in the first petition?*

A. In the first petition, which is, Hallowed be thy name, we pray that God would enable us, and others, to glorify him in all that whereby he maketh himself known; and that he would dispose all things to his own glory.

Question 102

Q. *What do we pray for in the second petition?*

A. In the second petition, which is, Thy kingdom come, we pray that Satan's kingdom may be destroyed; and that the kingdom of grace may be advanced, ourselves and others brought into it, and kept in it; and that the kingdom of glory may be hastened.

Question 103

Q. *What do we pray for in the third petition?*

A. In the third petition, which is, Thy will be done in earth, as it is in heaven, we pray that God, by his grace, would make us able and willing to know, obey, and submit to his will in all things, as the angels do in heaven.

Question 104

Q. What do we pray for in the fourth petition?

A. In the fourth petition, which is, Give us this day our daily bread, we pray that of God's free gift we may receive a competent portion of the good things of this life, and enjoy his blessing with them.

Question 105

Q. *What do we pray for in the fifth petition?*

A. In the fifth petition, which is, And forgive us our debts, as we forgive our debtors, we pray that God, for Christ's sake, would freely pardon all our sins; which we are the rather encouraged to ask, because by his grace we are enabled from the heart to forgive others.

Question 106

Q. *What do we pray for in the sixth petition?*

A. In the sixth petition, which is, And lead us not into temptation, but deliver us from evil, we pray that God would either keep us from being tempted to sin, or support and deliver us when we are tempted.

Question 107

Q. *What doth the conclusion of the Lord's Prayer teach us?*

A. The conclusion of the Lord's Prayer, which is, For thine is the kingdom, and the power, and the glory, forever. Amen, teacheth us to take our encouragement in prayer from God only, and in our prayers to praise him, ascribing kingdom, power, and glory to him; and, in testimony of our desire, and assurance to be heard, we say, Amen.

4. Bible Memorization: 50 Great Passages[28]

The Psalmist writes, "Thy word have I hid in my heart, that I might not sin against Thee" (Psalm 119:11). As the word of God is "treasured" in our hearts, we meditate upon it, contemplate its application, and draw upon it in time of need. The following are among the best known and most beloved Bible passages, to which many more could be added. "O how I love Thy law!," says the Psalmist, "It is my meditation all the day" (Psalm 119:97). Locate other passages also for yourself and add them to this list.

Subject	Passage	First Line
1. The Lord's Prayer	Mt 6:9–13	"Our Father who art in heaven..."
2. The Ten Commandments	Ex 20:3–17	"You shall have no other gods before me..."
3. Christ's Commandment	Jn 13:34–35	"A new commandment I give to you..."
4. Two Great Laws	Mt 22:36–40	"Teacher...which is the great commandment in the law?..."
5. The Beatitudes	Mt 5:3–12	"Blessed are the poor in spirit..."
6. Faith in God	Ps 23	"The LORD is my shepherd..."
7. The Lord's Glory	Ex 34:6,7	"Then the LORD passed by..."
8. Call to Faith	Deut 6:4–7	"Hear, O Israel: The LORD our God is one LORD..."
9. Whom Does the LORD bless?	Ps 24:1–6	"The earth is the LORD's..."
10. Song of Faith	Ps 46	"God is our refuge and strength..."
11. Prayer for Renewal	Ps 51:10-2	"Create in me a clean heart..."
12. Abiding in God	Ps 91:1–6	"He who dwells in the shelter of the Most High..."
13. Thanksgiving	Ps 100	"Make a joyful noise to the LORD..."

---

[28]Adapted from *J. Gilchrist Lawson* (ed.), *The Christian Workers New Testament and Psalms* (Grand Rapids: Zondervan Bible Publishers, 1962, [1924]).

Subject	Passage	First Line
14. God's Mercy	Ps 103	"Bless the LORD, O my soul..."
15. Prayer of Praise	1 Chron 29:10–13	"So David blessed the LORD..."
16. Prophecy of the Messiah	Isa 9:6–7	"For to us a child is born..."
17. God Upholds His Own	Isa 40:28–31	"Have you not known?..."
18. Good Tidings	Isa 52:7–10	"How beautiful upon the mountains..."
19. The Servant of Men	Isa 53:4–9	"Surely he has borne our griefs..."
20. True Glory	Jer 9:23–24	"Let not the wise man glory in his wisdom..."
21. The New Covenant	Jer 31:31–34	"Behold, the days are coming..."
22. Vision of the Son of Man	Dan 7:13–14	"I saw in the night visions..."
23. What Does God Require?	Mic 6:8	"He has showed you, O man, what is good..."
24. Tithing	Mal 3:8–10	"Will a man rob God?..."
25. Love Your Enemies	Mt 5:43–48	"You have heard that it was said..."
26. Worry	Mt 6:25–33	"Therefore...do not be anxious about your life..."
27. Prayer Is Answered	Mt 7:7–8	"Ask, and it will be given you..."
28. Christ's Yoke	Mt 11:28–30	"Come to me, all who labor..."
29. Following Jesus	Mt 16:24–26	"If any man would come after me..."
30. Jesus Blesses Children	Mk 10:13–16	"And they were bringing children to him..."
31. Mary's Son	Lk 1:46–55	"My soul magnifies the LORD..."
32. Good News of Great Joy	Lk 2:8–14	"And in that region there were shepherds..."
33. Forgiveness on the Cross	Lk 23:34	"And Jesus said, 'Father, forgive them..."
34. In the Beginning	Jn1:1-5,14	"In the beginning was the Word...and the Word became flesh..."

Subject	Passage	First Line
35. Why Jesus Came	Jn 3:16	"For God so loved the world..."
36. The Light of the World	Jn 8:12	"I am the light of the world..."
37. The Good Shepherd	Jn 10:14–16	"I am the good shepherd..."
38. The Way, the Truth, and the Life	Jn 14:1–6	"Let not your hearts be troubled..."
39. Abiding in Christ	Jn 15:1–5	"I am the true vine..."
40. More than Conquerors	Rom 8:35–39	"Who shall separate us from the love of Christ?..."
41. How Should a Christian Live?	Rom 12:9–21	"Let love be without hypocrisy..."
42. Hymn of Love	1 Cor 13	"If I speak in the tongues of men and of angels..."
43. Fruit of the Spirit	Gal 5:22–23	"But the fruit of the Spirit is love..."
44. The Whole Armor of God	Eph 6:10–17	"Finally, be strong in the LORD..."
45. Peace	Phil 4:6–8	"Be anxious for nothing..."
46. Bible Study	2 Tim 3:16	"All scripture is inspired by God..."
47. What Is Faith?	Heb 11:1–3	"Now faith is the assurance of things hoped for..."
48. God Is Love	1 Jn 4:7–12	"Beloved, let us love one another..."
49. He Who Knocks	Rev 3:20	"Behold, I stand at the door and knock..."
50. God's People	Rev 21:3–7	"Behold, the dwelling of God is with men..."

Other passages for memorization:

Chapter Seven

HISTORICAL RESOURCES

The first of our historical resources is a condensed form of Isaac Watts' *A Guide to Prayer*, a work written to teach young men to pray. We have modernized the pronouns and verb endings for the convenience of the modern reader.

We also include as resources two documents associated with the work of the Westminster Assembly. The first is Thomas Manton's "Epistle to the Reader," which by order of the Assembly was bound with the Confession and Catechisms and which urged diligence in the practice of family religion generally and catechizing in particular. "Religion was first hatched in families," writes Manton, "and there the devil seeketh to crush it." Because it is "the seminary of the Church and State," he urges, "how careful should ministers and parents be to train up young ones while they are still pliable."

The second is the Church of Scotland's *Directory for Family Worship*, which though apparently not a product of the Westminster divines was approved for use within the Church of Scotland at the same time that approval was given for the *Confession of Faith* (August 1647) and like Manton's "Epistle" was bound together with it. The General Assembly included its instructions for the use of the Family Directory warnings of disciplinary action, beginning with admonition, and if "obstancy" continued, excommunication of heads of household who neglected "this necessary duty" of family worship. Such was the seriousness with which our forefathers took this responsibility!

1. A Condensed Version of *A Guide to Prayer* by Isaac Watts

I. Invocation, or calling upon God

A. Mention the names or titles of God

O Lord my God, most high and most holy God and Father. O God of Israel, that dwells between the cherubims. Almighty God and everlasting King, Our Father in heaven. O God, that keeps covenant...

B. Declare our desire and design to worship Him

Unto You do we lift up our souls. We draw near to you as our God. We come into Your presence. We that are but dust and ashes, take upon us to speak to Your Majesty. We bow ourselves before You in humble addresses.

C. Ask for His assistance and acceptance

Lord, quicken us to call upon Your name. Assist us by Your Spirit in our access to Your mercy seat. Raise our hearts to Yourself. Teach us to approach You as becomes creatures, and do draw near to us as a God of grace. Hearken to the voice of my cry, my King and my God, for unto You will I pray.

II. Adoration, or honor paid to God by the creature

A. Honor God for His nature

You are God, and there is none else; Your name alone is Jehovah the Most High. Who in the heavens can be compared to the Lord, or who among the sons of the mighty can be likened to our God? All nations before You are as nothing, and they are counted in Your sight less than nothing and vanity. You are the first and the last, the only true and living God; Your glorious name is exalted above all blessing and praise.

B. For His attributes

You are very great, O Lord, You are clothed with honor and majesty. You are the blessed and only Potentate, King of kings, and Lord of lords. All things are naked and open before Your eyes. You search the heart of man, but how unsearchable is Your understanding? and Your power is unknown. You are of purer eyes than to behold iniquity. Your mercy endures forever. You are slow to anger, abundant in goodness, and Your truth reaches to all generations.

C. For His works of creation, providence, and redemption

You, Lord, have made the heavens and the earth. The whole creation is the work of Your hands. You rule among the armies of heaven, and among the inhabitants of the earth. You do what pleases Yourself. You have revealed Your goodness towards mankind, and have magnified Your mercy above all You name. Your works of nature and of grace are full of wonder, and sought out by all those that have pleasure in them.

D. For His relation to us as a Creator, Father, Redeemer, King, almighty Friend, and everlasting portion

III. Confession

A. Of our lowliness as creatures

You, O Lord, are in heaven, but we on the earth; our being is but of yesterday, and our foundation is in the dust. What is man that You are mindful of him, and the son of man that You should visit him? Man, that is a worm, and the son of man that is but a worm! It is in You that we live, move, and have our being: You withhold Your breath and we die.

B. Of original sin and actual sins

We mourn before God because of our pride and vanity of mind, the violence of our passions, our earthly-mindedness and love of this world, our sensuality and indulgence of our flesh, our carnal security and unthankfulness under plentiful mercies, and our fretfulness and impatience, or sinful defection in a time of trouble: Our neglect of duty and want of love to God, our unbelief and hardness of heart, our slothfulness and decay in religion, the dishonors we have brought to God, and all our miscarriages towards our fellow-creatures. How often they have been repeated even before and since we knew God savingly; that we have committed them against much light; and that we have sinned against much love; and that after many rebukes of the word and providence, and many consolations from the gospel and Spirit of God. *We are ashamed, and blush to lift up our faces before You our God, for our iniquities are increased over our head, and our trespasses grown up to the heavens. Behold we are vile, what shall we answer You? We will lay our hands upon our mouth, and put our mouth in the dust, if so there may be hope.*

C. Of our deserving punishment and unworthiness of mercy

We deserve, O Lord, to be forever cast out of Your presence, and to be eternally cut off from all hope of mercy. We deserve to fall under the curse of that law which we have broken, and to be forever banished from the blessings of that gospel which we have so long refused. We have sinned against so much mercy, that we are no longer worthy to be called Your children. We are utterly unworthy of any of those favors that are promised in Your word, and which You have given us encouragement to hope for. If You contend with us for our transgressions, we are not able to answer You, O Lord, nor do we make excuse for one of a thousand; if You should mark our iniquities, O Lord, who shall stand? But there is forgiveness with You, there is mercy and plenteous redemption.

D.   Of our needs and sorrows of every kind

[see next section]

IV. Petition

A.   To be delivered from evil—temporal, spiritual, and eternal

O Lord, take away the guilt of our sins by the atonement of Your own Son. Subdue the power of our iniquities by Your own Spirit. Deliver us from the natural darkness of our own minds, from the corruption of our hearts, and perverse tendencies of our appetites and passions. Free us from the temptations to which we are exposed, and the daily snares that attend us. We are in constant danger while we are in this life, let the watchful eye of our God be upon us for our defense. Deliver us from Your everlasting wrath, and from that eternal punishment that is due to our sins in hell. Save us from the power of our enemies in this world, and from all the painful evils that we have justly exposed ourselves to by sinning against You.

B.   For good to be conferred—temporal, spiritual, and eternal

O You that has the hearts of all men in Your hand, form our hearts according to Your own will, and according to the image of Your own Son: Be our light and our strength, make us run in the way of holiness; and let all the means of grace be continued to us, and be made serviceable for the great end for which You have appointed them. Preserve Your gospel among us, and let all Your providences be sanctified. Let Your mercies draw us nearer to Yourself, as with the cords of love; and let the several strokes of Your afflicting hand wean us from sin, mortify us to this world, and make us ready for a departure hence, whensoever Your please to call us. Guide us by Your counsels, *and secure us by Your grace, in all our travels through this dangerous wilderness, and at last give us a triumph over death, and a rich and* abundant entrance into the kingdom of Your Son in glory. *But since we are here, we wear these bodies of flesh about us, and there are many things necessary to support our lives, and to make them easy and comfortable; we entreat You would bestow these conveniences and refreshment upon us, so far as is consistent with Your own glory and the designs for Your grace. Let our health, our strength, and our peace be maintained, and let* holiness to the Lord *be inscribed upon them all, that whatsoever we receive from Your hands, may be improved to Your honor, and our own truest advantage; heal our diseases, and pardon our iniquities, that our souls may ever bless you.*

C. For the church

That He would enlarge the borders of the dominion of Christ, that He would spread His gospel among the heathens, and make the name of Christ known and *glorious from the rising of the sun to its going down:* That He would call in the remainder of His ancient people the Jews, and that He would bring *the fullness of the gentiles* into His church: That He would pour down a more abundant measure of His own Spirit, to carry on His work upon the earth; that the Spirit may descend and be diffused in plentiful degrees upon churches, upon ministers, upon families, and upon all the saints; that God would deliver His church from the power of persecuting enemies; that He would restrain *the wrath of man, and suffer not the wicked to triumph over the righteous.*

D. For the nation

That liberty and peace may be established and flourish in it; for governors that rule over us, in places of supreme authority or subordinate; that wisdom and faithfulness may be conferred upon them from heaven, to manage those affairs God has entrusted them with on earth.

E. For friends and those near to us

That God would deliver them from all the evils they feel or fear, and bestow upon them all the good we wish for ourselves here or hereafter.

V. Pleading, or arguing our case with Him in a fervent, yet humble manner

A. Based upon the greatness of our needs

My sorrows, O Lord, are such as overpress me, and endanger my dishonoring of Your name and Your gospel. My pains and my weaknesses hinder me from Your service and I am rendered useless upon earth, and a cumberer of the ground: They have been already of so long continuance, that I fear my flesh will not be able to hold out, nor my spirit to bear up, if Your hand abide thus heavy upon me. If this sin be not subdued in me, or that temptation removed, I fear that I shall be turned aside from the paths of religion, and let go my hope.

B. Based upon the perfections of God's nature

For Your mercies' sake, O Lord, save me; Your lovingkindness is infinite, *let this infinite lovingkindness be displayed in my salvation. You are wise, O Lord, and though my enemies are crafty, You can disappoint their devices: And you know how by Your wondrous counsels to turn my sorrows to joy. You can find out a way for my relief, when all creatures stand afar off and say, that they see no way to help me. You are almighty and all-sufficient; Your power can suppress my adversaries at once, vanquish the tempter, break the powers of darkness to pieces, release me from the chains of my corruption, and bring me into* glorious liberty. *You are just and righteous and will You let the enemy oppress forever? You are sovereign, and all things are at Your command: You can say to pains and diseases, go, or come; speak therefore the sovereign word of healing, and my flesh and soul shall praise you. You delight in pardoning grace; it is the honor of our God to forgive; therefore let my iniquities be all canceled, through the abundance of Your rich mercy.*

C.   Based upon the various relations in which God stands to us

Lord, You are my Creator, will You not have a desire to the work of Your hands? Have you not made me and fashioned me, and will you now destroy me? *You are my Governor and my King; to whom should I fly for protection but to you, when the enemies of Your honor and my soul beset me around? Are You not my Father? and have You not called me one of Your children? and given me a* name and a place among Your sons and Your daughters? *Why should I look like one cast out of Your sight, or that belongs to the family of Satan? Are not the bowels of a father with You, and tender compassions? Why should not one of Your poor and weak helpless children be neglected or forgotten? Are you not my God in covenant, and* the God and Father of my Lord Jesus Christ, *by whom that covenant is ratified? Under that relation I would plead with You for all necessary mercies.*

D.   Based upon the promises of the covenant of grace

Enlighten me, O Lord, *and pardon me, and sanctify my soul; and bestow* grace and glory *upon me according to that word of Your promise* on which you have caused me to hope. Remember Your word *is past in heaven, it is recorded among the articles of Your sweet covenant, that I must receive light and love, and strength, and joy, and happiness and are You not a faithful God, to fulfill every one of those promises?* What if heaven and earth must pass away? *Yet Your covenant stands upon* two immutable *pillars, Your* promise *and Your* oath; *and now I have* fled for refuge to lay hold on this hope, let me have strong consolation. Remember the covenant *made with Your Son in the days of eternity, and let the mercies there promised to all His seed be bestowed upon me according to my various wants.*

E.   Based upon the name and honor of God in the world

What will you do for Your great name, *if Israel be cut off or perish? If Your saints go down to the grave in multitudes,* who shall praise You in the land of the living? The dead cannot celebrate You, *nor make mention of Your name and honors,* as I do this day.

F.   Based upon the former experiences of ourselves and others

Our fathers cried unto You, O Lord, and were delivered, they trusted in You, and they were not confounded; *let me be a partaker of the same favor while I cry unto You, and make You my trust:* You have never said to the seed of Jacob, seek my face in vain; *and let it not be said that Your poor servant has now sought Your face, and has not found You. Often have I received mercy in a way of return to prayer: Often has my soul drawn near to unto You, and been comforted in the midst of sorrow: Often have I taken out fresh supplies of grace according to my need from the treasures of Your grace that are in Christ; and shall the door of these treasures be shut against me now? Shall I receive no more favors from the hand of my God, that has heretofore dealt them so plentifully to me?*

G.   Based upon the name and mediation of our Lord Jesus Christ

Lord, let my sins be forgiven for the sake of that love which You bear Your own Son, for the sake of that love which Your Son bears to You; for the sake of His humble state, when He took flesh upon Him, that He might look like a sinner, and be made a sacrifice, though Himself was free from sin; *for the sake of His perfect and painful obedience, which has given complete honor to Your law; for the sake of* the curse which He bore, *and the death which He suffered, which has glorified Your authority, and honored Your justice more than it was possible for my sins to have affronted it: Remember His dying groans; remember His agonies when* the hour of darkness *was upon Him; and let not the powers of darkness prevail over me: Remember the day when You stood afar from Your own Son, and He cried out as one forsaken of God, and let me have Your everlasting presence with me; let me never be forsaken of God, since Your Son has borne that punishment.* Again, we plead the intercession of Jesus our High-Priest above: *Father, we would willingly ask You for nothing, but what Your Son already asks you for: We would willingly request nothing at Your hands, but what Your own Son requests beforehand for us: look upon* the Lamb, as He had been slain, in the midst of the throne: *Look upon His pure and perfect righteousness, and that* blood with which our High-Priest is entered into the highest heavens, and in which forever He appears before You to make intercession; and let every blessing be bestowed upon me, which that blood did purchase, and which that great, that infinite Petitioner pleads for at Your right hand. What can you deny Your own Son? for He has told us, *that You hear him always.* For the sake of that Son of Your love, deny us not.

VI. Self Dedication, or profession

A.   Profess our relation to God

Tell Him that we are the Lord's; that we belong to His family; that we are one of His household; that we stand among the number of His children; that our names are written in His covenant.

B.   Profess our former commitments to God

Lord, we have given ourselves up unto You, and chosen You for our eternal portion, and our highest good; we have seen the insufficiency of creatures to make us happy, and we have betaken ourselves to a higher hope; we have beheld Christ Jesus the Savior in His perfect righteousness, and in His all-sufficient grace; we have put our trust in Him, and we have made our covenant with the Father, by the sacrifice of the Son; we have often drawn near to You in Your ordinances; we have ratified and confirmed the holy covenant at Your table, as well as been devoted to You by the initial ordinance of baptism; we have given up our names to God in His house; and we have, as it were, subscribed with our hands to be the Lord's.

C.   Presently recommit ourselves to Him

Lord, I confirm all may former dedications of myself to You; and may all my covenantings be forever ratified. Or if I did never yet sincerely give myself up to the Lord, I do it now with the greatest solemnity, and from the bottom of my heart: I commit my guilty soul into the hands of Jesus my Redeemer, that He may sprinkle it with His atoning blood, that He may clothe it with His justifying righteousness, and make me, a vile sinner, accepted in the presence of a just and holy God: I appear, O Father, in the presence of Your justice and holiness, clothed in the garments of Your own Son, and I trust You behold not iniquity in me *to punish it. I give my soul, that has much corruption in it by nature, and much of the remaining power of sin, into the hands of my almighty Savior, that by His grace He may form all my powers anew; that He may subdue every irregular appetite, and root out every disorderly passion; that He may frame me* after His own image, *fill me with His own grace, and fit me for His own glory. I hope in You, my God, for* You are my refuge, my strength, and my salvation: *I love You above all things; and I know I love you.* Whom have I in heaven but you? And there is nothing upon earth that I desire in comparison of you: *I desire you with my strongest affections, and I delight in You above all delights:* My soul stands in awe, and fears before You; *and I rejoice to love such a God who is almighty, and the object of my highest reverence.*

D.   Profess our resolutions to be the Lord's forever

To love Him above all things; to fear Him, to hope in Him, to walk in His ways, *in a course of holy obedience, and to wait for His mercy unto eternal life.*

E.   Renounce all that is inconsistent with self-dedication

As I am Yours, O Lord, and I belong not to this world: I have given myself to You, and I have given myself away from sin and from the creature: I have renounced the world as my portion, and chosen the Father. I have renounced all other saviors, and all my own duties and righteousness as the foundation of my interest in the favor of God, and chosen Christ Jesus, as my only way to the Father. *I have renounced my own strength as the ground of my hope; for my understanding is dark, my will is impotent, and my affections are insufficient to carry me onwards to heaven; I now again renounce dependence upon all of them, that I may receive greater light and strength and love from God.* I am dead to the law, *I am mortified to sin, I am crucified to the world, and all by the cross of Jesus my Savior. I bid Satan get behind me; I renounce him and his works; I will neither fear him nor love him; nor lay a confederacy with the men of this world, for I love my God, for I fear my God, in my God is my eternal help and hope:* I will say, what have I to do any more with idols? *And I will banish the objects of temptation from my sight. Thus I abandon every thing that would divide me from God, to whom I have made a surrender of myself. And should you see fit to scourge and correct me, O my God, I submit to Your hand; should You deny the particular requests I have presented to You, I leave myself in Your hands, trusting You will choose better for me. And because I know my own frailty of heart, and the inconstancy of my will, I humbly put all these my vows and solemn engagements into the hands of my Lord Jesus to fulfill them in me, and by me, through all the days of my infirmity and this dangerous state of trial.*

VII.   Thanksgiving, or to acknowledge the bounty of God

A.   For benefits given without our asking

We praise You, O Lord, for Your original designs of love to fallen man; that you should make a distinction between us and the angels that sinned: What is man, that You are thoughtful *about His salvation; and suffer the angels to perish forever without remedy: that You should choose a certain number of the race of Adam, and give them into the hands of Christ before all worlds, and make a covenant of grace with them in Christ Jesus, that their happiness might be secured, that You should reveal this mercy in various types and promises to our fathers by the prophets, and that in Your own appointed time You should send Your Son* to take our nature upon Him, and to redeem us by His death? *We give glory to Your justice and to Your grace for this work of terror and compassion, this work of reconciling sinners to Yourself by the punishment of Your Son: We praise You for the gospel which You have established to the world, the gospel of pardon and peace; and that You have confirmed it by such abundant testimonies, to raise and establish our faith: We give glory to that power of Yours that has guarded Your gospel in all ages, and through ten thousand oppositions of Satan has delivered it down safe to our age, and has proclaimed* the glad tidings of peace *in our nation: We bless You that You have built habitations for Yourself amongst us, and that we should be born in such a land of light as this is: It is a distinguishing favor of Yours, that among the works of Your creation we should be placed in the rank of rational beings; but it is more distinguishing goodness, that we should be born of religious parents under the general promises of grace. We give thanks unto Your goodness for our preservation from many dangers which we could never foresee, and which we could not ask You to prevent: How infinitely we are indebted to You, O Lord, that You have not cut us off in a state of nature and sin, and that our portion is not at this time amongst* the children of *eternal* wrath! *That our education should be under religious care, and that we should have so many conveniences and comforts of life conferred upon us, as well as the means of grace brought near to us; and all this before we began to know you, or sought any of the mercies of this life or the other at Your hands!*

B.   For benefits given as an answer to prayer

We give thanks to You, O Lord, for our deliverance from evils temporal and spiritual, and our hopes of deliverance from the evils that are eternal; for the communication of good for soul and body, and our comfortable expectation of the eternal happiness of both; for mercies bestowed on churches, on nations, on our governors, on relatives and our friends, as well as ourselves. Truly You are a God that hears prayer, and You have not despised the cry of those that sought You: we ourselves are witnesses, that You do not bid Your people seek Your face in vain.

All these our thanksgivings are yet further heightened by the consideration of the mercies that we have received, of their greatness, and of their continuance: when we consider the glory and the self-sufficiency of God the giver, that He is happy in Himself, and stands in no need of us, and yet He condescends to confer perpetual benefits upon us; that He is sovereign, and might dispose of His favors to thousands, and leave us out of the number of His favorites. That we are as vile and unworthy as others, and that our God beholds all our unworthiness, all our guilt, our repeated provocations, and His past mercies abused, and yet He continues to have mercy upon us, and waits to be gracious.

VIII.   Blessing of God

A.   Expressing our pleasure in the attributes and glories of God

We delight, O Lord, to see Your name honored in the world, and we rejoice in Your real excellencies: We take pleasure to seek You exalted above all: We triumph in the several perfections of Your nature, and we give thanks at the remembrance of Your holiness.

B.   Wishing that the glories of God may continue forever

May the name of God be forever blest: May the kingdom, and the power, and the glory be forever ascribed to Him: May all generations call Him honorable, and make His name glorious in the earth. To You, O Father, Son, and Holy Spirit, belong everlasting power and honor.

IX. Amen

A.   Thereby affirming that all that we have prayed is true

B.   Thereby asserting that we wish and desire "to obtain all that we have prayed for."

Lord, let it be thus as we have said, is the language of this little word.

2. Thomas Manton's *Epistle to the Reader of the Westminster Confession of Faith and Larger and Shorter Catechisms*[29]

Christian Reader,

I cannot suppose that you are such a stranger in England as to be ignorant of the general complaint concerning the decay of the power of godliness, and especially of the great corruption of youth. Wherever you go, you will hear men crying out about how bad youth are. But indeed the source of the problem must be sought a little higher: it is bad parents that make bad children! We cannot blame children so much for their unruliness, for the greater weight of the blame lies in our own negligence in their education.

The devil has great spite toward the kingdom of Christ, and he knows no better way to crush it in the egg, than by the perversion of youth, and supplanting of family-duties. Granted, he strikes at all those pubic duties in the assemblies of the saints, but they are too well guarded by the solemn injunctions and the dying charge of Jesus Christ as that he could totally subvert and undermine them. But at family duties he strikes with the more success, because the institution is not so solemn, and the practice of family duties is not so seriously and conscientiously regarded. Therefore the omission of family duties is not so liable to be noticed, and public censure to be executed. Religion was first hatched in families, and there the devil seeks to crush it. The families of the Patriarchs were the only Churches God had in the world for the time. Therefore, (I suppose,) when Cain went out from Adam's family, it was said he went out from the presence of the Lord, Gen. 4:16. Now, the devil knows that this is a blow at the root, and a ready way to prevent the succession of Churches. If he can subvert families, other societies and communities will not flourish long and subsist with any power and vigor. For there is the stock from which all societies are supplied, both for the present and for the future.

For the present: A family is the seminary of Church and State. If children are not well principled in the home, then everything miscarries! A error in the first mixture is not mended in the second! If youth are ill-bred in the family, then they will be ill-mannered in Church and society. It is in the home where making or marring of one's character first takes place, which early character is the presage of their future lives (Proverb 20:11). By family discipline officers are trained up for the Church (1 Timothy 3:4, One that ruleth well his own house, etc.), for there are men bred up in subjection and obedience. It is noted

---

[29]This edition has been updated for the modern reader by the Presbyterian Heritage Foundation.

in Acts 21:5 that the disciples brought Paul on his way with their wives and children. Their children are probably mentioned to imply that their parents would by their example and affectionate farewell to Paul raise them up in a way of reverence and respect to the pastors of the Church.

For the future: As it is certainly encouraging to see a thriving nursery of young plants, even so we are greatly comforted by the hope that God will have a people to serve him when we are dead and gone. In this way the people of God comforted themselves in that hope in Psalm 102:28, "the Children of thy servants shall continue, &c."

By reason of all these considerations, how careful should ministers and parents be to train up young ones while they are still pliable. Like wax they are capable of any form and impression in the knowledge and fear of God. We ought diligently to instil the principles of our most holy faith, as they are reduced to short summaries in Catechisms, and so completely laid in the view of conscience! Surely these seeds of truth planted in the field of memory, if they accomplish nothing else, will at least be a great check and bridle to them. And as the casting in of cold water stops the boiling of the pot, the truths may somewhat allay the fervours of youthful lusts and passions.

I had purposed to recommend the work of catechizing to you with great earnestness. Particularly, I had planned to prove what adequate, and useful books our catechisms and confession are, especially as they are printed here with the Scriptures proofs. But coming across an unpublished letter of a very learned and godly divine, in which my aforesaid purpose is excellently written, I will be bold to transcribe a part of it, and offer it to public view.

The author having cried out concerning the great distractions, corruptions, and divisions that are in the Church, he now offers the cause and cure: "Among others, a principal cause of these mischiefs is the great and common neglect of the governors of families, in the discharge of that duty which they owe to God for the souls that are under their charge, especially in teaching them the doctrine of Christianity. Families are societies that must be sanctified to God as well as Churches; and the governors of families have as true a charge of the souls that are in them, as pastors have of the Churches. But, alas, how little is this considered or regarded! But while negligent ministers are (deservedly) cast out of their places, the negligent masters of families take themselves to be almost blameless. They...promise to teach their children the doctrine of the gospel, and bring them up in the nurture of the Lord, but they easily promise, and easily break it. Thereby they educate their children for the world and the flesh although they have renounced these and dedicated them to God. This covenant-breaking with God, and betraying the souls of their children to the devil, must lie heavy on them here or hereafter. They beget children, and keep families, merely for the world and the flesh, but little consider the greatness of the charge that is committed to them, and what it is to bring up a child for God, and govern a family as a sanctified society.

"O how sweetly and successfully the work of God would go on, if we would just all join together in our several places to promote it! Men would not so often run off to be preachers(uncalled), but would find that part of the kingdom's work that belongs to them to be enough, and not only enough, but the best that they can be employed in. Especially women should be careful of this duty; because as they spend the most time with their children, and have early and frequent opportunities to instruct them. This is the principal service they can do to God in this world, being restrained from more public work. And doubtless many excellent magistrates have been sent into the Commonwealth, and many excellent pastors into the Church, and many precious saints to heaven, through the happy preparations of a holy education, and perhaps by a woman that thought herself useless and unserviceable to the Church.

"If parents would begin immediately, and labor to affect the hearts of their children with the great matters of everlasting life, and to acquaint them with the substance of the doctrine of Christ, and when they find in them the knowledge and love of Christ, bring them then to the pastors of the Church to be tried, confirmed, and admitted to the further privileges of the Church, O what happy, well-ordered Churches we might have! Then one pastor be forced to do the work of two or three hundred or thousand governors of families, to teach their children those principles which they should have taught them long before. Nor would we be forced to preach to so many miserable ignorant souls, that are not prepared by education to understand us. Nor would we have need to bar so many from holy communion on the account of ignorance, because they do not have the grace to feel it and lament it. Nor do they have the understanding and patience to wait in a learning state until they are ready to be fellow citizens with the saints, and of the household of God. But now they come to us with aged self-conceitedness, being past children, and yet worse than children still...having the ignorance of children, but having outgrown the teachableness of children. They think that they are wise, even wise enough to quarrel with the wisest of their teachers because they have lived long enough to have been wise. But the evidence of their knowledge is their aged ignorance. They are readier to demand Church privileges to our faces, than they are to learn from us, and obey our instructions until they are prepared for those privileges that they may do them good. But like snapping dogs, that will bite us on the fingers for their meat, and snatch it out of our hands rather than be like children that wait until we give it to them.

"Parents have raised so many that are unruly, that ministers have hardly any to deal with but the unruly. And it is because of this lack of laying the foundation well at first, that so many believers themselves are so ignorant. This is why so many, specially of the younger sort, swallow down almost any error that is offered to them. How they follow any false prophet that will entice them with earnestness and plausibility.

"For, alas! though by the grace of God their hearts may be changed in an hour, (whenever they understand but the essentials of the faith,) yet these who have been deprived of a holy education in the home need much time to understand. Only with great diligence are they furnished with such knowledge as will establish them, and fortify them against deceits. Upon these, and many the similar considerations, we should urge all Christian families to take more pains in this necessary work, and to get better acquainted with the substance of Christianity. And to that end, (together with some moving treatises to awaken the heart,) I do not know what book would be more appropriate for their use than the one compiled by the Assembly at Westminster. In spite of all the bitter words which they have received from self-conceited men, I truly think that they were a Synod of as godly and judicious divines as England ever saw.

"Though they had the unhappiness to live in calamitous times, when the noise and the licentiousness of wars set every wanton tongue and pen at liberty to reproach and dishonor them. I dare say, if in the days of old, when councils were in power and account, they had but such a council of bishops equal to these presbyters, the fame of it for learning and holiness, and all ministerial abilities, would, with very great honor, have been transmitted to posterity.

"I do therefore desire, that all masters of families would first study well this work themselves, and then teach it their children and servants, according to their several capacities. And, if they once understand these grounds of religion, they will be able to read other books more understandingly, and hear sermons more profitably, and confer more judiciously, and hold fast the doctrine of Christ more firmly, than ever you are like to do by any other course. First, let them read and learn the Shorter Catechism, and next the Larger, and lastly, read the Confession of Faith."

Thus far he, whose name I shall conceal, (though the excellency of the matter, and present style, will easily discover him,) because I have published it without his privity and consent, though, I hope, not against his liking and approbation. I shall add no more, but that I am, Thy servant, in the Lord's work,

—Thomas Manton

3. The Directory For Family Worship

Directions of the General Assembly,

Concerning secret and private worship, and mutual edification; for cherishing piety, for maintaining unity, and avoiding schism and division.[The General Assembly, after mature deliberation, doth approve the following Rules and Directions for cherishing piety, and preventing division and schism; and doth appoint minsters and ruling elders in each congregation to take special care that these Directions be observed and followed; as likewise; that presbyteries and provincial synods enquire and make trial whether the said Directions be duly observed in their bounds; and to reprove or censure (according to the quality of the offense), such as shall be found reprovable or censurable therein. And, to the end that these directions may not be rendered ineffectual and unprofitable among some, through the usual neglect of the very substance of the duty of Family-worship, the Assembly doth further require and appoint ministers and ruling elders to make diligent search and enquiry, in the congregations committed to their charge respectively, whether there be among them any family or families which used to neglect this necessary duty; and if any such family be found, the head of the family is to be first admonished privately to amend his fault; and, in case of his continuing therein, he is to be gravely and sadly reproved by the session; after which reproof, if he be found still to neglect Family-worship, let him be, for his obstinacy in such an offence, suspended and debarred from the Lord's supper, as being justly esteemed unworthy to communicate therein, til he amend. Edinburgh, August 24, 1647.]

Besides the public worship in congregations, mercifully established in this land in great purity, it is expedient and necessary that secret worship of each person alone, and private worship of families, be pressed and set up; that, with national reformation, the profession and power of godliness, both personal and domestic, be advanced.

I.   And first, for secret worship, it is most necessary, that every one apart, and by themselves, be given to prayer and meditation, the unspeakable benefit whereof is best known to them who are most exercised therein; this being the mean whereby, in a special way, communion with God is entertained, and right preparation for all other duties obtained: and therefore it becometh not only pastors, within their several charges, to press persons of all sorts to perform this duty morning and evening, and at other occasions; but also it is incumbent to the head of every family to have a care, that both themselves, and all within their charge, be daily diligent herein.

II.   The ordinary duties comprehended under the exercise of piety which should be in families, when they are convened to that effect, are these: First, Prayer and praises performed with a special reference, as well to the public condition of the kirk of God and this kingdom, as to the present case of the family, and every member thereof. Next, Reading of the scriptures, with catechising in a plain way, that the understandings of the simpler may be the better enabled to profit under the public ordinances, and they made more capable to understand the scriptures when they are read; together with godly conferences tending to the edification of all the members in the most holy faith: as also, admonition and rebuke, upon just reasons, from those who have authority in the family.

III.   As the charge and office of interpreting the holy scriptures is a part of the ministerial calling, which none (however otherwise qualified) should take upon him in any place, but he that is duly called hereunto by God and his kirk; so in every family where there is any that can read, the holy scriptures should be read ordinarily to the family; and it is commendable, that thereafter they confer, and by way of conference make some good use of what hath been read and heard. As, for example, if any sin be reproved in the word read, use may be made thereof to make all the family circumspect and watchful against the same; or if any judgement be threatened, or mentioned to have been inflicted in that portion of scripture which is read, use may be made to make all the family fear lest the same or a worse judgment befall them, unless they beware of the sin that procured it: and, finally, if any duty be required, or comfort held forth in a promise, use may be made to stir up themselves to employ Christ for strength to enable them for doing the commanded duty, and to apply the offered comfort. In all which the master of the family is to have the chief hand; and any member of the family may propone a question or doubt for resolution.

IV.   The head of the family is to take care that none of the family withdraw himself from any part of family-worship: and, seeing the ordinary performance of all the parts of family-worship belongeth properly to the head of the family, the minister is to stir up such as are lazy, and train up such as are weak, to a fitness to these exercises; it being always free to persons of quality to entertain one approved by the presbytery for performing family-exercise. And in other families, where the head of the family is unfit, that another, constantly residing in the family, approved by the minister and session, may be employed in that service, wherein the minister and session are to be accountable to the presbytery. And if a minster, by divine Providence, be brought to any family, it is requisite that at no time he convene a part of the family for worship, secluding the rest, except in singular cases especially concerning these parties, which (in Christian prudence) need not, or ought not, to be imparted to others.

V.   Let no idler, who hath no particular calling, or vagrant person under pretence of a calling, be suffered to perform worship in families, to or for the same; seeing persons tainted with errors, or aiming at division, may be ready (after that manner) to creep into houses, and lead captive silly and unstable souls.

VI. At family-worship, a special care is to be had that each family keep by themselves; neither requiring, inviting, nor admitting persons from divers families, unless it be those who are lodged with them, or at meals, or otherwise with them upon some lawful occasion.

VII. Whatsoever have been the effects and fruits of meetings of persons of divers families in the times of corruption or trouble, (in which cases many things are commendable, which otherwise are not tolerable,) yet, when God hath blessed us with peace and purity of the gospel, such meetings of persons of divers families (except in cases mentioned in these Directions) are to be disapproved, as tending to the hindrance of the religious exercise of each family by itself, to the prejudice of the public ministry, to the rending of the families of particular congregations, and (in progress of time) of the whole kirk. Besides many offences which may come thereby, to the hardening of the hearts of carnal men, and grief of the godly.

VIII. On the Lord's day, after every one of the family apart, and the whole family together, have sought the Lord (in whose hands the preparation of men's hearts are) to fit them for the public worship, and to bless to them the public ordinances, the master of the family ought to take care that all within his charge repair to the public worship, that he and they may join with the rest of the congregation: and the public worship being finished, after prayer, he should take an account what they have heard; and thereafter, to spend the rest of the time which they may spare in catechising, and in spiritual conferences upon the word of God: or else (going apart) they ought to apply themselves to reading, meditation, and secret prayer, that they may confirm and increase their communion with God: that so the profit which they found in the public ordinances may be cherished and promoted, and they more edified unto eternal life.

IX. So many as can conceive prayer, ought to make use of that gift of God; albeit those who are rude and weaker may begin at a set form of prayer, but so as they be not sluggish in stirring up in themselves (according to their daily necessities) the spirit of prayer, which is given to all the children of God in some measure: to which effect, they ought to be more fervent and frequent in secret prayer to God, for enabling of their hearts to conceive, and their tongues to express, convenient desires to God for their family. And, in the meantime, for their greater encouragement, let these materials of prayer be meditated upon, and made use of, as followeth.

"Let them confess to God how unworthy they are to come in his presence, and how unfit to worship his Majesty; and therefore earnestly ask of God the spirit of prayer.

"They are to confess their sins, and the sins of the family; accusing, judging, and condemning themselves for them, till they bring their souls to some measure of true humiliation.

"They are to pour out their souls to God, in the name of Christ, by the Spirit, for forgiveness of sins; for grace to repent, to believe, and to live soberly, righteously, and godly; and that they may serve God with joy and delight, walking before him.

"They are to give thanks to God for his many mercies to his people, and to themselves, and especially for his love in Christ, and for the light of the gospel.

"They are to pray for such particular benefits, spiritual and temporal, as they stand in need of for the time, (whether it be morning or evening,) as anent[30] health or sickness, prosperity or adversity.

"They ought to pray for the kirk of Christ in general, for all the reformed kirks, and for this kirk in particular, and for all that suffer for the name of Christ; for all our superiors, the king's majesty, the queen, and their children; for the magistrates, ministers, and whole body of the congregation whereof they are members, as well for their neighbors absent in their lawful affairs, as for those that are at home.

"The prayer may be closed with an earnest desire that God may be glorified in the coming of the kingdom of his Son, and in doing of his will and with assurance that themselves are accepted, and what they have asked according to his will shall be done."

X.   These exercises ought to be performed in great sincerity, without delay, laying aside all exercises of worldly business or hindrances, notwithstanding the mockings of atheists and profane men; in respect of the great mercies of God to this land, and of his severe corrections wherewith lately he hath exercised us. And, to this effect, persons of eminency (and all elders of the kirk) not only ought to stir up themselves and families to diligence herein, but also to concur effectually, that in all other families, where they have power and charge, the said exercises be conscionably performed.

XI. Besides the ordinary duties in families, which are above mentioned, extraordinary duties, both of humiliation and thanksgiving, are to be carefully performed in families, when the Lord, by extraordinary occasions, (private or public,) calleth for them.

---

[30]"anent" is an old English word meaning "in respect of; with reference it; concerning, about" (*The New Shorter Oxford English Dictionary*, Oxford University Press, 1993).

XII. Seeing the word of God requireth that we should consider one another, to provoke unto love and good works; therefore, at all times, and specially in this time, wherein profanity abounds, and mockers, walking after their own lusts, think it strange that others run not with them to the same excess of riot; every member of this kirk ought to stir up themselves, and one another, to the duties of mutual edification, by instruction, admonition, rebuke; exhorting one another to manifest the grace of God in denying ungodliness and wordly lusts, and in living godly, soberly, and righteously in this present world; by comforting the feeble-minded, and praying with or for one another. Which duties respectively are to be performed upon special occasions offered by Divine Providence; as namely, when under any calamity, cross, or great difficulty, counsel or comfort is sought; or when an offender is to be reclaimed by private admonition, and if that be not effectual, by joining one or two more in the admonition, according to the rule of Christ, that in the mouth of two or three witnesses every word may be established.

XIII. And, because it is not given to every one to speak a word in season to a wearied or distressed conscience, it is expedient, that a person (in that case,) finding no ease, after the use of all ordinary means, private and public, have their address to their own pastor, or some experienced Christian: but if the person troubled in conscience be of that condition, or of that sex, that discretion, modesty, or fear of scandal, requireth a godly, grave, and secret friend to be present with them in the said address, it is expedient that such a friend be present.

XIV. When persons of divers families are brought together by Divine Providence, being abroad upon their particular vocations, or any necessary occasions; as they would have the Lord their God with them whithersoever they go, they ought to walk with God, and not neglect the duties of prayer and thanksgiving, but take care that the same be performed by such as the company shall judge fittest. And that they likewise take heed that no corrupt communication proceed out of their mouths, but that which is good, to the use of edifying, that it may minister grace to the hearers.

The drift and scope of all these Directions is no other, but that, upon the one part, the power and practice of godliness, amongst all the ministers and members of this kirk, according to their several places and vocations, may be cherished and advanced, and all impiety and mocking of religious exercises suppressed: and, upon the other part, that, under the name and pretext of religious exercises, no such meetings or practices be allowed, as are apt to breed error, scandal, schism, contempt, or misregard of the public ordinances and ministers, or neglect of the duties of particular callings, or such other evils as are the works, not of the Spirit, but of the flesh, and are contrary to truth and peace.

Chapter Eight

FAMILY PSALTER/HYMNAL

Introduction

It would be difficult to overestimate the importance of the church's songs. Luther once remarked that it would be preferable to write hymn lyrics to books of theology since the former wields more influence than the latter. Through its songs the church learns both its theology (particularly its theology of worship) and the language of Christian experience. Instinctively we turn to our songs both in times of crisis and great joy to find adequate language to express our response. So Mary at the annunciation drew upon the Song of Hannah (Lk 1:46–55; *cf.*, 1 Sam 2:1–10); Solomon at the dedication of the temple incorporated Psalm 132:8, 9 (2 Chr 6:40–42); Jesus on the cross itself used the words of Psalm 22:1 and 31:5 (Mt 27:46; Lk 23:46); and the early Christians in the face of persecution "lifted their voices to God with one accord" and recited or sang Psalms 146 and 2 (Acts 4:24–30), all doing so in order to interpret and give expression to their experiences.

Consequently it is vital that the church's songs be substantial enough to accurately express the subtlety of Christian truth and experience. Simplistic, sentimental, repetitious songs will leave the people of God ill-equipped on occasions of great moment. Few of them, we are sure, will survive the present generation. For this reason we have a decided preference for the enduring, metrical Psalms (Psalms rhymed, metered, and set to music) and time-proven hymns, particularly those of the 18th century, the "golden age" of hymn writing.

The Psalter has served as the primary hymnal of the Christian church since the time of the Apostles. Protestants were exclusively or nearly exclusively Psalm-singing for over 300 years. They have slipped from view only in relatively recent times. A revival of Psalm-singing is one of the great needs of our day.[31]

Likewise hymns are valued insofar as they summarize or give expression to biblical truths. Robert Godfrey, President of Westminster Theological Seminary in California, has suggested that the reason why the 18th century hymn

---

[31]See introduction to the *Trinity Psalter* (Pittsburgh: Crown and Covenant Publications, 1994).

writers were so outstanding (*e.g.*, Isaac Watts, Charles Wesley, John Newton, Augustus Toplady, William Cowper, Philip Dodderidge) was that they grew up singing the Psalms. Thus they had in their blood, as it were, the sophistication, the balance, and subtlety of the Psalms and the whole of the biblical revelation as they wrote "Our God, Our Help in Ages Past," "When I Survey the Wondrous Cross," "Joy to the World" (to name three of Watts'), "Amazing Grace" (John Newton), "Rock of Ages" (Toplady), "O For a Thousand Tongues to Sing," and "Hark! the Herald Angels Sing" (Wesley).

We have also included in our collection lyrics written by representatives of the best of the medieval tradition, including Francis of Assisi and Bernard of Clairvaux, the Reformer Martin Luther, the 18th century men listed above, Bishop Reginald Heber, Timothy Dwight, Frances Ridley Havergal and several from the 20th century. The Psalm lyrics, of course, date to around 1000 B.C. Their translations date to more recent times, primarily the *Scottish Psalter* of 1650, the *Book of Psalms*, 1871, *The Psalter*, 1912, and *The Book of Psalms for Singing*, 1973.

The tunes selected are among the best of the Christian tradition, including selections written by Bach, Handel, Beethoven, Haydn, Mendelssohn, Louis Bourgeois, Lowell Mason, John B. Dykes, Arthur S. Sullivan, and 20th century composer Ralph Vaughan-Williams.

Thus, the following collection of sixty metrical Psalms and sixty hymns combines the very best in Christian lyrics and music. We have included a variety of Psalm and hymn types, including some not sung as frequently today, such as Psalms of lament (*e.g.*, Psalms 22, 38, 60, 129), and minor key hymnody (*e.g.*, hymns nos. 1 and 45). You may wish to introduce one song a month in your family worship over the next ten years. If you do so, you will in the case of the Psalms be committing to memory Scripture itself, and in the case of the hymns, be introducing your family to the richness of the church's heritage in devotional song. Most of the following Psalms were taken from the *Trinity Psalter* and the hymns from the *Trinity Hymnal*. The music for the Psalms may be found in the *Trinity Psalter Music Edition* and the hymns, of course, in the *Trinity Hymnal*. We have included in the back indices for the Psalms and hymns and tables for their introduction and use over a ten year period. For additional help in learning great hymns and Psalms we recommend the following:

> *Hymns Triumphant Vol 1 and 2*, Sparrow Records, 1981, 1984. These two CDs/tapes include almost all of our hymn selections.

> *Psalms of the Trinity Psalter Vol 1 and 2*, IPC Press, 1999, 2002. These two CDs/tapes include almost all of our Psalm selections.

> *The Psalms of Scotland*, SCS Music Limited, 1988. Includes five of our Psalm/tune combinations, and an additional three of our tunes.

Contents
Metrical Psalms – pp. 125–158

Hymns – pp. 159–189

Psalms

Psalm 1

Based on *Scottish Psalter*, 1650

1. O greatly blessed is the man
Who walketh not astray
In counsel of ungodly men,
Nor stands in sinners' way.

2. Nor sitteth in the scorner's chair,
But placeth his delight
Upon GOD's law, and meditates
On His law day and night.

3. He shall be like a tree that grows
Set by the water side,
Which in its season yields its fruit,
And green its leaves abide;

4. And all he does shall prosper well.
The wicked are not so,
But are like chaff which by the wind
Is driven to and fro.

5. In judgment therefore shall not stand
Such as ungodly are,
Nor in th'assembly of the just
Shall wicked men appear.

6. Because the way of godly men
Is to Jehovah known,
Whereas the way of wicked men
Shall quite be overthrown.

TUNE: ARLINGTON CM
("This is The Day the Lord Has Made")
Thomas A. Arne, 1762

Psalm 2

Based on the *Book of Psalms,* 1871 and
The Psalter, 1912

1. Why do heathen nations rage?
Why do peoples folly mind?

2. Kings of earth in plots engage,
Rulers are in league combined;
Then against Jehovah high,
And against Messiah's sway,

3. "Let us break their bands," they cry,
"Let us cast their cords away."

4. But the Lord will scorn them all;
He will laugh Who sits on high,

5. Then His wrath will on them fall;
Sore displeased He will reply:

6. "Yet according to My will
I have set My King to reign,
And on Zion's holy hill
My Anointed I'll maintain."

7. His decree I will make known:
Unto Me the LORD did say,
"Thou art My beloved Son;
I've begotten Thee this day.

8. Ask of Me, and Thee I'll make
Heir to earth and nations all;

9. Them with iron Thou shalt break,
Dashing them in pieces small."

10. Therefore, kings, be wise, give ear;
Hearken, judges of the earth;

11. Serve the Lord with godly fear;
Mingle trembling with your mirth.

12. Kiss the Son, His wrath to turn,
Lest ye perish in the way,
For His anger soon will burn.
Blessed are all that on Him stay.

TUNE: HINTZE 7777D
Jakob Hintze, 1678;
harm. Johann S. Bach

Psalm 5

Based on the *Book of Psalms*, 1871 and
The Psalter, 1912

1 O Jehovah, hear my words;
To my thoughts attentive be.
2 Hear my cry, my King, my God,
For I make my prayer to Thee.
3 With the morning light, O LORD,
Thou shalt hear my voice and cry;
In the morn my prayer arrange
And keep constant watch will I.

4 Truly Thou art not a God
That in sin doth take delight;
Evil shall not dwell with Thee,
5 Nor the proud stand in Thy sight.
Evildoers Thou dost hate;
6 Liars Thou wilt bring to naught.
GOD abhors the man who loves
Deed of blood or lying thought.

7 But in Thine abundant grace
To Thy house will I repair;
Looking to Thy holy place,
In Thy fear I'll worship there.
8 Since, O LORD, mine enemies
For my soul do lie in wait,
Lead me in Thy righteousness;
Make Thy way before me straight.

9 For they flatter with their tongue;
In their mouth no truth is found;
Like an open grave their throat;
All their thoughts with sin abound.
10 Hold them guilty, O my God;
Them for all their sins expel;
Let them fall by their own craft,
For against Thee they rebel.

11 But let all that trust Thy care
Ever glad and joyful be;
Let them joy who love Thy name,
For they guarded are by Thee.
12 And a blessing rich, O LORD,
To the righteous Thou wilt yield;
Thou wilt compass him about
With Thy favor as a shield.

TUNE: ABERYSTWYTH 7777D
("Jesus Lover of My Soul")
Joseph Parry, 1879

Psalm 8

Elements from *The Psalter*, 1912

1 LORD, our Lord, in all the earth
How excellent Your name!
You above the heav'ns have set
The splendor of Your fame.
2 From the mouths of infants young
You the power of praise compose
In the face of enemies
To stop avenging foes.

3 When I view the skies above
Which Your own fingers made,
When I see the moon and stars
Which You in order laid,
4 What is man so frail and weak
That You should remember him?
What can be the son of man
That You should care for him?

5 Next to God You have made man,
With light and honor crowned.
6 You placed him above Your works;
Beneath him all is found:
7 Oxen, sheep, and all wild beasts,
8 Birds, and fish the oceans claim.
9 LORD, our Lord, in all the earth
How excellent Your name!

TUNE: AMSTERDAM 76767776
Freylinghausen, *Gesangbuch*, 1704

Psalm 15

1 LORD, in Thy tent who will
  Abide with Thee,
  And on Thy holy hill
  A dweller be?
2 Who walks in uprightness,
  Who worketh righteousness,
  Who doth the truth express
  Unfeignedly;

3 Whose tongue doth not defame
  Nor harm his friend,
  Who to his neighbor's shame
  No ear doth lend,
4 Who has the vile abhorred
  But honor doth accord
  To those who fear the LORD
  And Him attend.

  When to his hurt he swears
  Naught changes he;
5 His gold no increase bears
  From usury;
  His hands no bribes receive
  The guiltless to aggrieve.
  Lo, he who thus doth live
  Unmoved shall be.

TUNE: LOWRY 64.64.66.64.
("Savior, Thy Dying Love")
Robert Lowry

Psalm 19

Based on the *Book of Psalms,* 1871 and
The Psalter, 1912

Verses 1–6

1 The spacious heav'ns declare
  The glory of our God;
  The firmament displays
  His handiwork abroad;
2 Day unto day doth utter speech,
  And night to night doth knowledge
  teach.

3 Aloud they do not speak;
  They utter forth no word,
  Nor into language break;
  Their voice is never heard;
4 Yet through the world their line
  extends,
  Their words to earth's remotest ends.

  In heav'n He set a tent
  A dwelling for the sun,
5 Which as a mighty man
  Delights his course to run.
  He, bridegroomlike in his array,
  Comes from his chamber, bringing
  day.

6 His daily going forth
  Is from the end of heav'n:
  The firmament to him
  Is for his circuit giv'n;
  And everywhere from end to end,
  His radiant heat he doth extend.

(continued next page)

Verses 7–14

7 Jehovah's perfect law
Restores the soul again;
His testimony sure
Gives wisdom unto men;
8 The precepts of the LORD are right,
And fill the heart with great delight.

The Lord's command is pure,
Enlightening the eyes;
9 Jehovah's fear is clean,
More lasting than the skies.
The judgments of the LORD express
His truth and perfect righteousness.

10 They're more to be desired
Than stores of finest gold;
Than honey from the comb
More sweetness far they hold.
11 With warnings they Thy servant guard;
In keeping them is great reward.

12 His errors who can know?
Cleanse me from hidden stain.
13 Keep me from willful sins,
Nor let them o'er me reign.
And then I upright shall appear
And be from great transgression clear.

14 Let all the words I speak
And all the thoughts within
Come up before Thy sight
And Thine approval win.
O Thou Jehovah, unto me
My rock and my Redeemer be.

TUNE: COLUMBIA 66.66.88.
("Praise Ye, Praise Ye the Lord")
Leonard Cooper Blanton, 1951; alt.

Psalm 22

Verses 1–12

1 My God, my God, O why have You
Forsaken me? O why
Are You so far from giving help
And from my groaning cry?
2 By day and night, my God, I call;
Your answer still delays.
3 And yet You are the Holy One
Who dwells in Israel's praise.

4 Our fathers put their trust in You;
From you their rescue came.
5 They begged You and You set them
free;
They were not put to shame.
6 But as for me, I am a worm
And not a man at all.
To men I am despised and base;
Their scornings on me fall.

7 All those who look at me will laugh
And cast reproach at me.
Their mouths they open wide: they
wag
Their heads in mockery.
8 "The LORD was his reliance once;
Now see what God will send.
Yes, let God rise and set him free,
This man that was His friend."

9 You took me from my mother's womb
To safety at the breast.
10 Since birth when I was cast on You
In You, my God, I rest.
11 Be not far off, for grief is near,
And none to help is found;
12 For bulls of Bashan in their strength
Now circle me around.

TUNE: HORSLEY CM
William Horsley, 1844

Psalm 23

Based on *Scottish Psalter*, 1650

1 The LORD's my Shepherd, I'll not want;
2 He makes me down to lie
In pastures green; He leadeth me
The quiet waters by.

3 My soul He doth restore again;
And me to walk doth make
Within the paths of righteousness,
Ev'n for His own name's sake.

4 Yea, though I walk in death's dark vale,
Yet will I fear no ill;
For thou art with me, and Thy rod
And staff me comfort still.

5 A table Thou has furnished me
In presence of my foes;
My head Thou dost with oil anoint,
And my cup overflows.

6 Goodness and mercy all my life
Shall surely follow me;
And in GOD's house forevermore
My dwelling place shall be.

TUNE: CRIMOND CM
Jessie Seymour Irvine, 1871

Psalm 24

Based on the *Book of Psalms*, 1871
and *The Psalter*, 1912

1 The earth and the riches with which it
is stored,
The world and its dwellers, belong to
the LORD.
2 For He on the seas its foundation has
laid,
And firm on the waters its pillars has
stayed.

3 O who shall the mount of Jehovah
ascend?
Or who in the place of His holiness
stand?
4 The man of pure heart and of hands
without stain,
Who has not sworn falsely nor loved
what is vain.

5 He shall from Jehovah a blessing
receive;
The God of salvation shall
righteousness give.
6 Thus looking to Him is a whole blessed
race,
All those who, like Jacob, are seeking
Your face.

7 O gates, lift your heads! Ageless
doors, lift them high!
The great King of glory to enter draws
nigh!
8 O who is the King that in glory draws
near?
The LORD, mighty LORD of the battle is
here!

9 O gates, lift your heads! Ageless
doors, lift them high!
The great King of glory to enter draws
nigh!
10 This great King of glory, O Who can
He be?
Jehovah of hosts, King of glory is He!

TUNE: GREYFRIARS 11.11.11.11.
S. A. Sterrett Metheny, 1909

Psalm 25

Based on *Scottish Psalter*, 1650

Verses 1–7

1 To Thee I lift my soul,
2 O LORD; I trust in Thee,
   My God; let me not be ashamed
   Nor foes exult o'er me.
3 Yea, none that wait on Thee
   Shall be ashamed at all;
   But those that wantonly transgress,
   Upon them shame shall fall.

4 Show me Thy ways, O LORD;
   Thy paths, O teach Thou me,
5 And do Thou lead me in Thy truth;
   Therein my teacher be.
   For Thou art God that dost
   To me salvation send,
   And I upon Thee all the day
   Expecting do attend.

6 Thy tender mercies, LORD,
   To mind do Thou recall,
   And lovingkindnesses, for they
   Have been through ages all.
7 My sins of youth, my faults,
   Do Thou, O LORD, forget;
   In lovingkindness think on me
   And for Thy goodness great.

TUNE: TRENTHAM SM
("Breathe on Me, Breath of God")
Robert Jackson, 1888

Psalm 27

Based on *The Psalter*, 1912

Verses 1–6

1 The LORD's my shining light
   And my salvation sure;
   Who can fill me with fright
   Or move my heart secure?
   The LORD's my stronghold ever near;
   Of Whom then shall I stand in fear?

2 When adversaries came
   To eat my flesh away,
   Those wicked tripped in shame,
   And fell to their dismay.
3 Though hosts surround, I will not quail;
   And still I trust, though war assail.

4 My one desire has been,
   Still to the LORD I'll pray,
   That all my days within
   The LORD's house I may stay,
   The LORD's own beauty to admire,
   And in His temple to inquire.

5 When troubles fill my day,
   When fears and dangers throng,
   Securely hid I'll stay
      In His pavilion strong.
   He'll hide me in His tent always;
   And high upon a rock me raise.

6 My head shall lifted be
   Above my enemies.
   Within His tent with glee
   I'll offer sacrifice.
   With shouts of joy my song I'll bring;
   There praises to the LORD I'll sing.

TUNE: ST. JOHN 66.66.88.
("Within Your Temple, Lord")
William H. Havergal, 1853

Psalm 32

1 What blessedness for him whose guilt
Has all forgiven been!
When his transgressions pardoned are,
And covered is his sin.
2 O blessed the man 'gainst whom the LORD
Counts no iniquity,
And in whose spirit there is not
Deceit or treachery.

3 When I kept silent, my bones aged;
My groaning filled each day.
4 Your hand oppressed me day and night;
My moisture dried away.
5 Then I to You admitted sin,
Hid not my guiltiness;
I said, "I will before the LORD
Transgressions now confess."

Then You did all my sin forgive
And take my guilt away.
6 For this when You are near at hand
Let all the godly pray.
The rising floods will harm him not.
7 You are my hiding place.
And You will comfort me with songs
Of victory and grace.

8 Instruction I will give to you
And teach you as you go.
My watchful eye will guide your steps;
My counsel you will know.
9 Be not like senseless horse or mule
Which if you would subdue
You must with bit and bridle hold
To bring him close to you.

10 The wicked many pangs endure,
But steadfast cov'nant love
Encircles every man whose trust
Is in the LORD above.
11 Be glad and shout, you righteous ones,
And in the LORD rejoice!
And all whose hearts are just and true
Sing out with joyful voice.

TUNE: VOX DILECTI CMD
("I Heard the Voice of Jesus Say")
John B. Dykes, 1868

Psalm 34

Verses 1–14

1 In every time I'll always bless the
LORD;
His praise will ever be within my mouth.
2 My soul will make its boasting in the
LORD;
Let all the humble hear it and be glad.
3 O join with me to magnify the LORD!
Let us together raise His name on
high!

4 I sought the LORD and He has
answered me,
And He from all my terrors set me
free.
5 O look to Him, be radiant, unashamed!
6 This poor man cried; the Lord from
trouble saved.
7 The LORD'S own angel constantly
encamps
Around those fearing Him, and
rescues them.

8 O taste and you will see the LORD is
good!
How happy is the man who trusts in
Him!
9 O fear the LORD, all you He has
redeemed!
For those who fear Him never suffer
want.
10 Young lions hunger; they may lack
their food;
But those who seek the LORD shall
have no want.

11 O come, you children, listen unto me;
And I will teach you how to fear the
LORD.
12 Who longs for life and loves to see
good days?
13 From evil keep your tongue, your lips
from lies.
14 Depart from evil and be doing good;
Seek peace and strive for it with all
your heart.

TUNE: YORKSHIRE 10.10.10.10.10.10.
John Wainwright, 1750

Psalm 37

Elements from *Scottish Psalter*, 1650

Verses 1–9

1 Have no disturbing thoughts about
 Those doing wickedly,
 And be not envious of those
 Who work iniquity.
2 For even like the growing grass
 Soon be cut down shall they;
 And like the green and tender plant
 They all shall fade away.

3 Set thou thy trust upon the LORD;
 Continue doing good.
 Dwell thou securely in the land;
 Make faithfulness thy food.
4 Joy in the LORD; He'll grant each gift
 For which thy heart may call.
5 Commit thy way unto the LORD;
 Trust Him; He'll do it all.

6 And like the morning light He shall
 Thy righteousness display;
 And He thy judgment shall bring forth
 Like noontide of the day.
7 Rest in the LORD; wait patiently;
 Fret not for anyone
 Who prospers in his wicked way,
 Completing schemes begun.

8 Cease being thou by anger stirred;
 Make thou of wrath an end.
 Fret not thyself, for fretting will
 To evildoing tend.
9 For evildoers soon shall be
 Cut off, no more to stand;
 But those who wait upon the LORD
 Inherit shall the land.

TUNE: FOREST GREEN CMD
English melody

Psalm 38

Based on the *Book of Psalms*, 1871

Verses 1–10

1 LORD, do not in hot displeasure
 Speak in stern reproof to me;
 Let Thy chast'ning be in measure
 And Thy stroke from anger free.
2 For Thy hand most sorely presses;
 Fast Thine arrows stick within;
3 Wrath my weary flesh distresses,
 Gives my bones no rest for sin.

4 For my manifold transgressions
 Have gone up above my head;
 Like a burden their oppressions
 Weigh me down with constant dread.
5 Loathsome are my wounds neglected;
 My own folly makes it so;
6 Bowed with pain, with grief dejected,
 All day long I mourning go.

7 For my loins are filled with burning,
 All my flesh with sore distress;
8 Faint and bruised, I'm ever mourning
 In my heart's disquietness.
9 My desire and ceaseless wailing,
 Lord, unveiled before Thee lie;
10 Throbs my heart; my strength is failing;
 All the light has left my eye.

TUNE: MERTON 87.87.
William Henry Monk, 1850

Psalm 42

Based on *Scottish Psalter*, 1650

Verses 1–5

1 As in its thirst a fainting hart
To water brooks doth flee,
So pants my longing soul, O God,
That I may come to Thee.
2 My soul for God, the living God,
Is thirsting; shall I near
Before the face of God approach
And in His sight appear?

3 My tears have unto me been food
Both in the night and day,
While unto me continually,
"Where is your God?" they say.
4 Poured out within me is my soul
When this I think upon:
How often with the eager throng
I rev'rently had gone,

How to the house of God I went
With voice of joy and praise,
Yea, with the multitude that kept
The solemn holy days.
5 O why, my soul, art thou bowed down?
Why so discouraged be?
Hope now in God! I'll praise Him still!
My help, my God is He!

Verses 6–11

6 O God, my soul's cast down in me;
I Thee remember will
From Jordan land, from Hermon's
height,
And ev'n from Mizar hill.
7 With thunder of Thy waterfalls
Deep makes the deep its call;
Thy billows all roll over me;
On me Thy breakers fall.

8 And yet Jehovah will command
His mercy in the day;
By night His song shall be with me;
To God, my Life, I'll pray.
9 To God Who is my rock I'll say,
"O why forget me so?
Beneath oppression of my foes
Why do I mourning go?"

10 As with a sword within my bones
My enemies upbraid,
While unto me, "Where is Thy God?"
Continually is said.
11 O why, my soul, art thou bowed down?
Why so discouraged be?
Hope now in God! I'll praise Him still!
My Help, my God is He!

TUNE: ST. AGNES CM
("Jesus the Very Thought of Thee")
John B. Dykes, 1866

Psalm 46

Based on *Scottish Psalter*, 1650

1 God is our refuge and our strength,
2 In straits a present aid;
And, therefore, tho' the earth remove
We will not be afraid;
3 Tho' hills amidst the seas be cast,
Tho' troubled waters roar,
Yea, tho' the swelling billows shake
The mountains on the shore.

4 A river is whose streams make glad
The city of our God,
The holy place wherein the Lord
Most High has His abode.
5 Yea, God is in the midst of her;
Unmoved she stands for aye;
And God will surely grant her help
Before the break of day.

6 The nations raged; the kingdoms
moved;
And when the earth had heard
The mighty voice He sent abroad
It melted at His word.
7 The LORD of hosts is on our side
Our safety to secure;
The God of Jacob is for us
A refuge strong and sure.

8 O come, behold what wondrous works
Have by the LORD been wrought;
Come, see what desolations great
He on the earth has brought.
9 To utmost ends of all the earth
Wars into peace He turns;
The bow He breaks, the spear He
cuts,
In fire the chariot burns.

10 Be still and know that I am God;
Among the nations I
Will be exalted; I on earth
Will be exalted high.
11 The LORD of hosts is on our side.
Our safety to secure;
The God of Jacob is for us
A refuge strong and sure.

TUNE: MATERNA CMD
("O Beautiful for Spacious Skies")
Samuel A. Ward, 1882; or
BETHLEHEM CMD
Gottfried W. Fink, 1842

Psalm 47

Based on *Scottish Psalter,* 1650

1 All peoples, clap your hands for joy;
To God in triumph shout;
2 For awesome is the LORD Most High,
Great King the earth throughout.
3 He brings the peoples under us
In mastery complete;
And He it is Who nations all
Subdues beneath our feet.

4 The land of our inheritance
He chooses out for us,
And He to us the glory gives
Of Jacob whom He loves.
5 God is ascended with a shout,
The LORD with trumpeting.
6 Sing praises unto God! Sing praise!
Sing praises to our King!

7 For God is King of all the earth;
Sing praise with skillfulness.
8 God rules the nations; God sits on
His throne of holiness.
9 Assemble, men of Abrah'm's God!
Come, people, princes, nigh!
The shields of earth belong to God;
He is exalted high.

TUNE: PETERSHAM CMD
Clement W. Poole, 1875

Psalm 51

Based on the *Book of Psalms,* 1871 and
The Psalter, 1912

Verses 1–11

1 God, be merciful to me;
On Thy grace I rest my plea;
In Thy vast, abounding grace,
My transgressions all erase.
2 Wash me wholly from my sin;
Cleanse from every ill within.

3 For my sins before me rise,
Ever present to my eyes.
4 I have sinned 'gainst Thee alone,
In Thy sight this evil done;
That Thy judgment may be clear,
And Thy sentence just appear.

5 Lo, brought forth was I in sin;
When conceived I was unclean.
6 Lo, Thou dost desire to find
Truth sincere within the mind:
And Thou wilt within my heart
Wisdom unto me impart.

7 Then with hyssop sprinkle me,
And from sin I clean shall be.
Wash me from its stain, and lo,
I shall whiter be than snow.
8 Make me hear joy's cheering voice;
Make my broken bones rejoice.

9 From my sins hide Thou Thy face;
My iniquities erase.
10 O my God, renew my heart,
And a spirit right impart.
11 Cast me not away from Thee,
Nor Thy Spirit take from me.

Verses 12–19

12 Give salvation's joy again,
And a willing mind sustain.
13 Then thy perfect ways I'll show
That transgressors may them know;
They converted then shall be;
Sinners shall be turned to Thee.

14 Free me from the guilt of blood,
God, of my salvation God;
Then with joy my tongue shall raise
Songs Thy righteousness to praise.
15 Open Thou my lips, O Lord;
Then my mouth shall praise accord.

16 Sacrifice Thou wilt not take,
Else would I the off'ring make.
Off'rings burnt bring no delight,
But a broken heart, contrite,
17 God's accepted sacrifice,
Thou, O God, wilt not despise.

18 Prosper Zion in Thy grace;
Salem's broken walls replace.
19 Then shall sacrifices right,
Whole burnt off'rings Thee delight;
So will men, their vows to pay,
Bullocks on Thine altar lay.

TUNE: REDHEAD / AJALON 77.77.77.
("Gracious Spirit, Dwell With Me")
Richard Redhead, 1853

Psalm 60

Elements from *The Psalter*, 1912

Verses 1–5

1 O God, Thou hast rejected us,
Hast broken us once more.
As Thou with us hast angry been,
O once again restore.

2 For Thou hast made the earth to
quake,
Hast torn it fearfully.
O heal its gaping cracks, for, lo,
It shakes in agony!

3 For Thou hast made the people see
The hardness of distress,
And Thou hast made them drink the
wine
Of reeling drunkenness.

4 But those that fear Thee Thou didst
give
A banner in their sight,
That they might rally and be firm,
Made strong by truth and right.

5 O grant that Thy beloved ones
May safe delivered be.
O save them with Thy strong right
hand,
And do Thou answer me.

TUNE: BANGOR CM
William Tans'ur, 1734

Psalm 63

1 God, Thee, my God, I'll early seek;
My soul's athirst for Thee.
On dry land, weary, waterless,
My flesh has longed for Thee.

2 Thus have I looked for Thee before
Within Thy holy place
That there I might behold Thy strength
And glory of Thy face.

3 Because Thy grace is more than life
My lips Thee praise shall give;

4 I in Thy name will lift my hands
And bless Thee while I live.

5 My soul with rich, abundant food
Shall be well satisfied;
With shouts of joy upon my lips
My mouth shall praise provide.

6 And when I turn my thought to Thee
Upon my bed at night,
As watches pass I meditate
On Thee with great delight.

7 Thou art my help; I sing for joy
In shadow of Thy wings.

8 For Thy right hand has held me fast;
To Thee my spirit clings.

9 But they go down to depths of earth
Who would my soul destroy;

10 They are delivered to the sword
For jackals to enjoy.

11 The king shall then rejoice in God
And all that by Him swear;
For stopped shall be the mouths of
those
Who do a lie declare.

TUNE: ST. COLUMBA CM
("How Sweet and Awful is the Place")
Old Irish hymn melody

Psalm 65

Based on the *Book of Psalms,* 1871 and
The Psalter, 1912

Verses 1–8, 11–13

1 Praise waits for Thee in Zion!
   To Thee vows paid shall be.
2 O God, of prayer the hearer,
   All flesh shall come to Thee.
3 Iniquities are daily
   Prevailing over me,
   But all of our transgressions
   Are covered o'er by Thee.

4 How blessed the man Thou choosest
   And bringest near to Thee,
   That in Thy courts forever
   His dwelling place may be.
   We shall within Thy temple
   Be wholly satisfied
   And filled with all the goodness
   Thy sacred courts provide.

5 O God of our salvation,
   Thou in Thy righteousness
   With awesome deeds and wonders
   Thine answer wilt express,
   O Thou in Whom confiding
   All ends of earth agree,
   And people who are sailing
   Upon the farthest sea.

6 Thy might has built the mountains;
   Power clothes Thee evermore,
7 To calm the nations' clamor
   And still the ocean's roar.
8 Thine awesome signs and wonders
   Fill distant lands with fear.
   Thou makest dawn and sunset
   For joy to shout and cheer.

11 Thou crownest years with goodness;
   Thy steps enrich the ground.
12 The desert pastures blossom.
   The hills with joy resound.
13 The fields with flocks are covered;
   The vales with grain are clad.
   They all rejoice with shouting!
   They all with songs are glad!

TUNE: WEBB 76.76.D
("Stand Up, Stand Up for Jesus")
George J. Webb, 1837

Psalm 66

Based on *Scottish Psalter,* 1650,
the *Book of Psalms,* 1871
and *The Psalter,* 1912

Verses 1–6

1 All lands to God in joyful sounds
   Aloft your voices raise;
2 Sing forth the honor of His name,
   And glorious make His praise,
   And glorious make His praise.

3 Say unto God, How terrible
   In all Thy works art Thou!
   Through Thy great power Thy foes to
     Thee
   Shall be constrained to bow,
   Shall be constrained to bow.

4 Yes, all the earth shall worship Thee,
   And unto Thee shall sing;
   And to Thy name most glorious
   Their songs of praise shall bring,
   Their songs of praise shall bring.

5 O come, behold the works of God,
   His mighty doings see;
   In dealing with the sons of men
   Most terrible is He,
   Most terrible is He.

   He turned the sea into dry land,
   So they a pathway had;
6 They through the river went on foot;
   There we in Him were glad,
   There we in Him were glad.

TUNE: MILES LANE CM
("All Lands to God")
William Shrubsole, 1779

Psalm 67

Based on the *Book of Psalms,* 1871,
and *The Psalter,* 1912

1 O God, to us show mercy,
And bless us in Thy grace;
Cause Thou to shine upon us
The brightness of Thy face;
2 That so Thy way most holy
On earth may soon be known,
And unto every people
Thy saving grace be shown.

3 O God, let peoples praise Thee;
Let all the people sing;
4 Let nations now be joyful;
Let songs of gladness ring;
For Thou wilt judge the peoples
In truth and righteousness;
And o'er the earth shall nations
Thy leadership confess.

5 O God, let peoples praise Thee;
Let all the people sing;
6 For earth in rich abundance
To us her fruit will bring.
God, our own God, will bless us;
Yea, God will blessing send;
And all the earth shall fear Him
To its remotest end.

TUNE: MISSIONARY HYMN 76.76.D
("From Greenland's Icy Mountains")
Lowell Mason, 1824

Psalm 68

Based on *Scottish Psalter,* 1650;
vv. 1–6, *The Book of Psalms
with Music,* 1950;
vv. 7, 8, *The Book of Psalms for
Singing,* 1973

Verses 1–8

1 Let God arise, and scattered far
Be all His enemies;
And let all those who do Him hate
Before His presence flee,
2 As smoke is driven, drive Thou them;
As wax melts by the fire,
Let wicked men before God's face
So perish in His ire.

3 But let all righteous men be glad;
Let them before God's sight
Be very joyful; yea, let them
Rejoice with all their might.
4 Sing praise to God; prepare His way;
Jehovah is His name,
Who rideth through the wilderness;
Before Him joy proclaim.

5 He takes a father's place to those
Who are left fatherless;
The widow's judge is God, within
His place of holiness.
6 Yea, God the solitary sets
In families; from bands
The chained doth free; but rebels do
Inhabit desert lands.

7 O God, the time Thy going forth
Was at Thy people's head,
The time when Thy majestic march
Into the desert led,
8 Then at God's presence trembled
earth;
The melting heavens fell;
This Sinai quaked, for God was there,
The God of Israel.

TUNE: WEYMOUTH CMD
Theodore P. Ferris, 1941

Psalm 72

Based on the *Book of Psalms*, 1871

Verses 1–12

1 O God, Thy judgments give the king,
His reigning son Thy righteousness;
2 He to Thy people right shall bring,
With justice shall Thy poor redress.
3 The heights shall bring prosperity,
The hills bring peace by righteousness;
4 He'll judge the poor, the wronged set free,
And crush the men who them oppress.

5 Till sun and moon no more are known
They shall Thee fear in ages all;
6 He'll come as rain on meadows mown
And showers upon the earth that fall.
7 The just shall flourish in his day;
While lasts the moon shall peace extend;
8 From sea to sea shall be his sway,
And from the River to earth's end.

9 The nomads bow to him as king,
And to the dust his foes descend;
10 The isles and Tarshish tribute bring,
And Sheba, Seba gifts shall send.
11 All kings shall down before him fall,
All nations his commands obey.
12 He'll save the needy when they call,
The poor, and those that have no stay.

TUNE: TRURO LM
("Lift Up Your Head, Ye Mighty Gates")
Thomas Williams,
Psalmodia Evangelica, 1789

Psalm 76

Elements from *The Psalter,* 1912

1 God the Lord is known in Judah;
Great His name in Israel;
2 His pavilion is in Salem;
His abode on Zion hill.
3 There he broke the bow and arrows,
Bade the sword and shield be still.

4 Excellent art Thou and glorious
Coming from the hills of prey.
5 Thou hast spoiled the valiant-hearted;
Wrapt in sleep of death are they.
Mighty men have lost their cunning;
None are ready for the fray.

6 Horse and chariot low are lying
In the sleep of death's dark night.
Jacob's God, Thou didst rebuke them;
7 Thou art fearful in Thy might.
When Thine anger once is risen,
Who may stand before Thy sight?

8 When from heav'n Thy sentence sounded,
All the earth in fear was still,
9 While to save the meek and lowly
God in judgment wrought His will.
10 Ev'n the wrath of man shall praise Thee;
What remains is kept from ill.

11 Make your vows now to Jehovah;
Pay your God what is His own.
All men, bring your gifts before Him;
Fear is due to Him alone;
12 He brings low the pride of princes;
Kings shall tremble at His frown.

TUNE: NEANDER 87.87.87.
("Christ is Coming")
Joachim Neander, 1680

Psalm 78

Elements from *Scottish Psalter*, 1650

Verses 1–8

1 O ye my people, to my law
Attentively give ear;
The words that from my mouth proceed
Incline yourselves to hear.
2 My mouth shall speak a parable,
The sayings dark of old,
3 Which we have listened to and known
As by our fathers told.

4 We will not hide them from their sons
But tell the race to come
Jehovah's praises and His strength,
The wonders He has done.
5 His word He unto Jacob gave,
His law to Israel,
And bade our fathers teach their sons
6 The coming race to tell,

That children yet unborn might know
And their descendants lead
7 To trust in God, recall God's works,
And His commandments heed,
8 And not be like their fathers were,
A race of stubborn mood,
Which never would prepare its heart
Nor keep its faith with God.

TUNE: ELLACOMBE CMD
("Hosanna, Loud Hosanna")
Gesangbuch der Herzogl. Wurttemberg.
Hofkapelle, 1784

Psalm 84

Book of Psalms, 1871

1 O Lord of hosts, how lovely
The place where thou dost dwell.
Thy tabernacles holy
In pleasantness excel.
2 My soul is longing, fainting,
Jehovah's courts to see;
My heart and flesh are crying,
O living God, for Thee.

3 Behold the sparrow findeth
A house in which to rest,
The swallow has discovered
Where she may build her nest;
And where, securely sheltered,
Her young she forth may bring;
So Lord of hosts, Thy altars
I seek, my God, my King.

4 Blest who Thy house inhabit,
They ever give Thee praise;
5 Blest all whom Thou dost strengthen,
Who love the sacred ways.
6 Who pass through Baca's valley,
And make in it a well;
There rains in shower abundant
The pools with water fill.

7 So they from strength unwearied
Go forward unto strength,
Till they appear in Zion,
Before the Lord at length.
8 O hear, Lord God of Jacob,
To me an answer yield;
9 The face of Thy Anointed,
Behold, O God, our Shield.

10 One day excels a thousand,
If spent Thy courts within;
I'll choose a threshold rather
Than dwell in tents of sin.
11 Our sun and shield Jehovah,
Will grace and glory give;
No good will He deny them
That uprightly do live.

12 O God of hosts, Jehovah,
How blest is every one
Who confidence reposes
On Thee, O Lord, alone.
1 O Lord of hosts, how lovely
The place where thou dost dwell.
Thy tabernacles holy
In pleasantness excel.

TUNE: LLANGLOFFAN 76.76.D
("O Lord of Hosts, How Lovely")
Welsh Melody

Psalm 86

The Psalter, 1912; altered 1993

Verses 1–11

1 Bow down Thy ear, O LORD, and hear,
For I am poor and great my need;
2 Preserve my soul, for Thee I fear;
O God, Thy trusting servant heed.
3 O LORD, be merciful to me,
For all the day to Thee I cry;
4 Rejoice Thy servant, for to Thee
I lift my soul, O Lord Most High.

5 For Thou, O Lord, art good and kind,
And ready to forgive Thou art;
Abundant mercy they shall find
Who call on Thee with all their heart.
6 O LORD, incline Thy ear to me,
My voice of supplication heed;
7 In trouble I will cry to Thee,
For Thou wilt answer when I plead.

8 There is no God but Thee alone,
Nor works like Thine, O Lord Most
High;
9 All nations, Lord, shall round Thy
throne
Their great Creator glorify.
10 In all Thy deeds how great Thou art!
Thou one true God, Thy way make
clear;
11 Teach me, O LORD, unite my heart
To trust Thy truth, Thy Name to fear.

TUNE: LLEF LM
Griffith Hugh Jones, 1849–1919

Psalm 87

1 Upon the holy hills the LORD
Has His foundation laid;
2 He loves the gates of Zion more
Than dwellings Jacob made.

3 O city of our God, there are
Things glorious said of thee.
4 I'll mention Egypt, Babylon,
Among those knowing me.

Include the land of Palestine;
Let Tyre the survey share,
With distant Ethiopia:
"This is a man born there!"

5 And so of Zion it is said,
"Each one was born in her;"
And He that is Himself Most High,
He has established her.

6 The LORD, when listing peoples, notes,
"This is a man born there!"
7 And singers with their minstrels say,
"Our fountains in thee are."

TUNE: RICHMOND CM
("City of God")
("O Praise the Lord, for He Is Good")
Thomas Haweis, 1794

Psalm 89

The Complete Book of Psalms for Singing, 1991; altered 1993

Verses 1–16

1 Of GOD's love I'll sing forever,
   To each age Your faithfulness.
2 I'll declare Your love's forever,
   Founded in the word from heav'n:
3 "With My Chosen I've made cov'nant,
   To My servant David sworn:
4 'I'll your line confirm forever,
   To each age build up your throne.'"

5 LORD, the heavens praise Your wonders,
   Angels sing your faithfulness.
6 For none matches GOD in heaven,
   Who's like GOD in heaven's throng?
7 God is feared among the angels,
   He's more awesome than they all.
8 LORD, O God of hosts, who's like You?
   Mighty God, You're girt with truth.

9 You rule over sea's proud surging;
   When its waves rise, bid them still.
10 You broke Egypt, left her dying;
   Your strong arm dispersed Your foes.
11 Yours the heavens, earth's bounds also;
   You have founded all the world.
12 North and south You have created;
   Tabor, Hermon, praise Your name.

13 You've an arm that's great in power;
   Your strong hand is all supreme.
14 Your rule's based on right and justice;
   Cov'nant love and truth are yours.
15 They are happy who acclaim you;
   In Your favour, LORD, they walk.
16 In Your name rejoicing ever;
   In Your righteousness raised high.

TUNE: ODE TO JOY 87.87.D
("God, All Nature Sings Thy Glory")
Ludwig van Beethoven, 1824

Psalm 90

Based on The Book of Psalms, 1871, and The Psalter, 1912

Verses 1–9

1 Lord, Thou hast been our dwelling place
   Through all the ages of our race.
2 Before the mountains had their birth,
   Or ever Thou hadst formed the earth,
   From years which no beginning had
   To years unending, Thou art God.

3 Thou turnest man to dust again,
   And say'st, "Return, ye sons of men."
4 As yesterday when past appears,
   So are to Thee a thousand years;
   They like a day are in Thy sight,
   Yes, like a passing watch by night.

5 Thou with a flood hast swept men on;
   They like a sleep are quickly gone.
   They are like grass which grows each morn;
6 Its blades of green the fields adorn.
   At morn its sprouts and blossoms rise;
   At eve, cut down, it withered lies.

7 For by Thine anger we're consumed,
   And by Thy wrath to terror doomed.
8 Our sins Thou in Thy sight dost place,
   Our secret faults before Thy face;
9 So in Thy wrath our days we end,
   And like a sigh our years we spend.

(continued next page)

Verses 10–17

10 For some life's years are seventy;
Perhaps the strong may eighty see;
Their best involves but toil and woe;
All quickly ends. How soon we go!
11 Who has Thine anger understood?
Who fears Thy fury as he should?

12 O teach Thou us to count our days
And set our hearts on wisdom's ways.
13 How long, O Lord? Return! Repent,
And toward Thy servants now relent.
14 Each morning fill us with Thy grace;
We'll sing for joy through all our days.

15 According to the days we spent
Beneath affliction Thou hast sent,
And all the years we evil know,
Now make us glad, our joy renew.
16 Thy work in all Thy servants show;
Thy glory on their sons bestow.

17 On us let there be shed abroad
The beauty of the Lord our God.
Our handiwork upon us be
Established evermore by Thee.
Yes, let our handiwork now be
Established evermore by Thee.

TUNE: ST. CATHERINE 88.88.88.
("Faith of Our Fathers")
Henry F. Hemy, 1864

Psalm 91

1 Who with God Most High finds shelter
In th'Almighty's shadow hides.
2 To the Lord I'll say, "My Refuge!"
3 In my God my trust abides.
From the fowler's snare He'll save
you,
From the deadly pestilence;
4 Cover you with outspread pinions,
Make His wings your confidence.

God's own truth, your shield and
buckler;
5 You will fear no ill by night,
Nor the shafts in daylight flying,
6 Nor disease that shuns the light,
Nor the plague that wastes at
noonday.
7 At your side ten thousand fall;
8 You will only see this judgment
Which rewards the wicked all.

9 You have made the Lord your refuge,
God Most High your dwellingplace;
10 Nothing evil shall befall you;
In your tent no scourge you'll face.
11 He will angels charge to keep you,
Guard you well in all your ways.
12 In their hands they will uphold you
Lest your foot a stone should graze.

13 You shall trample serpents, lions,
Tread on all your deadly foes.
14 For his love to Me I'll save him,
Keep him, for My name he knows;
15 When he calls Me I will answer,
Save and honor him will I.
16 I will show him my salvation,
With long life will satisfy.

TUNE: HYFRYDOL 87.87.D
("Jesus What a Friend for Sinners")
Rowland H. Pritchard, c. 1830;
harm. Ralph Vaughan–Williams

Psalm 95

Based on the *Book of Psalms*, 1871 and
The Psalter, 1912

Verses 1–7

1 O come and to Jehovah sing;
   Let us our voices raise;
   In joyful songs let us the Rock
   Of our salvation praise.
2 Before His presence let us come
   With praise and thankful voice;
   Let us sing psalms to Him with grace;
   With shouts let us rejoice.

3 The LORD's a mighty God and King;
   Above all gods He is.
4 The depths of earth are in His hand;
   The mountain peaks are His.
5 To Him the spacious sea belongs;
   'Twas made by His command;
   And by the working of His hands
   He formed the rising land.

6 O come and let us worship Him;
   Let us with one accord
   In presence of our Maker kneel,
   And bow before the Lord.
7 Because He only is our God,
   And we His chosen sheep,
   The people of His pasturage,
   Whom His own hand will keep.

TUNE: IRISH CM
Irish melody;
*A Collection of Hymns and Sacred
Poems*, 1749

Psalm 98

Based on *Scottish Psalter*, 1650

1 O sing a new song to the LORD
   For wonders He has done,
   His right hand and His holy arm
   The victory have won.

2 The great salvation wrought by Him
   Jehovah has made known.
   His justice in the nations' sight
   The Lord has clearly shown.

3 He mindful of His grace and truth
   To Is'rel's house has been.
   The great salvation of our God
   All ends of earth have seen.

4 O all the earth, sing to the LORD
   And make a joyful sound.
   Lift up your voice aloud to Him;
   Sing psalms! Let joy resound!

5 With harp make music to the LORD;
   With harp a psalm O sing!
6 With horn and trumpet raise a shout
   Before the LORD, the King.

7 Let seas in all their vastness roar,
   The world its living horde.
8 Let rivers clap, let mountains sing
   Their joy before the LORD!

9 Because He comes, He surely comes
   The judge of earth to be!
   With justice he will judge the world
   All men with equity.

TUNE: DESERT CM
Thomas Jarman

Psalm 100

Based on William Kethe and
Scottish Psalter, 1564

1 All people that on earth do dwell,
    Sing to the LORD with cheerful voice.
2 Him serve with mirth; His praise forth
        tell;
    Come ye before Him and rejoice.

3 Know that the LORD is God indeed;
    Without our aid He did us make.
    We are His folk; He doth us feed,
    And for His sheep He doth us take.

4 O enter then His gates with praise;
    Within His courts your thanks
        proclaim;
    With grateful hearts your voices raise
    To bless and magnify His name.

5 Because the LORD our God is good,
    His mercy is forever sure;
    His truth at all times firmly stood
    And shall for age to age endure.

TUNE: OLD 100TH LM
Louis Bourgeois, 1551

Psalm 103

Based on the *Book of Psalms,* 1871 and
The Psalter, 1912;
Verses 20–22 altered 1993

Verses 1–13

1 Bless the LORD, my soul; my whole
        heart
2 Ever bless His holy name.
    Bless the LORD, my soul; forget not
    All His mercies to proclaim.
3 Who forgives all thy transgressions,
    Thy diseases all Who heals;
4 Who redeems thee from destruction,
    Who with thee so kindly deals.

    Who with love and mercy crowns thee,
5 Satisfies thy mouth with good,
    So that even like the eagle
    Thou art blessed with youth renewed.
6 In His righteousness Jehovah
    Will deliver those distressed;
    He will execute just judgment
    In the cause of all oppressed.

7 He made known His ways to Moses,
    And His acts to Israel's race;
8 Tender, loving is Jehovah
    Slow to anger, rich in grace.
9 He will not forever chide us
    Nor will keep His anger still,
10 Has not dealt as we offended
    Nor requited us our ill.

11 For as high as is the heaven,
    Far above the earth below,
    Ever great to them that fear Him
    Is the mercy He will show.
12 Far as east from west is distant
    He has put away our sin;
13 Like the pity of a father
    Has Jehovah's pity been.

(continued on next page)

Verses 14–22

14 For our frame He well remembers;
   That we are but dust He knows;
15 As for man, like grass he rises;
   As the flower in field he grows;
16 Over it the wind now passes;
   In a moment it is gone;
   In the place where once it flourished
   It shall never more be known.

17 But Jehovah's loving kindness
   Unto them that fear His name
   From eternity abideth
   To eternity the same.
   And His righteousness remaineth
   To their children and their seed,
18 Who His covenant remember
   And His precepts hear and heed.

19 In the heavens has Jehovah
   Founded His eternal throne;
   Over all is His dominion;
   He is king and He alone.
20 Bless the LORD, all you His angels,
   You on whom He strength conferred,
   Who His orders are performing,
   Who obey His every word.

21 Bless the LORD, all you His servants,
   Hosts that know and do His will,
   Who forever wait upon Him,
   All His pleasure to fulfill.
22 Bless the LORD, all you His creatures,
   All His works with one accord
   In all parts of His dominion.
   O my soul, bless thou the Lord.

TUNE: BEECHER 87.87.D
("Love Divine All Loves Excelling")
John Zundell, 1870

Psalm 106

Verses 1–12

1 O praise the LORD! O thank the LORD!
   For bountiful is He;
   Because His lovingkindness lasts
   To all eternity.
2 Who can express Jehovah's praise
   Or tell His deeds of might?
3 O blessed are they who justice keep
   And ever do the right.

4 Regard me with the favor, LORD,
   Which Thou dost bear to Thine.
   O visit Thou my soul in love;
   Make Thy salvation mine;
5 That I may see Thy people's good
   And in their joy rejoice,
   And may with Thine inheritance
   Exult with cheerful voice.

6 With all our fathers we have sinned,
   Iniquity have done;
   We have gone on in wickedness,
   In evil ways have run.
7 Our fathers did not understand
   Thy works in Egypt done;
   Of all Thy many mercies shown,
   They did remember none.

   Though at the sea, the Sea of Reeds,
   They were rebellious grown,
8 He saved them for His own name's
   sake,
   To make His power known.
9 And so the Red Sea He rebuked;
   It dried at His command.
   And then He led them through the
   depths
   As through the desert land.

10 And from the hand that hated them,
   He did His people save,
   And from the hand of enemies
   To them redemption gave.
11 The water overwhelmed their foes;
   None lived of all their throng.
12 His people then believed His words
   And praised His name in song.

TUNE: LEVEQUE CMD
Edward Hamilton

Psalm 110

Based on *Scottish Psalter,* 1650

1 Jehovah to my Lord has said,
"Sit Thou at My right hand
Until I make Thy foes a stool
Whereon Thy feet may stand."
2 Jehovah shall from Zion send
The scepter of Thy power.
In battle with Thine enemies
Be Thou the conqueror.

3 A willing people in Thy day
Of power shall come to Thee.
Thy youth arrayed in holiness
Like morning dew shall be.
4 Jehovah swore, and from His oath
He never will depart:
"Of th'order of Melchizedek
A priest Thou ever art."

5 The Lord at Thy right hand shall smite
Earth's rulers in His wrath.
6 Among the nations He shall judge;
The slain shall fill His path.
In many lands He'll overthrow
Their kings with ruin dread;
7 And, marching, He'll drink from the
brook
And so lift up His head.

TUNE: ALL SAINTS NEW CMD
("The Son of God Goes Forth to War")
Henry S. Cutler, 1872

Psalm 113

1 Praise Jehovah; praise the Lord;
Ye His servants, praise accord;
2 Blessed be Jehovah's name;
Evermore His praise proclaim.

3 From the dawn to setting sun,
Praise the Lord, the Mighty One.
4 O'er all nations He is high;
Yea, His glory crowns the sky.

5 Who is like the Lord our God?
High in heav'n is His abode,
6 Who Himself doth humble low
Things in heav'n and earth to know.

7 He the lowly makes to rise
From the dust in which he lies,
8 That exalted he may stand
With the princes of the land.

9 He the childless woman takes
And a joyful mother makes;
Keeping house she finds reward.
Praise Jehovah; praise the Lord.

TUNE: MONKLAND 77.77.
("Let Us with A Gladsome Mind")
Anon., 1824

Psalm 117

Isaac Watts, *The Psalms of David
Imitated*, 1719, as altered in *Irish
Psalter*, 1880

1   From all that dwell below the skies,
    O let Jehovah's praise arise!
    Alleluia! Alleluia!
    And let His glorious name be sung
    In every land, by every tongue!
    Alleluia! Alleluia!

2   Great are the mercies of the LORD,
    And truth eternal is His word;
    Alleluia! Alleluia!
    Ye nations, sound from shore to shore
    Jehovah's praise for evermore!
    Alleluia! Alleluia!

TUNE: LAAST UNS ERFREUEN LM w/
ALLELUIA
("All Creatures of Our God and King")
Geistliche Kirchengesänge, Cologne,
1623

Psalm 118

Based on *Scottish Psalter*, 1650

Verses 17–29

17 I shall not die, but live and tell
    Jehovah's power to save;
18 The LORD has sorely chastened me,
19 But spared me from the grave.
    O set ye open unto me
    The gates of righteousness;
    Then will I enter into them
    And I the LORD will bless.

20 This is Jehovah's gate; by it
    The just shall enter in.
21 I'll praise Thee Who hast heard my
    prayer,
    And hast my safety been.
22 That stone is made head corner stone
    Which builders did despise.
23 This is the doing of the LORD,
    And wondrous in our eyes.

24 This is the day the LORD has made;
    Let us be glad and sing.
25 Hosanna, LORD! O give success!
    O LORD, salvation bring!
26 O blessed be the one who comes,
    Comes in Jehovah's name;
    The blessing from Jehovah's house
    Upon you we proclaim.

27 The LORD is God, and He to us
    Has made the light arise;
    O bind ye to the altar's horns
    With cords of sacrifice.
28 Thou art my God; I'll give Thee thanks.
    My God, I'll worship Thee.
29 O thank the LORD, for He is good;
    His grace will endless be.

TUNE: ST. ASAPH CMD
Giovanni M. Giornovichi

Psalm 119

Based on *The Psalter,* 1912

Aleph—Verses 1–8

1 How blest the blameless in their way
Who from GOD's law do not depart,
2 Who, holding fast the word of truth,
Seek Him with undivided heart.
3 Yea, they are kept from paths of sin
Who walk in His appointed way;
4 Thy precepts Thou hast given us
That we should faithfully obey.

5 My wav'ring heart is now resolved
Thy holy statutes to fulfill;
6 No more shall I be brought to shame
When I regard Thy holy will.
7 To Thee my praise sincere shall rise
When I Thy righteous judgments learn;
8 Forsake me not, but be my guide,
And from Thy statutes I'll not turn.

Beth—Verses 9–16

9 How shall a young man cleanse his
way?
Let him with care Thy word observe.
10 With all my heart I have Thee sought;
From Thy commands let me not
swerve.
11 Thy word I've treasured in my heart,
That I give no offense to Thee.
12 Thou, O Jehovah, blessed art;
Thy statutes teach Thou unto me.

13 I with my lips have oft declared
The judgments which Thy mouth has
shown,
14 More joy Thy testimonies gave
Than all the riches I have known.
15 I'll on Thy precepts meditate,
16 And have respect to all Thy ways.
I in Thy statutes will delight,
Thy word remember all my days.

TUNE: DUANE STREET LMD
("How Shall the Young Direct")
George Coles, 1835

Psalm 119

Mem—Verses 97–104

97 O how I love Thy law; it is
My study all the day.
98 It makes me wiser than my foes;
Its precepts with me stay.
99 More than my teachers or the old
Thy servant understands;
Thy testimonies I consult
100 And follow Thy commands.

101 I stayed my feet from evil ways
That I Thy word observe;
102 I have been taught by Thee and from
Thy judgments will not swerve.
103 How sweet in taste Thy promises,
Than honey far more sweet!
104 Thy precepts understanding give;
I therefore hate deceit.

Nun—Verses 105–112

105 Thy word is to my feet a lamp,
And to my path a light.
106 I sworn have, and I will confirm
To keep Thy judgments right.
107 I'm humbled much; LORD, quicken me
According to Thy word.
108 Accept the off'rings of my mouth;
Teach me Thy judgments, LORD.

109 My soul is ever in my hand;
Thy law I never spurn.
110 The wicked laid a snare, yet from
Thy precepts I'll not turn.
111 I'm to Thy testimonies heir;
They joy to my heart lend.
112 My heart Thy statutes longs to keep
Forever to the end.

TUNE: BETHLEHEM CMD
Gottfried W. Fink, 1842

Psalm 121

Based on *Scottish Psalter*, 1650

1 I to the hills will lift my eyes.
  From whence shall come my aid?
2 My safety cometh from the LORD
  Who heav'n and earth has made.

3 Thy foot He'll not let slide, nor will
  He slumber that thee keeps.
4 Lo, He that keepeth Israel,
  He slumbers not nor sleeps.

5 The LORD thee keeps; the LORD thy shade
  On thy right hand doth stay;
6 The moon by night thee shall not smite,
  Nor yet the sun by day.

7 The LORD shall keep thee from all ill;
  He shall preserve thy soul.
8 The LORD as thou shalt go and come
  Forever keeps thee whole.

TUNE: DUNDEE CM
Scottish Psalter, 1615

Psalm 124

Based on William Whittingham and
Scottish Psalter, 1564,
and *The Psalter*, 1912

1 Now Israel may say and that in truth,
  "If that the LORD had not our right maintained,
2 If that the LORD had not with us remained,
  When cruel men against us rose to strive,
3 We surely had been swallowed up alive.

  Yea, when their wrath against us fiercely rose,
4 Then as fierce floods before them all things drown,
  So had they brought our soul to death quite down;
5 The raging streams, with their proud swelling waves,
  Had then our soul o'erwhelmed as in the grave."

6 Blessed be the LORD Who made us not their prey;
7 As from the snare a bird escapeth free,
  Their net is rent and so escaped are we.
8 Our only help is in Jehovah's name,
  Who made the earth and all the heav'nly frame.

TUNE: OLD 124TH 10.10.10.10.10.
Louis Bourgeois, 1551

Psalm 127

Based on *Scottish Psalter*, 1650

1 Except the Lord shall build the house
The builders lose their pain;
Except the Lord the city keep
The watchmen watch in vain.

2 'Tis vain for you to rise betimes,
Or late from rest to keep,
To eat the bread of toil; for so
He gives His loved ones sleep.

3 Lo, children are the Lord's good gift;
Rich payment are men's sons.
4 The sons of youth as arrows are
In hands of mighty ones.

5 Who has his quiver filled with these,
O happy shall he be;
When foes they greet within the gate
They shall from shame be free.

TUNE: GLASGOW CM
Thomas Moore, 1756

Psalm 128

Based on the *Book of Psalms*, 1871 and
The Psalter, 1912

1 Blessed the man that fears Jehovah
And that walketh in His ways;
2 Thou shalt eat of thy hands' labor
And be prospered all thy days.
3 Like a vine with fruit abounding
In thy house thy wife is found,
And like olive plants thy children,
Compassing thy table round.

4 Lo, on him that fears Jehovah
Shall this blessedness attend;
5 For Jehovah out of Zion
Shall to thee His blessing send.
Thou shalt see Jerus'lem prosper
All thy days till life shall cease;
6 Thou shalt see thy children's children,
Unto Israel be peace.

TUNE: NETTLETON 87.87.D
("Come, Thou Fount of Every Blessing")
American melody; John Wyeth,
Repository of Sacred Music, II, 1813

Psalm 129

1 "Time and again they greatly did oppress me
From my youth up," let Israel declare;
2 "Time and again they greatly did oppress me
From my youth up, yet they did not prevail."

3 Upon my back, like plowmen plowing furrows,
So did they make their gouges deep and long.
4 Yet is Jehovah righteous in His dealings;
The ropes of lawless men He cuts apart.

5 Let them be shamed and fall back in confusion,
All those who bear for Zion bitter hate.
6 Let them become like grass upon the housetops
Which withers up before it can be pulled.

7 From such the reaper cannot get one hand full,
Nor can the one who binds fill up his arms.
8 None passing say, "Jehovah's blessing on you!
We give you blessing in Jehovah's name!"

TUNE: OLD 110TH 11.10.11.10.
Louis Bourgeois, 1551

Psalm 133

Based on *Scottish Psalter*, 1650

1 Behold how good a thing it is,
And how becoming well,
When those that brethren are delight
In unity to dwell.

2 For it is like the precious oil
Poured out on Aaron's head,
That, going down upon his beard,
Upon his garments spread.

3 Like Hermon's dew upon the hills
Of Zion that descends,
The LORD commands His blessing there,
Ev'n life that never ends.

TUNE: AZMON CM
("O, For a Thousand Tongues to Sing")
Carl G. Gläser, 1784–1829;
Arr. by Lowell Mason, 1839; or
MANOAH CM
Henry W. Greatorex, 1851

Psalm 135

1 Hallelujah! Praise the LORD's name!
Praise Him, servants of the LORD,
2 You that in the LORD's house serve Him,
In God's courtyard standing guard.
3 Praise the LORD! How good the LORD is!
Sing His name—how sweet its tone!
4 For the LORD has chosen Jacob,
Is-ra-el to be his own.

5 Well I know how great the LORD is;
Our Lord is above all gods.
6 For the LORD does what He pleases
In all heav'n, earth, deeps, and floods.
7 He it is Who lifts the vapors
From the ends of earth and sea,
Who with lightnings brings the rain down,
From His store the wind sets free,
(continued next page)

8 Who slew all of Egypt's firstborn,
9 On you, Egypt, wonders sent.
  Signs to Pharaoh and his servants,
10 Who killed kings, their kingdoms rent
11 Mighty Sihon, Og of Bashan
   Then the Kings of Canaan fell!
12 God their land gave to His people,
   Willed it all to Is-ra-el.

13 Your name, LORD, endures forever;
   Your fame, LORD, each age has known;
14 For the LORD acquits His people,
   Has compassion on His own.
15 Heathen idols, gold and silver,
   Work of human artistry:
16 Having mouths, they speak of nothing;
   Having eyes, they do not see.

17 Having ears, they never hearken;
   They do not breathe out or in.
18 Those who make them will be like
   them,
   All whose trust in them has been.
19 Bless the LORD, O house of Is-r'el!
   House of Aaron, bless the LORD!
20 Bless the LORD, O house of Levi!
   All who fear Him, bless the LORD!

   Blessings to the LORD you worship!
21 Blessed from Zion be the LORD,
   He whose dwelling is in Salem!
   Hallelujah! Praise the LORD!
1 Hallelujah! Praise the LORD's name!
   Praise Him, servants of the LORD,
2 You that in the LORD's house serve
   Him,
   In God's courtyard standing guard.

   TUNE: KIRKPATRICK 87.87.D
   William J. Kirkpatrick, 1890

Psalm 136

Based on John Craig and
Scottish Psalter, 1564

Verses 1–16

1 O thank the LORD, for good is He;
  His mercy lasts forever.
2 Thanks to the God of gods give ye;
  His mercy lasts forever.
3 O praises give the King of kings;
  His mercy lasts forever;
4 For He alone does wondrous things;
  His mercy lasts forever;

5 Who in His wisdom framed the skies;
  His mercy lasts forever;
6 Who made the earth from waters rise;
  His mercy lasts forever;
7 Who placed the great lights on display;
  His mercy lasts forever;
8 The sun to rule the sky by day;
  His mercy lasts forever;

9 The moon and stars to rule the night;
  His mercy lasts forever;
10 Who Egpyt's firstborn all did smite;
   His mercy lasts forever;
11 Who freed all Isr'el from their charm;
   His mercy lasts forever;
12 With mighty hand and outstretched
   arm;
   His mercy lasts forever;

13 Who by His wind the Red Sea clave;
   His mercy lasts forever;
14 Led Isr'el through the parted wave;
   His mercy lasts forever;
15 O'er Pharoah He the Red Sea spread;
   His mercy lasts forever;
16 Through desert wastes His people
   led;
   His mercy lasts forever;

   TUNE: CONSTANCE 87.87.D
   ("I've Found a Friend")
   Arthur S. Sullivan, 1875

Psalm 138

1 With all my heart my thanks I'll bring,
   Before the gods Thy praises sing;
2 I'll worship in Thy holy place
   And praise Thy name for truth and
   grace;

   For Thou above Thy name adored
   Has magnified Thy faithful word.
3 The day I called Thy help appeared;
   With inward strength my soul was
   cheered.

4 All kings of earth shall thanks accord
   When they have heard Thy words, O
   LORD;
5 Jehovah's ways they'll celebrate;
   The glory of the LORD is great.

6 Although Jehovah is most high,
   On lowly ones He bends His eye;
   But those that proud and haughty are
   He knoweth only from afar.

7 Through trouble though my pathway
   be,
   Thou wilt revive and comfort me.
   Thine outstretched hand Thou wilt
   oppose
   Against the wrath of all my foes.

   Thy hand, O LORD, shall set me free
8 And perfect what concerneth me;
   Thy mercy, LORD, forever stands;
   Leave not the work of Thine own
   hands.

TUNE: HURSLEY LM
("Sun of My Soul")
Katholiches Gesangbuch,
Vienna, c. 1774

Psalm 139

Based on the *Book of Psalms,* 1871;
v. 13 altered 1994

Verses 1–12

1 Lord, Thou has searched me;
2   Thou has known
   My rising and my sitting down;
   And from afar Thou knowest well
   The very thoughts that in me dwell.

3 Thou knowest all the ways I plan,
   My path and lying down dost scan;
4 For in my tongue no word can be,
   But, lo, O LORD, 'tis known to Thee.

5 Behind, before me, Thou dost stand
   And lay on me Thy mighty hand;
6 Such knowledge is for me too strange
   And high beyond my utmost range.

7 Where shall I from Thy Spirit flee,
   Or from Thy presence hidden be?
8 In heav'n Thou art, if there I fly,
   In death's abode, if there I lie.

9 If I the wings of morning take
   And utmost sea my dwelling make,
10 Ev'n there Thy hand shall guide my
   way
   And Thy right hand shall be my stay.

11 If I say, "Darkness covers me,"
12 The darkness hideth not from Thee.
   To Thee both night and day are bright;
   The darkness shineth as the light.

(continued next page)

Verses 13–24

13 My inward parts were formed by Thee;
Within the womb, Thou fashioned me;
14 And I Thy praises will proclaim,
For strange and wondrous is my
frame.

Thy wondrous works I surely know;
15 When as in depths of earth below
My frame in secret first was made,
'Twas all before Thine eyes displayed.

16 Mine unformed substance Thou didst
see;
The days that were ordained to me
Were written in Thy book, each one,
When as of them there yet was none.

17 Thy thoughts, O God, to me are dear;
18 How great their sum! They more
appear
In number than the sand to me.
When I awake, I'm still with Thee.

19 The wicked Thou wilt slay, O God;
Depart from me, ye men of blood,
20 They speak of thee in words profane,
The foes who take Thy name in vain.

21 Do not I hate Thy foes, O LORD?
And thine assailants hold abhorred?
22 I truly hate all foes of Thine;
I count them enemies of mine.

23 Search me, O God; my heart discern;
And try me, every thought to learn,
24 And see if any sin holds sway.
Lead in the everlasting way.

TUNE: MARYTON LM
("O Master Let Me Walk)
H. Percy Smith, 1874

Psalm 146

Based on the *Book of Psalms*, 1871,
and *The Psalter*, 1912

1 Hallelujah! Praise Jehovah!
O my soul, Jehovah praise!
2 I will sing the glo-rious praises
Of my God through all my days.
3 Put no confidence in princes,
Nor for help on man depend;
4 He shall die, to dust returning,
And his purposes shall end.

5 Happy is the man that chooses
Jacob's God to be his aid;
He is blessed whose hope of blessing
On the LORD his God is stayed.
6 He has made the earth and heaven,
Seas, and all that they contain;
He will keep His truth forever,
7 Rights of those oppressed maintain.

Food Jehovah gives the hungry,
Sight Jehovah gives the blind,
Freedom gives He to the pris'ner,
8 Cheer to those bowed down in mind.
Well Jehovah loves the righteous
9 To the stranger is a stay,
Helps the fatherless and widow,
But subverts the sinner's way.

1 *Hallelujah! Praise Jehovah!*
O my soul, Jehovah praise!
2 *I will sing the glo-rious praises*
Of my God through all my days.
10 Over all GOD reigns for ever,
Through all ages he is King;
Unto him, thy God, O Zion,
Joyful hallelujahs sing.

TUNE: RIPLEY 87.87.D
Gregorian chant;
Arr. by Lowell Mason, 1839

Psalm 147

Based on the *Book of Psalms,* 1871;
Verses 19 and 20 altered 1993

1 Praise GOD! 'tis good and pleasant,
And comely to adore;
2 Jehovah builds up Salem,
Her outcasts doth restore.
3 He heals the broken hearted,
And makes the wounded live;
4 The starry hosts He numbers,
And names to all doth give.

5 Our Lord is great and mighty;
His wisdom none can know;
6 The LORD doth raise the lowly
And sinners overthrow.
7 O thank and praise Jehovah!
Praise Him on harp with mirth,
8 The heaven with clouds Who covers,
And sends His rain on earth.

9 He clothes with grass the mountains,
And gives the beasts their food;
He hears the crying ravens,
And feeds their tender brood.
10 In horse's strength delights not,
Nor speed of man loves He;
11 The LORD loves all who fear Him,
And to His mercy flee.

12 O Salem, praise Jehovah,
Thy God, O Zion, praise;
13 For He thy gates has strengthened,
And blessed thy sons with grace.
14 With peace He'll bless thy borders,
The finest wheat afford;
15 He sends forth His commandment,
And swiftly speeds His word.

16 Like wool the snow he giveth,
Spreads hail o'er all the land,
17 Hoarfrost like ashes scatters;
Who can His cold withstand?
18 Then forth His word he sendeth,
He makes His wind to blow;
The snow and ice are melted,
Again the waters flow.

19 The words that He has spoken
To Jacob He makes known;
His judgments and His statutes
To Israel has shown.
20 Not so to any nation
Did He His grace accord.
For they've not known His judgments.
O do ye praise the LORD.

TUNE: LANCASHIRE 76.76.D
("Lead on O King Eternal")
Henry Smart, 1836

Psalm 148

Elements from George Wither and
Scottish Psalter, 1650

1 From heav'n O praise the Lᴏʀᴅ;
   Ye heights, His glory raise.
2 All angels, praise accord;
   Let all His host give praise.
3 Praise Him on high,
   Sun, moon, and star,
   Sun, moon, and star,
4 Ye heav'ns afar,
   And cloudy sky.

5 Yea, let them glorious make
   Jehovah's matchless name;
   For when the word He spake
   They into being came.
6 And from that place
   Where fixed they be,
   Where fixed they be,
   By His decree
   They cannot pass.

7 From earth O praise the Lᴏʀᴅ;
   Ye deeps and all below;
8 Wild winds that do His word,
   Ye clouds, fire, hail, and snow;
9 Ye mountains high,
   Ye cedars tall.
   Ye cedars tall,
10 Beasts great and small,
   And birds that fly.

11 Let all the people praise,
   And kings of every land;
   Let all their voices raise
   Who judge and give command.
12 By young and old,
   By maid and youth,
   By maid and youth,
13 His name in truth
   Should be extolled.

   Jehovah's name be praised
   Above the earth and sky.
14 For He His saints has raised
   And set their power on high.
   Him praise accord,
   O Israel's race,
   O Israel's race,
   Near to His grace.
   Praise ye the Lᴏʀᴅ.

TUNE: ST. CATHERINE'S 66.66.44.44.
Horatio R. Palmer

Psalm 149

The *Book of Psalms,* 1871

1 O praise ye the LORD! Prepare your
glad voice,
New songs with His saints assembled
to sing;
2 Before His Creator let Israel rejoice,
And children of Zion be glad in their
King.

3 And let them His name extol in the
dance;
With timbrel and harp His praises
express;
4 Jehovah takes pleasure His saints to
advance,
And with His salvation the humble to
bless.

5 His saints shall sing loud with glory
and joy,
And rest undismayed; with songs in
the night
6 In praises to God they their lips shall
employ;
A sword in their right hand, two-edged
for the fight;

7 The heathen to judge, their pride to
consume,
8 To bind kings with chains, due
vengeance record,
9 To execute on them their long-decreed
doom:
His saints have this honor. O praise
ye the LORD!

TUNE: LAUDATE DOMINIUM
10.10.11.11.
("O Praise Ye the Lord")
C. Hubert H. Parry, 1894

Psalm 150

Altered 1993

1 Praise ye the LORD! Praise unto God
Within His sanctuary raise.
Within His firmament of power
To Him on high O give ye praise.
2 O praise Him for His mighty deeds,
For all His acts of providence.
O praise Him for His glory great
And for His matchless excellence.

3 O praise Him with the trumpet sound.
Praise Him with rippling harp and
lyre.
4 Praise Him with timbrels in the dance.
Praise Him with organ and string choir.
5 Praise Him with cymbals sounding
high.
Praise Him with cymbals clashing
chord.
6 O praise the LORD, all things that
breathe!
O do ye praises give the LORD.

TUNE: CREATION LMD
From Franz Joseph Haydn,
The Creation, 1798

Hymns

1. A Debtor to Mercy Alone

Augustus M. Toplady, 1740–1778 Mod.

A debtor to mercy alone,
Of covenant mercy, I sing;
Nor fear, with your righteousness on,
My person and off'ring to bring.
The terrors of law and of God
With me can have nothing to do;
My Savior's obedience and blood
Hide all my transgressions from view.

The work which his goodness began,
The arm of his strength will complete;
His promise is yea and amen,
And never was forfeited yet.
Things future, nor things that are now,
Nor all things below or above,
Can make him his purpose forgo,
Or sever my soul from his love.

My name from the palms of his hands
Eternity will not erase;
Impressed on his heart it remains,
In marks of indelible grace.
Yes, I to the end shall endure,
As sure as the earnest is giv'n;
More happy, but not more secure,
The glorified spirits in heav'n.

TUNE: TREWEN 8.8.8.8.D.
David Emlyn Evans, 1843–1913

2. A Mighty Fortress Is Our God

Martin Luther, 1529
From Psalm 46

A mighty fortress is our God,
A bulwark never failing;
Our helper he amid the flood
Of mortal ills prevailing.
For still our ancient foe
Doth seek to work us woe;
His craft and pow'r are great;
And armed with cruel hate,
On earth is not his equal.

Did we in our own strength confide,
Our striving would be losing;
Were not the right man on our side,
The man of God's own choosing.
Dost ask who that may be?
Christ Jesus, it is he,
Lord Sabaoth His name,
From age to age the same,
And He must win the battle.

And though this world with devils filled,
Should threaten to undo us,
We will not fear for God hath willed
His truth to triumph through us.
The prince of darkness grim,
We tremble not for him;
His rage we can endure,
For lo! his doom is sure;
One little word shall fell him.

That Word above all earthly pow'rs,
No thanks to them, abideth;
The Spirit and the gifts are ours
Through Him who with us sideth.
Let goods and kindred go,
This mortal life also;
The body they may kill:
God's truth abideth still;
His kingdom is forever.

TUNE: EIN' FESTE BURG 8.7.8.7.6.6.6.7.
Martin Luther, 1529

3. Abide With Me: Fast Falls the Eventide

Henry F. Lyte, 1847

Abide with me: fast falls the eventide;
The darkness deepens;
   Lord, with me abide:
When other helpers fail,
   and comforts flee,
Help of the helpless, O abide with me.

Swift to its close ebbs out life's little day;
Earth's joys grow dim,
   its glories pass away;
Change and decay in all around I see;
O thou who changest not, abide with me.

I need thy presence every passing hour;
What but thy grace can
   foil the tempter's pow'r?
Who like thyself my
   guide and stay can be?
Through cloud and sunshine,
   O abide with me.

I fear no foe, with thee at hand to bless:
Ills have no weight, and tears no
   bitterness.
Where is death's sting?
   Where grave, thy victory?
I triumph still, if thou abide with me.

Hold thou thy cross
   before my closing eyes;
Shine through the gloom,
   and point me to the skies:
Heav'n's morning breaks,
   and earth's vain shadows flee:
Iin life, in death, O Lord, abide with me.

TUNE: EVENTIDE (MONK) 10.10.10.10.
William H. Monk, 1861

4. Alas! and Did My Savior Bleed

Isaac Watts, 1707; Alt. 1961

Alas! and did my Savior bleed,
And did my Sovereign die!
Would He devote that sacred head
For such a worm as I!

Was it for crimes that I had done
He groaned upon the tree!
Amazing pity! Grace unknown!
And love beyond degree!

Well might the sun in darkness hide,
And shut His glories in,
When Christ, the mighty Maker, died
For man the creature's sin.

Thus might I hide my blushing face
While His dear cross appears;
Dissolve my heart in thankfulness,
And melt my mine eyes in tears.

But drops of grief can ne'er repay
The debt of love I owe;
Here, Lord, I give myself away,
'Tis all that I can do.

TUNE: MARTYRDOM C.M.
Hugh Wilson, c. 1800

5. All Hail the Power of Jesus' Name!

St. 1–5, Edward Perronet, 1779; alt.
St. 6, John Rippon, 1787

All hail the pow'r of Jesus' name!
Let angels prostrate fall;
Bring forth the royal diadem,
And crown Him Lord of all;
Bring forth the royal diadem,
And crown Him Lord of all.

Crown him, ye martyrs of your God,
Whom from His altar call;
Extol the Stem of Jesse's rod,
And crown Him Lord of all;
Extol the Stem of Jesse's rod,
And crown Him Lord of all.

Ye seed of Israel's chosen race,
Ye ransomed from the fall,
Hail Him who saves you by His grace,
And crown Him Lord of all;
Hail Him who saves you by His grace,
And crown Him Lord of all.

Sinners, whose love can ne'er forget
The wormwood and the gall,
Go, spread your trophies at His feet,
And crown Him Lord of all;
Go, spread your trophies at His feet,
And crown Him Lord of all.

Let ev'ry kindred, ev'ry tribe,
On this terrestrial ball,
To Him all majesty ascribe,
And crown Him Lord of all;
To Him all majesty ascribe,
And crown Him Lord of all.

(O that with yonder sacred throng
We at His feet may fall;
We'll join the everlasting song,
And crown Him Lord of all;
We'll join the everlasting song,
And crown Him Lord of all.

TUNE: CORONATION C.M., rep.
Oliver Holden, 1793
or DIADEM 8.6.6.8.ref.
James Ellor, 1838

6. Amazing Grace!
John Newton, 1779

Amazing grace!—how sweet the sound—
That saved a wretch like me!
I once was lost, but now am found,
Was blind, but now I see.

'Twas grace that taught my heart to fear,
And grace my fears relieved;
How precious did that grace appear
The hour I first believed!

Thro' many dangers, toils, and snares,
I have already come;
'Tis grace has brought me safe thus far,
And grace will lead me home.

The Lord has promised good to me,
His Word my hope secures;
He will my shield and portion be,
As long as life endures.

And when this flesh and heart shall fail,
And mortal life shall cease,
I shall possess within the veil
A life of joy and peace.

When we've been there ten thousand
     years,
Bright shining as the sun,
We've no less days to sing God's praise
Than when we've first begun.

TUNE: NEW BRITAIN C.M.
Virginia Harmony, 1831

See also Psalms 87, 133

7. And Can It Be
Charles Wesley, 1738

And can it be that I should gain
An int'rest in the Savior's blood?
Died He for me, who caused His pain?
For me, who Him to death pursued?
Amazing love! how can it be
That Thou, my God, shouldst die for me?
Amazing love! how can it be
That Thou, my God, shouldst die for me?

'Tis myst'ry all! Th'Immortal dies:
Who can explore His strange design?
In vain the firstborn seraph tries
To sound the depths of love divine.
'Tis mercy all! let earth adore,
Let angel minds inquire no more.
'Tis mercy all! let earth adore,
Let angel minds inquire no more.

He left His Father's throne above,
So free, so infinite His grace,
Emptied Himself of all but love,
And bled for Adam's helpless race.
'Tis mercy all, immense and free;
For, O my God, it found out me!
'Tis mercy all, immense and free;
For, O my God, it found out me!

Long my imprison'd spirit lay
Fast bound in sin and nature's night;
Thine eye diffused a quick'ning ray,
I woke, the dungeon flamed with light;
My chains fell off, my heart was free,
I rose, went forth, and followed Thee.
My chains fell off, my heart was free,
I rose, went forth, and followed Thee.

No condemnation now I dread;
Jesus, and all in Him, is mine!
Alive in Him, my living Head,
And clothed in righteousness divine,
Bold I approach th'eternal throne,
And claim the crown, through Christ, my own.
Bold I approach th'eternal throne,
And claim the crown, through Christ, my own.

TUNE: SAGINA L.M.D.
Thomas Campbell, 1825

8. Angels We Have Heard On High
Traditional French Carol

Angels we have heard on high,
Sweetly singing o'er the plains,
And the mountains in reply
Echo back their joyous strains.
Gloria in excelsis Deo,
Gloria in excelsis Deo.

Shepherds, why this jubilee?
Why your joyous strains prolong?
Say what may the tidings be,
Which inspire your heav'nly song?
Gloria in excelsis Deo,
Gloria in excelsis Deo.

Come to Bethlehem and see
Him whose birth the angels sing;
Come, adore on bended knee
Christ the Lord, the newborn King.
Gloria in excelsis Deo,
Gloria in excelsis Deo.

TUNE: GLORIA 7.7.7.7.ref.
Traditional French Melody;
Arr. by Edward S. Barnes, 1937

9. Beneath the Cross of Jesus

Elizabeth C. Clephane, 1872

Beneath the cross of Jesus
I fain would take my stand,
The shadow of a mighty Rock
Within a weary land;
A home within the wilderness,
A rest upon the way,
From the burning of the noontide heat
And the burden of the day.

Upon the cross of Jesus
Mine eye at times can see
The very dying form of One
Who suffered there for me:
And from my stricken heart with tears
Two wonders I confess,
The wonders of redeeming love
And my own worthlessness.

I take, O cross, thy shadow
For my abiding place:
I ask no other sunshine
Than the sunshine of his face;
Content to let the world go by,
To know no gain nor loss;
My sinful self my only shame,
My glory all the cross.

TUNE: ST. CHRISTOPHER
7.6.8.6.8.6.8.6.
Frederick C. Maker, 1881

10. Christ is Made the Sure Foundation

Latin, 7th cent.
Tr. by John Mason Neale, 1851
Alt. in *Hymns Ancient and Modern*, 1861

Christ is made the sure foundation,
Christ the head and cornerstone,
Chosen of the Lord and precious,
Binding all the church in one;
Holy Zion's help forever,
And her confidence alone.

All that dedicated city,
Dearly loved of God on high,
In exultant jubilation
Pours perpetual melody;
God the One in Three adoring
In glad hymns eternally.

To this temple, where we call thee,
Come, O Lord of hosts, today:
With thy wonted lovingkindness
Hear thy people as they pray;
And thy fullest benediction
Shed within its walls alway.

Here vouchsafe to all thy servants
What they ask of these to gain,
What they gain from thee forever
With the blessed to retain,
And hereafter in thy glory
Evermore with thee to reign.

Laud and honor to the Father,
Laud and honor to the Son,
Laud and honor to the Spirit,
Ever Three and ever One,
One in might, and One in glory,
While unending ages run.

TUNE: REGENT SQUARE 8.7.8.7.8.7
Henry Smart, 1876

11. Christ Shall Have Dominion

From Psalm 72:8-14, 17-19
The Psalter, 1912

Christ shall have dominion over land and sea,
Earth's remotest regions shall his empire be;
They that wilds inhabit
    shall their worship bring,
Kings shall render tribute,
    nations serve our King.
Christ shall have dominion over land and sea,
Earth's remotest regions shall his empire be.

When the needy seek him,
    he will mercy show;
Yea, the weak and helpless
    shall his pity know;
He will surely save them from oppression's
    might,
For their lives are precious in his holy sight.
Christ shall have dominion over land and sea,
Earth's remotest regions
    shall his empire be.

Ever and forever shall his name endure,
Long as suns continue it shall stand secure;
And in him forever all men shall be blest,
And all nations hail him
    King of kings confessed.
Christ shall have dominion over land and sea,
Earth's remotest regions shall his empire be.

Unto God Almighty joyful Zion sings;
He alone is glorious, doing wondrous things.
Evermore, ye people, bless his glorious name,
His eternal glory through the earth proclaim.
Christ shall have dominion over land and sea,
Earth's remotest regions shall his empire be.

TUNE: ARMAGEDDON 6.5.6.5.D.ref.
German melody;
Adapted by John Goss, 1871

12. Christ the Lord Is Risen Today

Charles Wesley, 1739

"Christ the Lord is ris'n today," Alleluia!
Sons of men and angels say; Alleluia!
Raise your joys and triumphs high;
    Alleluia!
Sing ye heav'ns, and earth, reply, Alleluia!

Vain the stone, the watch, the seal;
    Alleluia!
Christ has burst the gates of hell: Alleluia!
Death in vain forbids Him rise; Alleluia!
Christ has opened paradise. Alleluia!

Lives again our glorious King; Alleluia!
Where, O death, is now thy sting? Alleluia!
Once He died, our souls to save; Alleluia!
Where thy victory, O grave? Alleluia!

Soar we now where Christ has led, Alleluia!
Foll'wing our exalted Head; Alleluia!
Made like Him, like Him we rise; Alleluia!
Ours the cross, the grave, the skies,
    Alleluia!

Hail, the Lord of earth and heav'n! Alleluia!
Praise to Thee by both be giv'n; Alleluia!
Thee we greet triumphant now; Alleluia!
Hail, the Resurrection, Thou! Alleluia!

TUNE: EASTER HYMN 7.7.7.7.al.
Lyra Davidica, 1708; alt.

13. Come, Christians, Join to Sing

Christian H. Bateman, 1843

Come, Christians, join to sing
Alleluia! Amen!
Loud praise to Christ our King;
Alleluia! Amen!
Let all with heart and voice,
Before his throne rejoice;
Praise is his gracious choice.
Alleluia! Amen!

Come, lift your hearts on high,
Alleluia! Amen!
Let praises fill the sky;
Alleluia! Amen!
He is our Guide and Friend;
To us he'll condescend;
His love shall never end.
Alleluia! Amen!

Praise yet our Christ again,
Alleluia! Amen!
Life shall not end the strain;
Alleluia! Amen!
On heaven's blissful shore,
His goodness we'll adore,
Singing for evermore,
"Alleluia! Amen!"

MADRID 6.6.6.6.D.
Traditional Spanish Melody;
Arr. by David Evans, 1927

14. Come, My Soul, Thy Suit Prepare

John Newton, 1779

Come, my soul, thy suit prepare:
Jesus loves to answer prayer;
He himself has bid thee pray,
Therefore will not say thee nay;
Therefore will not say thee nay.

Thou art coming to a King,
Large petitions with thee bring;
For his grace an pow'r are such,
None can ever ask too much;
None can ever ask too much.

With my burden I begin:
"Lord, remove this load of sin;
Let thy blood, for sinners spilt,
Set my conscience free from guilt;
Set my conscience free from guilt.

"Lord, I come to thee for rest,
Take possession of my breast;
There thy blood-bought right maintain,
And without a rival reign;
And without a rival reign.

"While I am a pilgrim here,
Let thy love my spirit cheer;
As my Guide, my Guard, my Friend,
Lead me to my journey's end;
Lead me to my journey's end.

"Show me what I have to do,
Ev'ry hour my strength renew:
Let me live a life of faith,
Let me die thy people's death;
Let me die thy people's death."

TUNE: HENDON 7.7.7.7.rep.
Henri A. Cesar Malan, 1827

15. Come, Thou Almighty King

Anonymous, ca. 1757

Come, thou Almighty King,
Help us thy name to sing,
Help us to praise.
Father, all glorious,
O'er all victorious,
Come and reign over us,
Ancient of Days.

Come, thou Incarnate Word,
Gird on thy mighty sword,
Our prayer attend.
Come, and thy people bless,
And give thy Word success;
Spirit of holiness,
On us descend.

Come, Holy Comforter,
Thy sacred witness bear
In this glad hour.
Thou who almighty art,
Now rule in every heart,
And ne'er from us depart,
Spirit of pow'r.

To the great One in Three
Eternal praises be,
Hence evermore.
His sovereign majesty
May we in glory see,
And to eternity
Love and adore.

TUNE: TRINITY 6.6.4.6.6.6.4.
Felice de Giardini, 1769

16. Come, Ye Thankful People, Come

Henry Alford, 1844, 1867

Come, ye thankful people, come,
Raise the song of harvest home:
All is safely gathered in,
Ere the winter storms begin;
God, our Maker, doth provide
For our wants to be supplied:
Come to God's own temple, come,
Raise the song of harvest home.

All the world is God's own field,
Fruit unto His praise to yield;
Wheat and tares together sown,
Unto joy or sorrow grown;
First the blade, and then the ear,
Then the full corn shall appear:
Lord of harvest, grant that we
Wholesome grain and pure may be.

For the Lord our God shall come,
And shall take His harvest home;
From his field shall in that day
All offenses purge away;
Give His angels charge at last
In the fire the tares to cast,
But the fruitful ears to store
In His garner evermore.

Even so, Lord, quickly come
To Thy final harvest home;
Gather Thou Thy people in,
Free from sorrow, free from sin;
There forever purified,
In Thy presence to abide:
Come, with all Thine angels, come,
Raise the glorious harvest home.

TUNE: ST. GEORGE'S, WINDSOR
7.7.7.7.D.
George J. Elvey, 1859

17. Crown Him with Many Crowns

Matthew Bridges, 1851

Crown Him with many crowns,
The Lamb upon His throne;
Hark! how the heav'nly anthem drowns
All music but its own:
Awake, my soul, and sing
Of Him who died for thee,
And hail Him as thy matchless King
Through all eternity.

Crown Him the Lord of love;
Behold His hands and side,
Rich wounds, yet visible above,
In beauty glorified:
No angel in the sky
Can fully bear that sight,
But downward bends his burning eye
At mysteries so bright.

Crown Him the Lord of peace;
Whose pow'r a scepter sways
From pole to pole, that wars may cease,
Absorbed in prayer and praise:
His reign shall know no end;
And round His pierced feet
Fair flow'rs of paradise extend
Their fragrance ever sweet.

Crown Him the Lord of years,
The Potentate of time;
Creator of the rolling spheres,
Ineffably sublime:
All hail, Redeemer, hail!
For Thou hast died for me:
Thy praise shall never, never fail
Throughout eternity.

TUNE: DIADEMATA S.M.D.
George J. Elvey, 1868

18. Eternal Father, Strong to Save

William Whiting, 1860, 1869

Eternal Father, strong to save,
Whose arm doth bind the restless wave,
Who bid'st the mighty ocean deep
Its own appointed limits keep:
O hear us when we cry to thee
For those in peril on the sea.

O Savior, whose almighty word
The winds and waves submissive heard,
Who walkedst on the foaming deep
And calm amid its rage didst sleep:
O hear us when we cry to thee
For those in peril on the sea.

O sacred Spirit, who didst brood
Upon the chaos dark and rude,
Who badd'st its angry tumult cease,
And gavest light and life and peace:
O hear us when we cry to thee
For those in peril on the sea.

O Trinity of love and pow'r,
Our brethren shield in danger's hour;
From rock and tempest, fire and foe,
Protect them where soe'er they go;
And ever let there rise to thee
Glad hymns of praise from land and sea.

TUNE: MELITA 8.8.8.8.8.8.
John B. Dykes, 1861

19. For all the Saints
William Walsham How, 1864, 1875

For all the saints
who from their labors rest,
Who thee by faith
before the world confessed,
Thy name, O Jesus, be forever blest.
Alleluia! Alleluia!

Thou wast their Rock,
their Fortress, and their Might;
Thou, Lord, their Captain
in the well fought fight;
Thou in the darkness drear,
their one true Light.
Alleluia! Alleluia!

O may thy soldiers, faithful, true, and
bold,
Fight as the saints who nobly fought of
old,
And win with them
the victors crown of gold.
Alleluia! Alleluia!

The golden evening brightens in the west;
Soon, soon to faithful
warriors comes their rest;
Sweet is the calm of Paradise the blest.
Alleluia! Alleluia!

But lo! There breaks
a yet more glorious day;
The saints triumphant rise in bright array;
The King of Glory passes on his way.
Alleluia! Alleluia!

From earth's wide bounds,
from ocean's farthest coast,
Through gates of pearl streams
in the countless host,
Singing to Father, Son, and Holy Ghost,
Alleluia! Alleluia!

TUNE: SINE NOMINE 10.10.10.al.
Ralph Vaughan Williams, 1906

20. Glorious Things of Thee Are Spoken
John Newton, 1779
From Psalm 87

Glorious things of Thee are spoken,
Zion, city of our God;
He whose word cannot be broken
Formed thee for His own abode:
On the Rock of Ages founded,
What can shake thy sure repose?
With salvation's walls surrounded,
Thou may'st smile at all thy foes.

See, the streams of living waters,
Springing from eternal love,
Well supply thy sons and daughters,
And all fear of want remove:
Who can faint, while such a river
Ever flows their thirst t'assuage?—
Grace which, like the Lord, the giver,
Never fails from age to age.

Round each habitation hov'ring,
See the cloud and fire appear
For a glory and a cov'ring,
Showing that the Lord is near:
Thus deriving from their banner
Light by night and shade by day,
Safe they feed upon the manna
Which he gives them when they pray.

Savior, if of Zion's city
I, through grace, a member am,
Let the world deride or pity,
I will glory in Thy name:
Fading is the worldling's pleasure,
All his boasted pomp and show;
Solid joys and lasting treasure
None but Zion's children know.

TUNE: AUSTRIAN HYMN 8.7.8.7.D.
Franz Joseph Haydn, 1797

21. God of Our Fathers

Daniel C. Roberts, 1876

God of our fathers, whose almighty hand
Leads forth in beauty all the starry band
Of shining worlds in splendor through the
    skies,
Our grateful songs before thy throne arise.

Thy love divine hath led us in the past;
In this free land by thee our lot is cast;
Be thou our ruler, guardian, guide, and
    stay;
Thy Word our law, thy paths our chosen
    way.

From war's alarms, from deadly
    pestilence,
Be thy strong arm our ever sure defense;
Thy true religion in our hearts increase,
Thy bounteous goodness nourish us in
    peace.

Refresh thy people on their toilsome way,
Lead us from night to never ending day;
Fill all our lives with love and grace divine,
And glory, laud, and praise be ever thine.

TUNE: NATIONAL HYMN 10.10.10.10.
George William Warren, 1892

See also Psalm 46

22. Great God, We Sing

Philip Doddridge, 1755
St. 5, line 4, alt.

Great God, we sing that mighty hand
By which supported still we stand;
The opening year thy mercy shows;
That mercy crowns it till it close.

By day, by night, at home abroad,
Still are we guarded by our God;
By his incessant bounty fed,
By his unerring counsel led.

With grateful hearts the past we own;
The future, all to us unknown,
We to thy guardian care commit,
And peaceful leave before thy feet.

In scenes exalted or depressed,
Thou art our Joy, and thou our Rest;
Thy goodness all our hopes shall raise,
Adored through all our changing days.

When death shall interrupt these songs,
And seal in silence mortal tongues,
Our helper God, in whom we trust,
Shall keep our souls and guard our dust.

TUNE: WAREHAM L.M.
William Knapp, 1738

See also Psalm 90

23. Great Is Thy Faithfulness

Thomas O. Chisholm, 1923

Great is Thy faithfulness, O God my
   Father;
There is no shadow of turning with Thee;
Thou changest not,
   Thy compassions, they fail not;
As Thou hast been Thou forever wilt be.
Refrain: Great is Thy faithfulness! Great
      is Thy faithfulness!
      Morning by morning new mercies
      I see:
      All I have needed Thy hand hath
      provided—
      Great is Thy faithfulness, Lord,
      unto me!

Summer and winter and
   springtime and harvest,
Sun, moon, and stars
   in their courses above,
Join with all nature in manifold witness
To Thy great faithfulness, mercy, and
   love.
Refrain

Pardon for sin and a peace that endureth,
Thine own dear presence
   to cheer and to guide,
Strength for today
   and bright hope for tomorrow,
Blessings all mine,
   with ten thousand beside!
Refrain

TUNE: FAITHFULNESS 11.10.11.10.ref.
   William M. Runyan, 1923

24. Guide Me, O Thou Great Jehovah

William Williams, 1745

Guide me, O Thou great Jehovah,
Pilgrim through this barren land;
I am weak, but Thou art mighty;
Hold me with Thy pow'rful hand;
Bread of heaven, Bread of heaven,
Feed me till I want no more,
Feed me till I want no more.

Open now the crystal fountain,
Whence the healing stream doth flow;
Let the fire and cloudy pillar
Lead me all my journey through;
Strong Deliv'rer, strong Deliv'rer,
Be Thou still my strength and shield,
Be Thou still my strength and shield.

When I tread the verge of Jordan,
Bid my anxious fears subside;
Death of death, and hell's Destruction,
Land me safe on Canaan's side;
Songs of praises, songs of praises,
I will ever give to Thee,
I will ever give to Thee.

TUNE: CWM RHONDDA
   8.7.8.7.8.7.rep.
   John Hughes, 1907

25. Hail the Day That Sees Him Rise

Charles Wesley, 1739

Hail the day that sees him rise, Alleluia!
To his throne above the skies; Alleluia!
Christ, the Lamb for sinners giv'n, Alleluia!
Enters now the hightest heav'n. Alleluia!

There for him high triumph waits; Alleluia!
Lift your heads, eternal gates, Alleluia!
He hath conquered death and sin, Alleluia!
Take the King of glory in! Alleluia!

See, he lifts his hands above! Alleluia!
See, he shows the prints of love! Alleluia!
Hark! his gracious lips bestow, Alleluia!
Blessings on his church below. Alleluia!

Lord, beyond our mortal sight, Alleluia!
Raise our hearts to reach thy height; Alleluia!
There thy face unclouded see, Alleluia!
Find our heav'n of heav'ns in thee! Alleluia!

TUNE: LLANFAIR 7.7.7.7.al.
Robert Williams, 1817

26. Hark! the Herald Angels Sing

Charles Wesley, 1739, 1753; alt.

Hark! the herald angels sing,
"Glory to the newborn King;
Peace on earth, and mercy mild,
God and sinners reconciled!"
Joyful, all ye nations, rise,
Join the triumph of the skies;
With th'angelic host proclaim,
"Christ is born in Bethlehem!"
Refrain: Hark! the herald angels sing,
        "Glory to the newborn King."

Christ, by highest heav'n adored,
Christ, the everlasting Lord!
Late in time behold Him come,
Offspring of the Virgin's womb.
Veiled in flesh the Godhead see;
Hail th'incarnate Deity,
Pleased as man with men to dwell,
Jesus, our Emmanuel.
Refrain

Hail the heav'n-born Prince of Peace!
Hail the Sun of Righteousness!
Light and life to all He brings,
Ris'n with healing in His wings.
Mild He lays His glory by,
Born that man no more may die,
Born to raise the sons of earth,
Born to give them second birth.
Refrain

Come, Desire of Nations, come!
Fix in us Thy humble home;
Rise, the woman's conquering seed,
Bruise in us the serpent's head.
Adam's likeness now efface,
Stamp Thine image in its place:
O, to all Thyself impart,
Formed in each believing heart.
Refrain

TUNE: MENDELSSOHN, 7.7.7.7.D.rep.
Felix Mendelssohn–Bartholdy, 1840

27. Here, O My Lord, I See Thee Face to Face

Horatius Bonar, 1855

Here, O my Lord, I see Thee face to face;
Here would I touch and handle things unseen,
Here grasp with firmer hand th'eternal grace,
And all my weariness upon Thee lean.

Here would I feed upon the bread of God,
Here drink with Thee the royal wine of heav'n;
Here would I lay aside each earthly load,
Here taste afresh the calm of sin forgiv'n.

This is the hour of banquet and of song;
This is the heav'nly table spread for me:
Here let me feast, and, feasting, still prolong
The brief, bright hour of fellowship with Thee.

I have no help but Thine, nor do I need
Another arm save Thine to lean upon:
It is enough, my Lord, enough indeed;
My strength is in Thy might, Thy might alone.

Mine is the sin, but Thine the righteousness;
Mine is the guilt, but Thine the cleansing blood;
Here is my robe, my refuge, and my peace,
Thy blood, Thy righteousness, O Lord my God.

TUNE: MORECAMBE 10.10.10.10.
Frederick C. Atkinson, 1870

28. Holy, Holy, Holy!

Reginald Heber, 1783-1826

Holy, holy, holy! Lord God Almighty!
Early in the morning our song shall rise to Thee.
Holy, holy, holy! Merciful and mighty!
God in three Persons, blessed Trinity!

Holy, holy, holy! All the saints adore Thee,
Casting down their golden crowns around the glassy sea;
Cherubim and seraphim falling down before Thee,
Who wert, and art, and evermore shalt be.

Holy, holy, holy! Though the darkness hide Thee,
Though the eye of sinful man Thy glory may not see,
Only Thou art holy; there is none beside Thee
Perfect in pow'r, in love, and purity.

Holy, holy, holy! Lord God Almighty!
All Thy works shall praise Thy name in earth and sky and sea.
Holy, holy, holy! Merciful and mighty!
God in three Persons, blessed Trinity!

TUNE: NICAEA 11.12.12.10.
John B. Dykes, 1861

29. How Great Thou Art

Stuart K. Hine, 1949; alt.

O Lord my God, when I in awesome wonder
Consider all the worlds Thy hands have made,
I see the stars, I hear the rolling thunder,
Thy pow'r thro' out the universe displayed.
Refrain: Then sings my soul, my Savior God, to Thee:
    How great Thou art, how great Thou art!
    Then sings my soul, my Savior God, to Thee:
    How great Thou art, how great Thou art!

When thro' the woods and forest glades I wander
And hear the birds sing sweetly in the trees,
When I look down from lofty mountain grandeur,
And hear the brook and feel the gentle breeze;
Refrain

And when I think that God, His Son, not sparing,
Sent Him to die, I scarce can take it in,
That on the cross, my burden gladly bearing,
He bled and died to take away my sin.
Refrain

When Christ shall come with shout of acclamation
And take me home, what joy shall fill my heart!
Then I shall bow in humble adoration,
And there proclaim, my God, how great Thou art.
Refrain

TUNE: O STORE GUD 11.10.11.10.ref.
Swedish folk melody;
Arr. Stuart K. Hine, 1949

30. I Love Thy Kingdom, Lord

Timothy Dwight, 1800
From Psalm 137

I love thy kingdom, Lord,
The house of thine abode,
The church our blest Redeemer saved
With his own precious blood.

I love thy church, O God:
Her walls before thee stand,
Dear as the apple of thine eye,
And graven on thy hand.

For her my tears shall fall,
For her my prayers ascend;
To her my cares and toils be giv'n,
Till toils and cares shall end.

Beyond my highest joy
I prize her heav'nly ways,
Her sweet communion, solemn vows,
Her hymns of love and praise.

Jesus, thou Friend divine,
Our Savior and our King,
Thy hand from ev'ry snare and foe
Shall great deliv'rance bring.

Sure as thy truth shall last,
To Zion shall be giv'n
The brightest glories earth can yield,
And brighter bliss of heav'n.

TUNE: ST. THOMAS S.M.
Aaron Williams, 1763

31. Immortal, Invisible, God Only Wise

Walter Chalmers Smith, 1867

Immortal, invisible, God only wise,
In light inaccessible hid from our eyes,
Most blessed, most glorious, the Ancient
of Days,
Almighty, victorious, Thy great name we
praise.

Unresting, unhasting and silent as light,
Nor wanting, nor wasting, Thou rulest in
might;
Thy justice like mountains high soaring
above
Thy clouds which are fountains of
goodness and love.

Great Father of glory, pure Father of light,
Thine angels adore Thee, all veiling their
sight;
All praise we would render; O help us to
see
'Tis only the splendor of light hideth Thee!

TUNE: JOANNA (or ST. DENIO)
11.11.11.11
Traditional Welsh hymn melody

32. It Is Well with My Soul

Horatio G. Spafford, 1873

When peace, like a river, attendeth my
way,
When sorrows like sea billows roll;
Whatever my lot, Thou hast taught me to
say,
"It is well, it is well with my soul."
Refrain: It is well with my soul;
It is well, it is well with my soul.

Though Satan should buffet, though trials
should come,
Let this blest assurance control,
That Christ has regarded my helpless
estate,
And has shed His own blood for my soul.
Refrain

My sin—O the bliss of this glorious
thought!—
My sin, not in part, but the whole,
Is nailed to the cross and I bear it no more;
Praise the Lord, praise the Lord, O my
soul!
Refrain

O Lord, haste the day when the faith shall
be sight,
The clouds be rolled back as a scroll,
The trump shall resound and the Lord
shall descend,
"Even so"—it is well with my soul.
Refrain

TUNE: VILLE DU HAVRE 11.8.11.9.ref.
Philip P. Bliss, 1876

33. Jesus Shall Reign

Isaac Watts, 1719
From Psalm 72

Jesus shall reign where'er the sun
Does his successive journeys run;
His kingdom stretch from shore to shore,
Till moons shall wax and wane no more.

To Him shall endless prayer be made,
And praises throng to crown His head;
His name, like sweet perfume, shall rise
With every morning sacrifice.

People and realms of every tongue
Dwell on His love with sweetest song;
And infant voices shall proclaim
Their early blessings on His name.

Blessings abound where'er He reigns;
The pris'ner leaps to lose his chains,
The weary find eternal rest,
And all the sons of want are blest.

Let every creature rise and bring
Peculiar honors to our King;
Angels descend with songs again,
And earth repeat the loud amen!

TUNE: DUKE STREET L.M.
John Hatton, 1793

34. Joy to the World! The Lord Is Come

Isaac Watts, 1719
From Psalm 98

Joy to the world! The Lord is come:
Let earth receive her King;
Let every heart prepare Him room,
And heav'n and nature sing,
And heav'n and nature sing,
And heav'n, and heav'n and nature sing.

Joy to the earth! The Savior reigns:
Let men their songs employ;
While fields and floods, rocks, hills, and plains
Repeat the sounding joy,
Repeat the sounding joy,
Repeat, repeat the sounding joy.

No more let sins and sorrows grow,
Nor thorns infest the ground;
He comes to make His blessings flow
Far as the curse is found,
Far as the curse is found,
Far as, far as the curse is found.

He rules the world with truth and grace,
And makes the nations prove
The glories of His righteousness
And wonders of His love,
And wonders of His love,
And wonders, wonders of His love.

TUNE: ANTIOCH C.M.rep.
George Frederick Handel, 1742;
Arr. by Lowell Mason, 1836

35. Let us Love and Sing and Wonder

John Newton, 1774; Mod.

Let us love and sing and wonder,
Let us praise the Savior's name!
He has hushed the law's loud thunder,
He has quenched Mount Sinai's flame:
He has washed us with his blood,
He has brought us nigh to God.

Let us love the Lord who bought us,
Pitied us when enemies,
Called us by his grace, and taught us,
Gave us ears and gave us eyes;
He has washed us with his blood,
He presents our souls to God.

Let us sing, though fierce temptation
Threaten hard to bear us down!
For the Lord, our strong salvation,
Holds in view the conqu'ror's crown:
He who washed us with his blood
Soon will bring us home to God.

Let us wonder; grace and justice
Join and point to mercy's store;
When through grace in Christ our trust is,
Justice smiles and asks no more:
He who washed us with his blood
Has secured our way to God.

Let us praise, and join the chorus
Of the saints enthroned on high;
Here they trusted him before us,
Now their praises fill the sky:
"You have washed us with your blood;
You are worthy, Lamb of God!"

TUNE: ALL SAINTS OLD 8.7.8.7.7.7.
Darmstadt Gesangbuch, 1698

36. Lord of the Sabbath, Hear us Pray

Philip Doddridge, 1737
alt. by Thomas Cotterill, 1819, and
others; mod.

Lord of the Sabbath, hear us pray,
In this your house, on this your day;
And own, as grateful sacrifice,
The songs which from your temple rise.

Now met to pray and bless your name,
Whose mercies flow each day the same,
Whose kind compassions never cease,
We seek instruction, pardon, peace.

Your earthly Sabbaths, Lord, we love,
But there's a nobler rest above;
To that our lab'ring souls aspire
With ardent hope and strong desire.

In your blest kingdom we shall be
From ev'ry mortal trouble free;
No sighs shall mingle with the songs
Resounding from immortal tongues;

No rude alarms of raging foes;
No cares to break the long repose;
No midnight shade, no waning moon,
But sacred, high, eternal noon.

O long expected day, begin,
Dawn on these realms of woe and sin!
Break, morn of God, upon our eyes;
And let the world's true Sun arise!

TUNE: GERMANY L.M.
William Gardiner's *Sacred Melodies*,
1815

37. My Faith Looks up to Thee

Ray Palmer, 1830

My faith looks up to thee,
Thou Lamb of Calvary,
Savior divine:
Now hear me while I pray,
Take all my guilt away,
O let me from this day be wholly thine.

May thy rich grace impart
Strength to my fainting heart,
My zeal inspire;
As thou hast died for me,
O may my love to thee
Pure, warm, and changeless be, a living
fire.

While life's dark maze I tread,
And griefs around me spread,
Be thou my guide;
Bid darkness turn today,
Wipe sorrow's tears away,
Nor let me ever stray from thee aside.

When ends life's transient dream,
When death's cold, sullen stream
Shall o'er me roll,
Blest Savior, then, in love,
Fear and distrust remove;
O bear me safe above, a ransomed soul.

TUNE: OLIVET 6.6.4.6.6.6.4.
Lowell Mason, 1832

38. Not What My Hands Have Done

Horatius Bonar, 1861; alt.

Not what my hands have done
Can save my guilty soul;
Not what my toiling flesh has borne
Can make my spirit whole.
Not what I feel or do
Can give me peace with God;
Not all my prayers and sighs and tears
Can bear my awful load.

Thy work alone, O Christ,
Can ease this weight of sin;
Thy blood alone, O Lamb of God,
Can give me peace within.
Thy love to me O God,
Not mine, O Lord to thee,
Can rid me of this dark unrest,
And set my spirit free.

Thy grace alone, O Christ,
Can ease this weight of sin;
Thy pow'r lone, O Son of God,
Can this sore bondage break.
No other work, save thine,
No other blood will do;
No strength save that which is divine,
Can bear me safely through.

I bless the Christ of God;
I rest on love divine;
And with unfalt'ring lip and heart,
I call this Savior mine.
His cross dispels each doubt;
I bury in his tomb
Each thought of unbelief and fear,
Each ling'ring shade of gloom.

I praise the God of grace;
I trust his truth and might;
He calls me his, I call him mine,
My God, my joy, my light.
'Tis he who saveth me,
And freely pardon gives;
I love because he loveth me,
I live because he lives.

TUNE: LEOMINSTER S.M.D.
George William Martin, 1862

39. Now Thank We All Our God

Martin Rinkart, 1636

Now thank we all our God
With heart and hands and voices,
Who wondrous things hath done,
In whom His world rejoices;
Who from our mothers' arms,
Hath blessed us on our way
With countless gifts of love,
And still is ours today.

O may this bounteous God
Through all our life be near us,
With ever-joyful hearts
And blessed peace to cheer us;
And keep us in His grace,
And guide us when perplexed,
And free us from all ills
In this world and the next.

All praise and thanks to God
The Father now be given
The Son, and Him who reigns
With Them in highest heaven--
The One eternal God,
Whom earth and heav'n adore;
For thus it was is now,
And shall be evermore.

TUNE: NUN DANKET 6.7.6.7.6.6.6.6.
Johann Crüger, 1647

40. O Come, All Ye Faithful

Latin hymn, attr. to
John Francis Wade, 1751

O come, all ye faithful,
Joyful and triumphant,
O come ye, O come ye to Bethlehem;
Come and behold Him
Born the King of angels;
Refrain: O come, let us adore Him,
O come, let us adore Him,
O come, let us adore Him,
Christ the Lord.

God of God,
Light of Light;
Lo, He abhors not the Virgin's womb:
Very God,
Begotten, not created.
Refrain

Sing, choirs of angels,
Sing in exultation,
Sing, all ye citizens of heav'n above;
Glory to God
In the highest;
Refrain

Yea, Lord, we greet Thee,
Born this happy morning:
Jesus, to Thee be all glory giv'n;
Word of the Father,
Late in flesh appearing;
Refrain

TUNE: ADESTE FIDELES
6.6.10.5.6.ref.
John Francis Wade's *Cantus Diversi*,
1751

41. O Come, O Come Emmanuel

Latin antiphons, 12th cent.
Latin hymn, 1710
Tr. by John Mason Neale, 1851, alt.
1961

O come, O come Emmanuel,
And ransom captive Israel,
That mourns in lonely exile here,
Until the Son of God appear.
Refrain: Rejoice! Rejoice! Emmanuel
          Shall come to thee, O Israel.

O come, O come, thou Lord of might,
Who to thy tribes, on Sinai's height,
In ancient times didst give the law
In cloud and majesty and awe.
Refrain

O come, thou Rod of Jesse, free
Thine own from Satan's tyranny;
From depths of hell thy people save,
And give them vict'ry o'er the grave.
Refrain

O come, thou Day-spring from on high,
And cheer us by thy drawing nigh;
Disperse the gloomy clouds of night,
And death's dark shadow put to flight.
Refrain

O come, thou Key of David, come
And open wide our heavn'ly home;
Make safe the way that leads on high,
And close the path to misery.
Refrain

TUNE: VENI EMMANUEL L.M.ref.
Plainsong, 13th cent.;
Arr. by Thomas Helmore, 1856

42. O For a Thousand Tongues to Sing

Charles Wesley, 1739; alt.
Alt. 1961

O for a thousand tongues to sing
My great Redeemer's praise,
The glories of my God and King,
The triumphs of His grace.

My gracious Master and my God,
Assist me to proclaim,
To spread through all the earth abroad
The honors of thy name.

Jesus, the name that charms our fears,
That bids our sorrows cease;
'Tis music in the sinner's ears,
'Tis life and health and peace.

He breaks the pow'r of reigning sin,
He sets the pris'ner free;
His blood can make the foulest clean,
His blood availed for me.

He speaks and, list'ning to His voice,
New life the dead receive;
The mournful, broken hearts rejoice;
The humble poor believe.

Hear him, ye deaf; His praise, ye dumb,
Your loosen'd tongues employ;
Ye blind, behold your Savior come;
And leap, ye lame, for joy.

TUNE: AZMON C.M.
Carl G. Gläser, 1784–1829;
Arr. by Lowell Mason, 1839

43. O God, Our Help in Ages Past

Isaac Watts, 1719, Alt. 1990, mod.
From Psalm 90

O God, our help in ages past,
Our hope for years to come,
Our shelter from the stormy blast,
And our eternal home.

Under the shadow of your throne
Your saints have dwelt secure,
Sufficient is your arm alone,
And our defense is sure.

Before the hills in order stood,
Or earth received her frame,
From everlasting you are God,
To endless years the same.

A thousand ages in Your sight
Are like an evening gone;
Short as the watch that ends the night
Before the rising sun.

The busy tribes of flesh and blood,
With all their lives and cares,
Are carried downward by your flood,
And lost in foll'wing years.

Time, like an ever-rolling stream,
Bears all its sons away;
They fly forgotten, as a dream
Dies at the op'ning day.

O God, our help in ages past,
Our hope for years to come:
O be our God while troubles last,
And our eternal home.

TUNE: ST. ANNE C.M.
Attr. to William Croft, 1678–1727;
Tate and Brady's *Supplement to the New Version*, 1708

44. O Sacred Head, Now Wounded

Bernard of Clairvaux, 1091–1153

O sacred Head, now wounded,
With grief and shame weighed down;
Now scornfully surrounded
With thorns, Thine only crown;
O sacred Head, what glory,
What bliss till now was Thine!
Yet, though despised and gory,
I joy to call Thee mine.

What Thou, my Lord, hast suffered,
Was all for sinners' gain:
Mine, mine was the transgression,
But Thine the deadly pain.
Lo, here I fall, my Savior!
'Tis I deserve Thy place;
Look on me with Thy favor,
Vouchsafe to me Thy grace.

What language shall I borrow
To thank Thee, dearest Friend,
For this, Thy dying sorrow,
Thy pity without end?
O make me Thine forever;
And should I fainting be,
Lord, let me never, never
Outlive my love to Thee.

TUNE: PASSION CHORALE 7.6.7.6.D.
Hans Leo Hassler, 1601;
Arr. by Johann Sebastian Bach, 1729

45. O the Deep, Deep Love of Jesus!

Samuel Trevor Francis, 1834–1925

O the deep, deep love of Jesus!
Vast, unmeasured, boundless, free;
Rolling as a mighty ocean
In its fullness over me.
Underneath me, all around me,
Is the current of thy love;
Leading onward,
Leading homeward,
To thy glorious rest above.

O the deep, deep love of Jesus!
Spread his praise from shore to shore;
How he loveth, ever loveth,
Changeth never, nevermore;
How he watches o'er his loved ones,
Died to call them all his own;
How for them he intercedeth,
Watcheth o'er them from the throne.

O the deep, deep love of Jesus!
Love of ev'ry love the best:
'Tis an ocean vast of blessing,
'Tis an haven sweet of rest.
O the deep, deep love of Jesus!
'Tis a hev'n of heav'ns to me;
And it lifts me up to glory,
For it lifts me up to thee.

TUNE: EBENEZER 8.7.8.7.D.
Thomas John Williams, 1819

46. Onward, Christian Soldiers

Sabine Baring-Gould, 1865

Onward, Christian soldiers
Marching as to war,
With the cross of Jesus
Going on before:
Christ the royal Master
Leads against the foe;
Forward into battle,
See, His banners go.
Refrain: Onward, Christian soldiers,
Marching as to war,
With the cross of Jesus
Going on before.

At the sign of triumph
Satan's host doth flee;
On then, Christian soldiers,
On to victory:
Hell's foundations quiver
At the shout of praise;
Brothers, lift your voices,
Loud your anthems raise.
Refrain

Like a mighty army
Moves the church of God;
Brothers, we are treading
Where the saints have trod;
We are not divided,
All one body we,
One in hope and doctrine,
One is charity.
Refrain

Crowns and thrones may perish,
Kingdoms rise and wane,
But the church of Jesus
Constant will remain;
Gates of hell can never
'Gainst the church prevail;
We have Christ's own promise,
And that cannot fail.
Refrain

(continued next page)

Onward, then, ye people,
Join our happy throng,
Blend with ours your voices
In the triumph song;
Glory, laud, and honor
Unto Christ the King:
This through countless ages
Men and angels sing.
Refrain

TUNE: ST. GERTRUDE 6.5.6.5.D.ref.
Arthur S. Sullivan, 1871

47. Praise, My Soul, the King of Heaven
From Psalm 103
Henry F. Lyte, 1834; mod.

Praise, my soul, the King of heaven,
To his feet your tribute bring;
Ransomed, healed, restored forgiven,
Who, like me, his praise should sing?
Praise him, praise him, praise him, praise
him,
Praise the everlasting King.

Praise him for his grace and favor
To our fathers in distress;
Praise him, still the same forever,
Slow to chide and swift to bless;
Praise him, praise him, praise him, praise
him,
Glorious in his faithfulness.

Fatherlike, he tends and spares us;
Well our feeble frame he knows;
In his hands he gently bears us,
Rescues us from all our foes;
Praise him, praise him, praise him, praise
him,
Widely as his mercy goes.

Frail as summer's flow'r we flourish,
Blows the wind and it is gone;
But while mortals rise and perish,
God endures unchanging on.
Praise him, praise him, praise him, praise
him,
Praise the High Eternal One.

Angels, help us to adore him;
You behold him face to face;
Sun and moon, bow down before him,
Dwellers all in time and space,
Praise him, praise him, praise him, praise
him,
Praise with us the God of grace.

TUNE: LAUDA ANIMA 8.7.8.7.8.7.
John Goss, 1869

48. Praise to the Lord, the Almighty
Joachim Neander, 1680

Praise to the Lord, the Almighty, the King
of creation!
O my soul, praise Him, for He is thy health
and salvation!
All ye who hear, now to His temple draw
near,
Join me in glad adoration.

Praise to the Lord, who o'er all things so
wondrously reigneth,
Shelters Thee under His wings, yea, so
gently sustaineth!
Hast thou not seen how thy desires e'er
have been
Granted in what He ordaineth?

Praise to the Lord, who doth prosper thy
work and defend thee!
Surely His goodness and mercy here
daily attend thee;
Ponder anew what the Almighty will do,
If with His love He befriend thee.

Praise to the Lord, who with marvelous
wisdom hath made thee,
Decked thee with health, and with loving
hand guided and stayed thee.
How oft in grief hath not He brought thee
relief,
Spreading His wings to o'ershade thee!

(continued next page)

Praise to the Lord! O let all that is in me
adore Him!
All that hath life and breath, come now
with praises before Him!
Let the amen sound from His people
again;
Gladly fore'er we adore Him.

TUNE: LOBE DEN HERREN 14.14.4.7.8
Stralsund Gesangbuch, 1665;
Arr. in *Praxis Pietatis Melica*, 1668

49. Rejoice, the Lord is King

Charles Wesley, 1746; alt.

Rejoice, the Lord is King;
Your Lord and King adore!
Rejoice, give thanks, and sing,
And triumph evermore.
Refrain: Lift up your heart, lift up your
voice!
Rejoice, again I say, rejoice!

Jesus the Savior reigns,
The God of truth and love;
When He had purged our stains,
He took His seat above.
Refrain

His kingdom cannot fail,
He rules o'er earth and heav'n;
The keys of death and hell
Are to our Jesus giv'n.
Refrain

He sits at God's right hand
Till all His foes submit,
And bow to His command,
And fall beneath His feet.
Refrain

Rejoice in glorious hope!
Our Lord, the Judge, shall come,
And take His servants up
To their eternal home.
Refrain

TUNE: DARWALL 6.6.6.6.8.8.
John Darwall, 1770

50. Rock of Ages, Cleft for Me

Augustus M. Toplady, 1776

Rock of Ages, cleft for me,
Let me hide myself in Thee;
Let the water and the blood,
From Thy riven side which flowed,
Be of sin the double cure,
Cleanse me from its guilt and pow'r.

Not the labors of my hands
Can fulfill Thy laws demands;
Could my zeal no respite know,
Could my tears forever flow,
All for sin could not atone;
Thou must save, and Thou alone.

Nothing in my hand I bring,
Simply to Thy cross I cling;
Naked, come to Thee for dress;
Helpless look to Thee for grace;
Foul, I to Thy fountain fly;
Wash me, Savior, or I die.

While I draw this fleeting breath,
When mine eyelids close in death,
When I soar to worlds unknown,
See Thee on Thy judgment throne,
Rock of Ages, cleft for me,
Let me hide myself in Thee.

TUNE: TOPLADY 7.7.7.7.7.7.
Thomas Hastings, 1830

51. The Church's One Foundation

Samuel J. Stone, 1866

The church's one foundation
Is Jesus Christ, her Lord;
She is His new creation
By water and the Word:
From heav'n He came and sought her
To be His holy bride;
With His own blood He bought her,
And for her life He died.

Elect from ev'ry nation,
Yet one o'er all the earth,
Her charter of salvation
One Lord, one faith, one birth;
One holy name she blesses,
Partakes one holy food,
And to one hope she presses,
With ev'ry grace endued.

Though with a scornful wonder
Men see her sore oppressed,
By schisms rent asunder,
By heresies distressed,
Yet saints their watch are keeping,
Their cry goes up, "How long?"
And soon the night of weeping
Shall be the morn of song.

The church shall never perish!
Her dear Lord to defend,
To guide, sustain, and cherish,
Is with her to the end;
Though there be those that hate her,
And false sons in her pale,
Against or foe or traitor
She ever shall prevail.

'Mid toil and tribulation,
And tumult of her war,
She waits the consummation
Of peace forevermore;
(continued next page)
Till with the vision glorious
Her longing eyes are blest,
And the great church victorious
Shall be the church at rest.

Yet she on earth hath union
With God the Three in One,
And mystic sweet communion
With those whose rest is won:
O happy ones and holy!
Lord, give us grace that we,
Like them, the meek and lowly,
On high may dwell with Thee.

TUNE: AURELIA 7.6.7.6.D.
Samuel S. Wesley, 1864

52. The First Noel

Old English Carol

The first Noel the angel did say
Was to certain poor shepherds in fields as
  they lay;
In fields where they lay akeeping their
  sheep,
On a cold winter's night that was so deep.
Refrain: Noel, Noel, Noel, Noel,
    Born is the King of Israel.

They looked up and saw a star
Shining in the east beyond them far,
And to the earth it gave great light,
And so it continued both day and night.
Refrain

And by the light of that same star,
Three wise men came from country far;
To seek for a king was their intent,
And to follow the star wherever it went.
Refrain

This star drew nigh to the north-west;
O'er Bethlehem it took its rest;
And there it did both stop and stay,
Right over the place where Jesus lay.
Refrain

Then entered in those wise men three,
Fell reverently upon their knee,
And offered there in his presence,
Their gold, and myrrh, and frankincense.
Refrain

(continued next page)

Then let us all with one accord
Sing praises to our heavenly Lord,
That hath made heaven and earth of
    nought,
And with his blood mankind hath bought.
Refrain

TUNE: THE FIRST NOEL: Irregular with
    Refrain
Traditional Melody
In Sandys' *Christmas Carols*, 1833

53. The God of Abraham Praise
Thomas Olivers, 1770

The God of Abraham praise,
Who reigns enthroned above,
Ancient of everlasting days
And God of love.
Jehovah! Great I AM!
By earth and heav'n confessed;
I bow and bless the sacred name,
Forever blest.

The God of Abraham praise,
At whose supreme command
From earth I rise, and seek the joys
At his right hand.
I all on earth forsake,
Its wisdom, fame, and pow'r,
And him my only portion make,
My shield and tow'r.

He by himself hath sworn,
I on his oath depend;
I shall, on eagles' wings upborne,
To heav'n ascend.
I shall behold his face,
I shall his pow'r adore,
And sing the wonders of his grace
Forevermore.

The goodly land I see,
With peace and plenty blest,
A land of sacred liberty
And endless rest.
There milk and honey flow,
And oil and wine abound,
And trees of life forever grow,
With mercy crowned.

There dwells the Lord our King,
The Lord our Righteousness,
Triumphant o'er the world and sin,
The Prince of Peace.
On Zion's sacred height
His kingdom he maintains,
And glorious with his saints in light
Forever reigns.

The whole triumphant host
Gives thanks to God on high;
"Hail, Father, Son, and Holy Ghost!"
They ever cry.
Hail, Abraham's God and mine!
I join the heav'nly lays;
All might and majesty are thine,
And endless praise.

TUNE: LEONI 6.6.8.4.D.
Jewish Melody;
Arr. by Meyer Lyon, 1770

54. This is My Father's World

Maltbie D. Babcock, 1901

This is my Father's world,
And to my list'ning ears,
All nature sings, and round me rings
The music of the spheres.
This is my Father's world:
I rest me in the thought
Of rocks and trees, of skies and seas;
His hand the wonders wrought.

This is my Father's world,
The birds their carols raise,
The morning light, the lily white,
Declare their Maker's praise.
This is my Father's world:
He shines in all that's fair;
In the rustling grass I hear him pass,
He speaks to me everywhere.

This is my Father's world,
O let me ne'er forget
That though the wrong seems oft so
strong,
God is the Ruler yet.
This is my Father's world:
The battle is not done;
Jesus who died shall be satisfied,
And earth and heav'n be one.

TUNE: TERRA BEATA S.M.D.
Franklin L. Sheppard, 1915;
Arr. by Edward Shippen Barnes, 1926

55. 'Twas on That Night When Doomed to Know

John Morison, 1781

'Twas on that night when doomed to
know
The eager rage of every foe,
That night in which he was betrayed,
The Savior of the world took bread;

And after thanks and glory giv'n
To him that rules in earth and heav'n,
That symbol of his flesh he broke,
And thus to all his foll'wers spoke:

"My broken body thus I give
For you, for all. Take, eat, and live.
And oft the sacred rite renew
That brings my saving love to view."

Then in his hands the cup he raised,
And God a new he thanked and praised,
While kindness in his bosom glowed,
And from his lips salvation flowed.

"My blood I thus pour forth," he cries,
"To cleanse the soul in sin that lies;
In this the covenant is sealed,
And heav'n's eternal grace revealed.

"With love to man this cup is fraught;
Let all partake the sacred draught;
Through latest ages let it pour,
In mem'ry of my dying hour."

TUNE: ROCKINGHAM OLD L.M.
Arr. by Edward Miller, 1790

56. When I Survey the Wondrous Cross

Isaac Watts, 1707, 1709

When I survey the wondrous cross
On which the Prince of Glory died,
My richest gain I count but loss,
And pour contempt on all my pride.

Forbid it, Lord, that I should boast,
Save in the death of Christ my God:
All the vain things that charm me most,
I sacrifice them to His blood.

See, from His head, His hands, His feet,
Sorrow and love flow mingled down:
Did e'er such love and sorrow meet,
Or thorns compose so rich a crown?

Were the whole realm of nature mine,
That were a present far too small:
Love so amazing, so divine,
Demands my soul, my life, my all.
Amen.

TUNE: HAMBURG L.M.
Gregorian chant;
Arr. by Lowell Mason, 1824

57. When Morning Gilds the Skies

German, ca. 1800
Tr. by Edward Caswall, 1853, 1858

When morning gilds the skies,
My heart awaking cries:
May Jesus Christ be praised.
Alike at work and prayer
To Jesus I repair:
May Jesus Christ be praised.

When sleep her balm denies,
My silent spirit sighs:
May Jesus Christ be praised.
When evil thoughts molest,
With this I shield my breast:
May Jesus Christ be praised.

Does sadness fill my mind?
A solace here I find:
May Jesus Christ be praised.
Or fades my earthly bliss?
My comfort still is this:
May Jesus Christ be praised.

In heav'n's eternal bliss
The loveliest strain is this:
May Jesus Christ be praised.
The pow'rs of darkness fear,
When this sweet chant they hear:
May Jesus Christ be praised.

Let earth's wide circle round
In joyful notes resound:
May Jesus Christ be praised.
Let air and sea and sky,
From depth to height, reply:
May Jesus Christ be praised.

Be this, while life is mine,
My canticle divine:
May Jesus Christ be praised.
Be this th'eternal song,
Through all the ages long:
May Jesus Christ be praised.

TUNE: LAUDES DOMINI 6.6.6.D.
Joseph Barnby, 1868

58. Who is on the Lord's Side?

Frances R. Havergal, 1877

Who is on the Lord's side?
Who will serve the King?
Who will be his helpers, other lives to
　bring?
Who will leave the world's side?
Who will face the foe?
Who is on the Lord's side?
Who for him will go?
By thy call of mercy,
By thy grace divine,
We are on the Lord's side, Savior,
We are thine.

Not for weight of glory,
Not for crown and palm,
Enter we the army, raise the warrior psalm;
But for Love that claimeth
Lives for whom he died:
He whom Jesus nameth must be on his
　side.
By thy love constraining,
By thy grace divine,
We are on the Lord's side, Savior,
We are thine.

Jesus, thou hast bought us,
Not with gold or gem,
But with thine own lifeblood,
For thy diadem:
With thy blessing filling
Each who comes to thee,
Thou hast made us willing,
Thou hast made us free,
By thy grand redemption,
By thy grace divine,
We are on the Lord's side, Savior,
We are thine.

Fierce may be the conflict,
Strong may be the foe,
But the King's own army none can
　overthrow:
Round his standard ranging,
Vict'ry is secure;
For his truth unchanging
Makes the triumph sure.
Joyfully enlisting
By thy grace divine,
We are on the Lord's side, Savior,
We are thine.

TUNE: RACHIE 6.5.6.5.6.5.D.
Caradog Roberts, 1878–1935

59. Who is This That Comes From Edom

Thomas Kelly, 1809
From Isaiah 63

Who is this that comes from Edom,
All his raiment stained with blood;
To the slave proclaiming freedom;
Bringing and bestowing good:
Glorious in the garb he wears,
Glorious in the spoils he bears?

'Tis the Savior, now victorious,
Trav'ling onward in his might;
'Tis the Savior, O how glorious
To his people is the sight!
Jesus now is strong to save,
Mighty to redeem the slave.

Why that blood his raiment staining?
Tis the blood of many slain;
Of his foes there's none remaining,
None the contest to maintain:
Fall'n they are, no more to rise,
All their glory prostrate lies.

Mighty Victor, reign for ever,
Wear the crown so dearly won;
Never shall thy people, never
Cease to sing what thou hast done:
Thou hast fought thy people's foes;
Thou wilt heal thy people's woes.

TUNE: EDOM 8.7.8.7.7.7.
Albert L. Peace, 1885

60. Ye Servants of God, Your Master Proclaim

Charles Wesley, 1744; alt.

Ye servants of God, your Master proclaim,
And publish abroad his wonderful name;
The name, all victorious, of Jesus extol;
His kingdom is glorious and rules over all.

God ruleth on high, almighty to save;
And still he is nigh his presence we have.
The great congregation his triumph shall
sing,
Ascribing salvation to Jesus, our King.

Salvation to God, who sits on the throne!
Let all cry aloud and honor the Son.
The praises of Jesus the angels proclaim,
Fall down on their faces and worship the
Lamb.

Then let us adore, and give him his right,
All glory and pow'r and wisdom and might,
All honor and blessing, with angels above,
And thanks never ceasing for infinite love.

TUNE: HANOVER OR
LYONS 10.10.11.11.
Johann Michael Haydn, 1737–1836
Arr. in William Gardiner's Sacred
Melodies, 1815

PSALTER/HYMNAL INDEX

Topical Listing of Hymns

Praise to God

1. A Mighty Fortress Is Our God .... #2 159
2. Come, Thou Almighty King .... #15 166
3. Great Is Thy Faithfulness .... #23 170
4. Holy, Holy, Holy .... #28 172
5. How Great Thou Art .... #29 173
6. Immortal, Invisible, God Only Wise .... #31 174
7. Praise, My Soul, the King of Heaven .... #47 182
8. Praise to the Lord, the Almighty .... #48 182
9. The God of Abraham Praise .... #53 185
10. This Is My Father's World .... #54 186

See also Psalms 8, 19, 89, 95, 100, 106, 113, 117, 138, 146–150

Jesus Christ the Savior

11. All Hail the Power of Jesus' Name .... #5 160
12. Christ Is Made the Sure Foundation .... #10 163
13. Come, Christians, Join to Sing .... #13 165
14. Crown Him with Many Crowns .... #17 167
15. Hail the Day that Sees Him Rise .... #25 171
16. Let Us Love and Sing and Wonder .... #35 176
17. O for a Thousand Tongues to Sing .... #42 179
18. Rejoice, the Lord Is King .... #49 183
19. When Morning Gilds the Skies .... #57 187
20. Who Is This That Comes From Eden .... #59 189

See also all the Psalms, especially the Messianic Psalms 2, 72, 110, 118

Salvation

21. A Debtor to Mercy Alone .... #1 159
22. Alas! and Did My Savior Bleed .... #4 160
23. And Can It Be .... #7 162
24. Beneath the Cross of Jesus .... #9 163
25. Not What My Hands Have Done .... #38 177
26. O Sacred Head, Now Wounded .... #44 180
27. O The Deep, Deep Love of Jesus! .... #45 181

Christmas:

See also Psalms 24, 72, 98

Alphabetical Index of First Lines of Psalms and Hymns

First Line:

Calendar for Learning Psalms and Hymns—Years 1–5

Month	Year 1	Year 2	Year 3	Year 4	Year 5
January	Psalm 1	Psalm 139	Psalm 32	Guide Me O	O for a Thousand
	Amazing Grace	Jesus Shall Reign	Onward Christian	Psalm 67	Psalm 110
February					
March	Psalm 23	Psalm 47	Psalm 118:17-29	Alas and Did	Here, O My Lord
April	When I Survey	Christ the Lord	O Sacred Head	Psalm 24	Psalm 2
May	Psalm 51	Psalm 119:1-16	Psalm 127	Praise to the Lord	All Hail the Power
June	O God Our Help	It is Well	Holy, Holy, Holy	Psalm 42	Psalm 95
July	Psalm 91	Psalm 46	Psalm 63	Glorious Things	Rejoice the Lord is King
August	Great Is Thy Faithfulness	The Church's One Foundation	Rock of Ages	Psalm 19	Psalm 8
September	Psalm 100	Psalm 68	Psalm 78	Immortal, Invisible	How Great Thou Art
October	A Mighty Fortress	Now Thank We All	Psalm 121	Psalm 124	Psalm 84
November	Psalm 103	Psalm 146	Come Ye Thankful	Crown Him With Many Crowns	And Can It Be
December	Joy to the World	Hark the Herald	O Come All Ye	Psalm 37	Psalm 128